The Quest

THE QUEST
HISTORY AND MEANING IN RELIGION

MIRCEA ELIADE

The University of Chicago Press

CHICAGO AND LONDON

Library of Congress Catalog Card Number: 68–19059

THE UNIVERSITY OF CHICAGO PRESS, CHICAGO 60637
THE UNIVERSITY OF CHICAGO PRESS, LTD., LONDON W.C.1

Preface

It is unfortunate that we do not have at our disposal a more precise word than "religion" to denote the experience of the sacred. This term carries with it a long, although culturally rather limited, history. One wonders how it can be indiscriminately applied to the ancient Near East, to Judaism, Christianity, and Islam, or to Hinduism, Buddhism, and Confucianism as well as to the so-called primitive peoples. But perhaps it is too late to search for another word, and "religion" may still be a useful term provided we keep in mind that it does not necessarily imply belief in God, gods, or ghosts, but refers to the experience of the sacred, and, consequently, is related to the ideas of *being, meaning,* and *truth.*

Indeed, it is difficult to imagine how the human mind could function without the conviction that there is something irreducibly *real* in the world, and it is impossible to imagine how consciousness could arise without conferring *meaning* on man's drives and experiences. The awareness of a real and meaningful world is intimately related to the discovery of the sacred. Through the experience of the sacred, the human mind grasped the difference between that which reveals itself as real, powerful, rich, and meaningful, and that which does not — i.e., the chaotic and dangerous flux of things, their fortuitous, meaningless appearances and disappearances.

I have discussed the dialectics of the sacred and its morphology in previous publications, and I do not need to take it up again. It suffices to say that the "sacred" is an element in the structure of consciousness, not a stage in the history of consciousness. A meaningful world — and man cannot live in "chaos" — is the result of a dialectical process which may be called the manifestation of the sacred. Human life becomes meaningful by imitating the paradigmatic models revealed by supernatural beings. The imitation of transhuman models constitutes one of the primary characteristics of "religious" life, a structural characteristic which is indifferent to culture and epoch. From the most archaic religious documents that are accessible to Christianity and Islam, *imitatio dei* as a norm and guideline of human existence was never interrupted; as a matter of fact, it could not have been otherwise. On the most archaic levels of culture, *living as a human being* is in itself a *religious act*, for alimentation, sexual life, and work have a sacramental value. In other words, to be — or, rather, to become — a man means to be "religious."

Thus, philosophical reflection was confronted from the very beginning with a world of meaning which was, genetically and structurally, "religious" — and this is true generally, not only with regard to the "primitives," the Orientals, and the pre-Socratics. The dialectics of the sacred preceded and served as a model for all the dialectical movements subsequently discovered by the mind. The experience of the sacred, by disclosing being, meaning, and truth in an unknown, chaotic, and fearful world, prepared the way for systematic thought.

This may be enough to arouse the interest of philosophers in the work of historians and phenomenologists of religion, but there are other aspects of the religious experience which are no less interesting. The hierophanies — i.e., the manifestations of the sacred expressed in symbols, myths, supernatural beings, etc. — are grasped as structures, and constitute a prereflective language that requires a special hermeneutics. For more than a quarter of a century, historians and phenomenologists of religion have attempted to elaborate such a hermeneutics. This type of work does not resemble the antiquarian's endeavor, although it may utilize documents from cultures long since vanished and from spacially remote peoples. By means of a competent hermeneutics, history of religions ceases to be a museum of fossils, ruins, and obsolete *mirabilia* and becomes what it should have been from the beginning for any investigator: a series of "messages" waiting to be deciphered and understood.

The interest in such "messages" is not exclusively historical. They do not only "speak" to us about a long-dead past, but they disclose fundamental existential situations that are directly relevant to modern man. As I have pointed out in one of the chapters of this book, a considerable enrichment of consciousness results from the hermeneutical effort of deciphering the meaning of myths, symbols, and other traditional religious structures; in a certain sense, one can even speak of the inner transformation of the researcher and, hopefully, of the sympathetic reader. What is called the phenomenology and history of religions can be considered among the very few humanistic disciplines that are at the same time propaedeutic and spiritual techniques.

In a progressively secularized society, these types of studies will probably become even more relevant. Seen from a Judeo-Christian perspective, the secularization may be at least partially misinterpreted. It may be considered, for example, a continuation of the process of demythologizing, which is in itself a late prolongation of the prophets' struggle to empty the Cosmos and cosmic life of the sacred. But this is not the whole truth. In the most radically secularized societies and among the most iconoclastic contemporary youth movements (such as the "hippie" movement, for example), there are a number of apparently nonreligious phenomena in which one can decipher new and original recoveries of the sacred — although, admittedly, they are not recognizable as such from a Judeo-Christian perspective. I do not refer to the "religiosity" evident in so many social and political movements, such as civil rights, antiwar manifestations, etc. More significant are the religious structures and (as yet unconscious) religious *values* of modern art, of some important and immensely popular films, of a number of phenomena related to youth culture, especially the recovery of the religious dimensions of an authentic and meaningful "human existence in the Cosmos" (the rediscovery of Nature, the uninhibited sexual mores, the emphasis on "living in the present" and freedom from social "projects" and ambitions, etc.).

Most of these recoveries of the sacred point to a type of cosmic religion that disappeared after the triumph of Christianity, surviving only among the European peasants. Rediscovering the sacredness of Life and Nature does not necessarily imply a return to "paganism" or "idolatry." Although in the eyes of a Puritan the cosmic religion of the southeastern European peasants could have been considered a form of paganism, it was still a "cosmic, Christian liturgy." A similar process occurred in medieval Judaism. Thanks mainly to the tradition embodied in the Kabbalah, a "cosmic sacrality," which seemed to have been irretrievably lost after the rabbinical reform has been successfully recovered.

These remarks are not intended as an argument for the crypto-Christianity of some of the more recent expressions of youth culture. What I am saying is that in a period of religious crisis one cannot anticipate the *creative*, and, as such, probably unrecognizable, answers given to such a crisis. Moreover, one cannot predict the expressions of a potentially new experience of the sacred. The "total man" is never completely desacralized, and one even doubts that this is possible. Secularization is highly successful at the level of conscious life: old theological ideas, dogmas, beliefs, rituals, institutions, etc. are progressively expunged of meaning. But no living, normal man can be reduced to his conscious, rational activity, for modern man still dreams, falls in love, listens to music, goes to the theater, views films, reads books — in short, lives not only in a historical and natural world but also in an existential, private world and in an imaginary Universe. It is primarily the historian and phenomenologist of religions who is capable of recognizing and deciphering the "religious" structures and meanings of these private worlds or imaginary Universes.

It is pointless to restate here the arguments developed in the present book. In sum, the interest in analyzing archaic and exotic religions is not restricted to their historical significance. The philosopher, the theologian, and the literary critic may equally profit by discovering these forgotten, misrepresented, or neglected worlds of meaning. For this reason I have tried to present and discuss documents drawn from less familiar religions. Important progress has recently been made in the understanding of the three monotheistic religions, of Buddhism, and even of the religious philosophies of India. Many well-known works on these themes are easily available to the interested reader.

The essays brought together in this book have not been written primarily for the "specialist," but rather for the *honnête homme* and the intelligent reader. Thus, I did not hesitate to quote examples that are known, or at least accessible, to the historian of religions, the anthropologist, and the orientalist, but which are probably ignored by the nonspecialist reader. I hope, however, that what may be called a "new humanism" will be engendered by a confrontation of modern Western man with unknown or less familiar worlds of meaning. These essays, as well as my previous publications, are intended to stress the cultural function which the history of religions could play in a desacralized society and also to develop a systematic hermeneutics of the sacred and its historical manifestations.

Most of the essays in this book have already appeared in different publications, but I have corrected and enlarged them. I am happy to thank three of my former students, Mr. Harry Partin, who translated a first draft of chapter 3 from the French manuscript, Mr. Alfred Hiltebeitel, who corrected and stylistically improved chapters 5, 7, and 8, and Norman Girardot, who prepared the index.

MIRCEA ELIADE

Contents

1

A New Humanism

Despite the manuals, periodicals, and bibliographies today available to scholars, it is progressively more difficult to keep up with the advances being made in all areas of the history of religions.[1] Hence it is progressively more difficult to become a historian of religions. A scholar regretfully finds himself becoming a specialist in *one* religion or even in a particular period or a single aspect of that religion.

This situation has induced us to bring out a new periodical. Our purpose is not simply to make one more review available to scholars (though the lack of a periodical of this nature in the United States would be reason enough for our venture) but more especially to provide an aid to orientation in a field that is constantly widening and to stimulate exchanges of views among specialists who, as a rule, do not follow the progress made in other disciplines. Such an orientation and exchange of views will, we hope, be made possible by summaries of the most recent advances achieved concerning certain key problems in the history of religions, by methodological discussions, and by attempts to improve the hermeneutics of religious data.

This chapter is a revised and expanded version of an article originally entitled "History of Religions and a New Humanism," which was first published in *History of Religions*, 1 (1961): 1–8. (© 1961 by The University of Chicago.)
   1. Since *Religionswissenschaft* is not easily translatable into English, we are obliged to use "history of religions" in the broadest sense of the term, including not only history properly speaking but also the comparative study of religions and religious morphology and phenomenology.

Hermeneutics is of preponderant interest to us because, inevitably, it is the least-developed aspect of our discipline. Preoccupied, and indeed often completely taken up, by their admittedly urgent and indispensable work of collecting, publishing, and analyzing religious data, scholars have sometimes neglected to study their meaning. Now, these data represent the expression of various religious experiences; in the last analysis they represent positions and situations assumed by men in the course of history. Like it or not, the scholar has not finished his work when he has reconstructed the history of a religious form or brought out its sociological, economic, or political contexts. In addition, he must understand its meaning — that is, identify and elucidate the situations and positions that have induced or made possible its appearance or its triumph at a particular historical moment.

It is solely insofar as it will perform this task — particularly by making the meanings of religious documents intelligible to the mind of modern man — that the science of religions will fulfill its true cultural function. For whatever its role has been in the past, the comparative study of religions is destined to assume a cultural role of the first importance in the near future. As we have said on several occasions, our historical moment forces us into confrontations that could not even have been imagined fifty years ago. On the one hand, the peoples of Asia have recently reentered history; on the other, the so-called primitive peoples are preparing to make their appearance on the horizon of greater history (that is, they are seeking to become *active subjects* of history instead of its *passive objects,* as they have been hitherto). But if the peoples of the West are no longer the only ones to "make" history, their spiritual and cultural values will no longer enjoy the privileged place, to say nothing of the unquestioned authority, that they enjoyed some generations ago. These values are now being analyzed, compared, and judged by non-Westerners. On their side, Westerners are being increasingly led to study, reflect on, and understand the spiritualities of Asia and the archaic world. These discoveries and contacts must be extended through dialogues. But to be genuine and fruitful, a dialogue cannot be limited to empirical and utilitarian language. A true dialogue must deal with the central values in the cultures of the participants. Now, to understand these values rightly, it is necessary to know their religious sources. For, as we know, non-European cultures, both oriental and primitive, are still nourished by a rich religious soil.

This is why we believe that the history of religions is destined to play an important role in contemporary cultural life. This is not only because an understanding of exotic and archaic religions will significantly assist in a cultural dialogue with the representatives of such religions. It is more especially because, by attempting to understand the existential situations expressed by the documents he is studying, the historian of religions will inevitably attain to a deeper knowledge of man. It is on the basis of such a knowledge that a new humanism, on a world-wide scale, could develop. We may even ask if the history of religions cannot make a contribution of prime importance to its formation. For, on the one hand, the historical and comparative study of religions embraces all the cultural forms so far known, both the ethnological cultures and those that have played a major role in history; on the other hand, by studying the religious expressions of a culture, the scholar approaches it from within, and not merely in its sociological, economic, and political contexts. In the last analysis, the historian of religions is destined to elucidate a large number of situations unfamiliar to the man of the West. It is through an understanding of such unfamiliar, "exotic" situations that cultural provincialism is transcended.

But more is involved than a widening of the horizon, a quantitative, static increase in our "knowledge of man." It is the meeting with the "others" — with human beings belonging to various types of archaic and exotic societies — that is culturally stimulating and fertile. It is the personal experience of this unique hermeneutics that is creative (see below, p. 62). It is not beyond possibility that the discoveries and "encounters" made possible by the progress of the history of religions may have repercussions comparable to those of certain famous discoveries in the past of Western culture. We have in mind the discovery of the exotic and primitive arts, which revivified modern Western aesthetics. We have in mind especially the discovery of the unconscious by psychoanalysis, which opened new perspectives for our understanding of man. In both cases alike, there was a meeting with the "foreign," the unknown, with what cannot be reduced to familiar categories — in short, with the "wholly other." [2] Certainly this contact with the

2. Rudolf Otto described the sacred as the *ganz andere*. Although occurring

"other" is not without its dangers. The initial resistance to the modern artistic movements and to depth psychology is a case in point. For, after all, recognizing the existence of "others" inevitably brings with it the relativization, or even the destruction, of the official cultural world. The Western aesthetic universe has not been the same since the acceptance and assimilation of the artistic creations of cubism and surrealism. The "world" in which preanalytic man lived became obsolete after Freud's discoveries. But these "destructions" opened new vistas to Western creative genius.

All this cannot but suggest the limitless possibilities open to historians of religions, the "encounters" to which they expose themselves in order to understand human situations different from those with which they are familiar. It is hard to believe that experiences as "foreign" as those of a paleolithic hunter or a Buddhist monk will have no effect whatever on modern cultural life. Obviously such "encounters" will become culturally creative only when the scholar has passed beyond the stage of pure erudition — in other words, when, after having collected, described, and classified his documents, he has also made an effort to understand them *on their own plane of reference*. This implies no depreciation of erudition. But, after all, erudition by itself cannot accomplish the whole task of the historian of religions, just as a knowledge of thirteenth-century Italian and of the Florentine culture of the period, the study of medieval theology and philosophy, and familiarity with Dante's life do not suffice to reveal the artistic value of the *Divina Commedia*. We almost hesitate to repeat such truisms. Yet it can never be said often enough that the task of the historian of religions is not completed when he has succeeded in reconstructing the chronological sequence of a religion or has brought out its social, economic, and political contexts. Like every human phenomenon, the religious phenomenon is extremely complex. To grasp all its valences and all its meanings, it must be approached from several points of view.

It is regrettable that historians of religions have not yet sufficiently profited from the experience of their colleagues who are historians of literature or literary critics. The progress made in these disciplines would have enabled them to avoid unfortunate

on the nonreligious plane, the encounters with the "wholly other" brought about by depth psychology and modern artistic experiments can be reckoned as parareligious experiences.

misunderstandings. It is agreed today that there is continuity and solidarity between the work of the literary historian, the literary sociologist, the critic, and the aesthetician. To give but one example: If the work of Balzac can hardly be understood without a knowledge of nineteenth-century French society and history (in the broadest meaning of the term — political, economic, social, cultural, and religious history), it is nonetheless true that the *Comédie humaine* cannot be reduced to a historical document pure and simple. It is the work of an exceptional individual, and it is for this reason that the life and psychology of Balzac must be known. But the working-out of this gigantic *œuvre* must be studied in itself, as the artist's struggle with his raw material, as the creative spirit's victory over the immediate data of experience. A whole labor of exegesis remains to be performed after the his-torian of literature has finished his task, and here lies the role of the literary critic. It is he who deals with the work as an au-tonomous universe with its own laws and structure. And at least in the case of poets, even the literary critic's work does not exhaust the subject, for it is the task of the specialist in stylistics and the aesthetician to discover and explain the values of poetic universes. But can a literary work be said to be finally "explicated" when the aesthetician has said his last word? There is always a secret mes-sage in the work of great writers, and it is on the plane of philos-ophy that it is most likely to be grasped.

We hope we may be forgiven for these few remarks on the her-meneutics of literary works. They are certainly incomplete,[3] but they will, we believe, suffice to show that those who study literary works are thoroughly aware of their complexity and, with few exceptions, do not attempt to "explicate" them by reducing them to one or another origin — infantile trauma, glandular accident, or economic, social, or political situations, etc. It serves a purpose to have cited the unique situation of artistic creations. For, from a certain point of view, the aesthetic universe can be compared

3. It is also necessary to consider, for example, the vicissitudes of the work in the public consciousness, or even "unconscious." The circulation, assimila-tion, and evaluation of a literary work present problems that no discipline can solve *by itself*. It is the sociologist, but also the historian, the moralist, and the psychologist, who can help us to understand the success of *Werther* and the failure of *The Way of All Flesh*, the fact that such a difficult work as *Ulysses* became popular in less than twenty years, while *Senilità* and *Co-scienza di Zeno* are still unknown, and so on.

with the universe of religion. In both cases, we have to do at once with *individual experiences* (aesthetic experience of the poet and his reader, on the one hand, religious experience, on the other) and with *transpersonal realities* (a work of art in a museum, a poem, a symphony; a Divine Figure, a rite, a myth, etc.). Certainly it is possible to go on forever discussing what meaning one may be inclined to attribute to these artistic and religious *realities*. But one thing at least seems obvious: Works of art, like "religious data," have a mode of being that is peculiar to themselves; they *exist on their own plane of reference*, in their particular universe. The fact that this universe is not the physical universe of immediate experience does not imply their nonreality. This problem has been sufficiently discussed to permit us to dispense with reopening it here. We will add but one observation: A work of art reveals its meaning only insofar as it is regarded as an autonomous creation; that is, insofar as we accept its mode of being — *that of an artistic creation* — and do not reduce it to one of its constituent elements (in the case of a poem, sound, vocabulary, linguistic structure, etc.) or to one of its subsequent uses (a poem which carries a political message or which can serve as a document for sociology, ethnography, etc.).

In the same way, it seems to us that a religious datum reveals its deeper meaning when it is considered on its plane of reference, and not when it is reduced to one of its secondary aspects or its contexts. To give but one example: Few religious phenomena are more directly and more obviously connected with sociopolitical circumstances than the modern messianic and millenarian movements among colonial peoples (cargo-cults, etc.). Yet identifying and analyzing the conditions that prepared and made possible such messianic movements form only a part of the work of the historian of religions. For these movements are equally creations of the human spirit, in the sense that they have become what they are — *religious movements*, and not merely gestures of protest and revolt — through a creative act of the spirit. In short, a religious phenomenon such as primitive messianism must be studied just as the *Divina Commedia* is studied, that is, by using all the possible tools of scholarship (and not, to return to what we said above in connection with Dante, merely his vocabulary or his syntax, or simply his theological and political ideas, etc.). For, if the his-

tory of religions is destined to further the rise of a new humanism, it is incumbent on the historian of religions to bring out the
autonomous value — the value as *spiritual creation* — of all these
primitive religious movements. To reduce them to sociopolitical
contexts is, in the last analysis, to admit that they are not sufficiently "elevated," sufficiently "noble," to be treated as creations
of human genius like the *Divina Commedia* or the *Fioretti* of St.
Francis.[4] We may expect that sometime in the near future the intelligentsia of the former colonial peoples will regard many social
scientists as camouflaged apologists of Western culture. Because
these scientists insist so persistently on the sociopolitical origin
and character of the "primitive" messianic movements, they may
be suspected of a Western superiority complex, namely, the conviction that such religious movements cannot rise to the same level
of "freedom from sociopolitical conjuncture" as, for instance, a
Gioachino da Fiore or St. Francis.

This does not mean, of course, that a religious phenomenon
can be understood outside of its "history," that is, outside of its
cultural and socioeconomic contexts. There is no such thing as
a "pure" religious datum, outside of history, for there is no such
thing as a human datum that is not at the same time a historical
datum. Every religious experience is expressed and transmitted in
a particular historical context. But admitting the historicity of religious experiences does not imply that they are reducible to nonreligious forms of behavior. Stating that a religious datum is always
a historical datum does not mean that it is reducible to a nonreligious history — for example, to an economic, social, or political
history. We must never lose sight of one of the fundamental
principles of modern science: *the scale creates the phenomenon.*
As we have recalled elsewhere,[5] Henri Poincaré asked, not without irony, "Would a naturalist who had never studied the elephant
except through the microscope consider that he had an adequate
knowledge of the creature?" The microscope reveals the structure
and mechanism of cells, which structure and mechanism are ex-

4. We may even wonder if, at bottom, the various "reductionisms" do not
betray the superiority complex of Western scholars. They have no doubt that
only science — *an exclusively Western creation* — will resist this process of
demystifying spirituality and culture.
5. *Traité d'histoire des religions* (Paris, 1949, p. ii (English translation:
Patterns in Comparative Religion [New York, 1958], p. xi).

actly the same in all multicellular organisms. The elephant is certainly a multicellular organism, but is that all that it is? On the microscopic scale, we might hesitate to answer. On the scale of human vision, which at least has the advantage of presenting the elephant as a zoölogical phenomenon, there can be no doubt about the reply.

We have no intention of developing a methodology of the science of religions here. The problem is far too complex to be treated in a few pages.[6] But we think it useful to repeat that the *homo religiosus* represents the "total man"; hence, the science of religions must become a total discipline in the sense that it must use, integrate, and articulate the results obtained by the various methods of approaching a religious phenomenon. It is not enough to grasp the meaning of a religious phenomenon in a certain culture and, consequently, to decipher its "message" (for every religious phenomenon constitutes a "cipher"); it is also necessary to study and understand its "history," that is, to unravel its changes and modifications and, ultimately, to elucidate its contribution to the entire culture. In the past few years a number of scholars have felt the need to transcend the alternative *religious phenomenology* or *history of religions*[7] and to reach a broader perspective in which these two intellectual operations can be applied together. It is toward the integral conception of the science of religions that the efforts of scholars seem to be orienting themselves today. To be sure, these two approaches correspond in some degree to different philosophical temperaments. And it would be naïve to suppose that the tension between those who try to understand the

6. Certain preliminary suggestions will be found in some of our preceding publications. See especially *Patterns in Comparative Religion*, pp. 1–33; *Images et symboles* (Paris, 1951), pp. 33–52, 211–35 (English translation: *Images and Symbols* [New York, 1961], pp. 27–41, 16–78); *Mythes, rêves et mystères* (Paris, 1957), pp. 7–15, 133–64 (English translation: *Myths, Dreams and Mysteries* [New York, 1961], pp. 13–20, 99–122); "Methodological Remarks on the Study of Religious Symbolism," in *The History of Religion: Essays in Methodology*, ed. M. Eliade and Joseph M. Kitagawa (Chicago, 1959), pp. 86–107.

7. These terms are used here in their broadest sense, including under "phenomenology" those scholars who pursue the study of structures and meanings, and under "history" those who seek to understand religious phenomena in their historical context. Actually, the divergences between these two approaches are more marked. In addition there are a certain number of differences — sometimes quite perceptible — within the groups that, for the sake of simplification, we have termed "phenomenologists" and "historians."

essence and the *structures* and those whose only concern is the *history* of religious phenomena will one day be completely done away with. But such a tension is creative. It is by virtue of it that the science of religions will escape dogmatism and stagnation.

The results of these two intellectual operations are equally valuable for a more adequate knowledge of *homo religiosus*. For, if the "phenomenologists" are interested in the meanings of religious data, the "historians," on their side, attempt to show how these meanings have been experienced and lived in the various cultures and historical moments, how they have been transformed, enriched, or impoverished in the course of history. But if we are to avoid sinking back into an obsolete "reductionism," this history of religious meanings must always be regarded as forming part of the history of the human spirit.[8]

More than any other humanistic discipline (i.e., psychology, anthropology, sociology, etc.), history of religions can open the way to a philosophical anthropology. For the sacred is a universal dimension and, as we shall see later (p. 68), the beginnings of culture are rooted in religious experiences and beliefs. Furthermore, even after they are radically secularized, such cultural creations as social institutions, technology, moral ideas, arts, etc., cannot be correctly understood if one does not know their original religious matrix, which they tacitly criticized, modified, or rejected in becoming what they are now: secular cultural values. Thus, the historian of religions is in a position to grasp the permanence of what has been called man's specific existential situation of "being in the world," for the experience of the sacred is its correlate. In fact, man's becoming aware of his own mode of being and assuming his *presence* in the world together constitute a "religious" experience.

8. In one of his last works, the great historian of religions Raffaele Pettazzoni reached similar conclusions. "Phenomenology and history complement each other. Phenomenology cannot do without ethnology, philology and other historical disciplines. Phenomenology, on the other hand, gives the historical disciplines that sense of the religious which they are not able to capture. So conceived, religious phenomenology is the religious understanding (*Verständniss*) of history; it is history in its religious dimension. Religious phenomenology and history are not two sciences but are two complementary aspects of the integral science of religion, and the science of religion as such has a well-defined character given to it by its unique and proper subject matter" ("The Supreme Being: Phenomenological Structure and Historical Development," in *History of Religion*, ed. Eliade and Kitagawa, p. 66).

Ultimately, the historian of religions is forced by his hermeneutical endeavor to "relive" a multitude of existential situations
and to unravel a number of presystematic ontologies. A historian
of religions cannot say, for example, that he has understood the
Australian religions if he has not understood the Australians' *mode
of being in the world*. And as we shall see later on, even at that
stage of culture we find the notion of a plurality of modes of being
as well as the awareness that the singularity of the human condition is the result of a primordial "sacred history" (see below,
p. 80).

Now, these points cannot be successfully realized if the investigator does not understand that every religion has a "*center*," in
other words, a central conception which informs the entire corpus of myths, rituals, and beliefs. This is evident in such religions
as Judaism, Christianity, and Islam, notwithstanding the fact that
the modifications introduced in the course of time tend, in some
cases, to obscure the "original form." For example, the central role
of Jesus as Christ is transparent no matter how complex and elaborated some contemporary theological and ecclesiastical expressions may seem in comparison to "original Christianity." But the
"center" of a religion is not always so evident. Some investigators
do not even suspect that there is a "center"; rather, they try to
articulate the religious values of a certain type of society in com-
pliance with a fashionable theory. Thus, for almost three-quarters
of a century the "primitive" religions were understood as illustrating one of the dominant theories of the day: animism, ancestor
cult, *mana*, totemism, and so on. Australia, for example, was considered almost the territory par excellence of totemism, and because of the supposed archaism of the Australians, totemism was
even proclaimed the most ancient form of religious life.

Whatever one may think of the various religious ideas and beliefs brought together under the name of "totemism," one thing
seems evident today, namely, that totemism does *not* constitute
the *center* of Australian religious life. On the contrary, the totemic
expressions, as well as other religious ideas and beliefs, receive
their full meaning and fall into a pattern only when the *center*
of religious life is sought where the Australians have untiringly
declared it to be: in the concept of the "Dreaming Time," that
fabulous primordial epoch when the world was shaped and man

became what he is today. We have discussed this problem at length elsewhere and it is unnecessary to take it up again here.[9]

This is only one example among many others, and perhaps not even the most illuminating, for the Australian religions do not present the complexity and the variety of forms that confront the student of Indian, Egyptian, or Greek religions. But it is easy to understand that the failure to search for the real center of a religion may explain the inadequate contributions made by the historians of religions to philosophical anthropology. As we shall see later (chap. 4), such a shortcoming reflects a deeper and more complex crisis. But on the other hand, there are also signs that this crisis is in the process of being resolved. We shall examine some aspects of the crisis and the subsequent renewal of our discipline in the following three chapters of this book.

9. "Australian Religion: An Introduction," *History of Religions*, 6 (1966); 108–34, 208–37.

2

The History of Religions in Retrospect: 1912 and After

The year 1912 was a significant date in the history of the scientific study of religion. Emile Durkheim published his *Formes élémentaires de la vie religieuse* and Wilhelm Schmidt finished the first volume of his monumental work *Ursprung der Gottesidee*, which was to be completed only after forty years, with vols. XI and XII appearing posthumously in 1954 and 1955. Also in 1912, Raffaele Pettazzoni brought out his first important monograph, *La religione primitiva in Sardegna*, and C. G. Jung published his *Wandlungen und Symbole der Libido*. Sigmund Freud was correcting the proofs of *Totem und Tabu*, to be issued in book form the following year.

Four different approaches to the study of religion — none really new — were illustrated by these works: the sociological, the ethnological, the psychological, and the historical. The only potentially new approach, that of the phenomenology of religion, was not to

In 1962 I was invited by the editors of *The Journal of Bible and Religion* to present, in no more than 7,000 words, a survey of the history of religions over the last fifty years. As other contributors were entrusted with discussing the progress of Old and New Testament scholarship, I did not include these areas in my essay. In preparing the present volume, I have revised and completed the text, but I have respected the original plan, notwithstanding the fact that some trends in biblical studies have been directly related to the discoveries of historians of religions working in other fields.

The original article was entitled "The History of Religions in Retrospect: 1912–1962," and was published in *The Journal of Bible and Religion*, 31 (1963): 98–107. (Copyright © 1963 by the American Academy of Religion, used with permission.)

be attempted for another ten years. But Freud, Jung, Durkheim, and Wilhelm Schmidt did apply new methods and claimed to have obtained more enduring results than their predecessors. Significantly enough, with the exception of Pettazzoni, none of these men was a historian of religions. Nevertheless, their theories were to play a considerable role in the cultural life of the following decades. Though very few historians of religion have been exclusively dependent on them, Freud, Jung, Durkheim, and Schmidt, and especially the first two, have contributed highly to the *Zeitgeist* of the last generations, and their interpretations of religion still enjoy a certain prestige among nonspecialists.

In the course of elaborating their hypotheses, all these authors were reacting, positively or negatively, to their immediate predecessors or contemporaries. Around 1910–12, the German astral-mythological and pan-Babylonian schools were declining. From a rather abundant production,[1] only P. Ehrenreich's *Die allgemeine Mythologie und ihre ethnologischen Grundlagen* (1910) and A. Jeremias' *Handbuch der altorientalischen Geisteskultur* (1913; 2d ed., 1929) retained a certain value for the ensuing generations of scholars. The most important contributions to the history of religions appearing in Germany between 1900 and 1912 depended, directly or indirectly, on E. B. Tylor's theory of animism.[2] But, as against the situation for the previous thirty years, this theory was no longer universally accepted. In 1900, R. R. Marett published his "Preanimistic Religion," an article destined to become famous, in which he tried to prove that the first stage of religion was not a universal belief in souls, but an emotion of awe and wonder aroused by the encounter with an impersonal power (*mana*).[3] A large number of scholars accepted and elaborated this theory. *Mana* (or *orenda, wakan,* and the like) became almost

1. More than one hundred volumes and pamphlets were published in about fifteen years. On these schools, cf. Wilhelm Schmidt, *The Origin and Growth of Religion: Facts and Theories*, trans. H. J. Rose (New York, 1931), pp. 91–102.

2. One might recall A. Dietrich, *Mutter Erde* (Leipzig, 1905); L. von Schroeder, *Mysterium und Mimus im Rig Veda* (Leipzig, 1908); W. Bousset, *Das Wesen der Religion dargestellt an ihrer Geschichte* (Halle, 1903); and W. Wundt, *Mythus und Religion*, 3 vols. (Leipzig, 1905–9).

3. In *Folklore* (1900): 162–82; republished in *The Threshold of Religion* (London, 1909), pp. 1–32.

a cliché, and, in spite of criticism by competent ethnologists,[4] it is still believed in many scientific circles to represent the primordial stage of religion.

Another very popular preanimistic hypothesis was brought forward by J. G. Frazer in his famous *Golden Bough* (2d ed., 1900). The learned anthropologist assumed that in the history of the human race magic preceded religion. In the same work Frazer adopted W. Mannhardt's concept of corn spirits and developed a very rich morphology of the dying and reviving gods of vegetation. With all its shortcomings, due mostly to his disregard of cultural stratification,[5] i.e., of history, Frazer's *Golden Bough* became a classic and exercised a tremendous influence on a multitude of fields of scholarship. Equally important, though less popular, was his *Totemism and Exogamy* (4 vols., 1910),[6] without which it is difficult to imagine Freud writing *Totem und Tabu.*

Durkheim, Freud, and Jung adopted and reelaborated the preanimistic hypotheses (i.e., *mana* and the precedence of magic) and insisted on the importance of totemism, which signified for the first two of these authors the initial manifestations of the religious life. The only one who rejected all the widely acclaimed theories of his time — Tylor's animism as well as preanimism, totemism, and vegetation gods — was Wilhelm Schmidt, who refused to see in these religious forms the source of religion or the most primitive religious experience. As we shall elaborate later, Schmidt thought that the most archaic form of religious life was the belief in a

4. Cf. P. Radin, "Religion of the North American Indians," *Journal of American Folk-Lore*, 27 (1914): 335–73, especially pp. 344 ff.; Schmidt, *Origin and Growth of Religion*, pp. 160–65; M. Eliade, *Patterns in Comparative Religion*, trans. R. Sheed (New York, 1958), pp. 19 ff., 35–36.

5. For a criticism of Frazer's theories, cf. Robert H. Lowie, *Primitive Religion* (New York, 1924), pp. 137–47; Lowie, *The History of Ethnological Theory* (New York, 1937), pp. 101–4; Schmidt, *Origin and Growth of Religion*, pp. 123–24; Eliade, *Patterns in Comparative Religion*, pp. 362–65. Theodor H. Gaster has recently summarized the main points on which Frazer's views were criticized or modified; cf. his Foreword to *The New Golden Bough* (New York, 1959), pp. xvi–xx. See also the discussion between Edmund Leach and I. C. Jarvie, "Frazer and Malinowski," *Current Anthropology*, 7 (1966): 560–75.

6. Frazer published his first contribution in a little book, *Totemism* (Edinburgh, 1887), followed by two important articles, "The Origin of Totemism," *Fortnightly Review*, April–May, 1899, and "The Beginnings of Religion and Totemism among the Australian Aborigines," in *ibid.*, July–September, 1905.

High God. He believed that he could prove this historically with the help of a new discipline: historical ethnology.

Sociological Approaches

For Durkheim, religion was a projection of social experience. Studying the Australians, he noticed that the totem symbolizes sacredness and the clan at the same time. He concluded that sacredness (or "God") and the social group are one and the same thing. Durkheim's explanation of the nature and origin of religion was emphatically criticized by some outstanding ethnologists. Thus, A. A. Goldenweiser pointed out that the simplest tribes do not have clans and totems. Whence, then, do nontotemist peoples derive their religion? Furthermore, Durkheim detected the origin of religious sentiment in the collective enthusiasm typified by the atmosphere of the Australian ritual. But Goldenweiser remarked that if the assembly itself gives rise to the sentiment of religion, why is it that the secular dances of North American Indians are not transformed into religious occasions?[7] Wilhelm Schmidt criticized the fact that Durkheim limited his information to the Central Australians, especially the Arunta, and ignored the Southeastern Australians, who form the oldest stratum and do not have totemism.[8] No less serious objections were brought forth by Robert Lowie.[9]

Notwithstanding these criticisms, *Les formes élémentaires* continued to enjoy a certain prestige in France. This was due especially to the fact that Durkheim was the founder of the French sociological school and the editor of *Année Sociologique*. Though Durkheim identified religion with society, *Les formes élémentaires* does not, properly speaking, represent a contribution to the sociology of religion. Later on, however, some of the most brilliant colleagues and pupils of Durkheim published important works in this area. Special reference must be made to Marcel

7. A. A. Goldenweiser, "Religion and Society: A Critique of Emile Durkheim's Theory of the Origin and Nature of Religion," *Journal of Philosophy, Psychology and Scientific Method*, 14 (1917): 113–24; *Early Civilization* (New York, 1922), pp. 360 ff.; *History, Psychology and Culture* (New York, 1933), p. 373.
8. Schmidt, *The Origin and Growth of Religion*, pp. 115 ff.
9. Lowie, *Primitive Religion*, pp. 153 ff.; *The History of Ethnological Theory*, pp. 197 ff.

Granet's interpretation of ancient Chinese religion [10] and to L. Gernet's studies on Greek religious institutions.[11]

As for Lucien Lévy-Bruhl, his position within the French sociological school is more peculiar.[12] A philosopher by vocation and training, he became famous for his notion of the "primitive mentality." He claimed that the "primitive" is engaged in a sort of *participation mystique* with the surrounding world and for that reason is unable to think correctly. Lévy-Bruhl believed that an understanding of this type of prelogical mind helps the modern scholar to grasp the meaning and the function of symbols and myths, and ultimately of primitive and archaic religions. The hypothesis of a prelogical mentality met with great success. Though never accepted by ethnologists,[13] it was passionately discussed by psychologists and philosophers. C. G. Jung thought that he found in the *participation mystique* one of the proofs for the existence of a collective unconscious. But Lévy-Bruhl was a very honest scholar. In his last years he meditated anew on his hypothesis and finally rejected it. He died without having had the opportunity to present his new views on the problem. (His *Carnets* were published posthumously by M. Leenhardt in 1948.) Though based on an erroneous hypothesis, Lévy-Bruhl's early works are not without merit; they helped to arouse interest in the spiritual creations of archaic societies.

Less manifest but even more profound and widespread was the influence of Marcel Mauss, one of the most learned and modest scholars of his time. His articles on sacrifice, magic, and the gift

10. *La Religion des Chinois* (1922); *Danses et Légendes de la Chine ancienne*, 2 vols. (Paris, 1926); *La Civilisation chinoise* (1929); and *La Pensée chinoise* (1934).

11. Cf. L. Gernet and A. Boulanger, *Le Génie grec dans la Religion* (Paris, 1932).

12. Lévy-Bruhl presented his hypothesis of a "prelogical mentality" in *Les Fonctions mentales dans les sociétés inférieures* (Paris, 1910), and *La mentalité primitive* (Paris, 1922). For the historian of religion some of his subsequent works are no less significant; cf. especially, *L'âme primitive* (1927); *Le surnaturel et la nature dans la mentalité primitive* (1931); and *La mythologie primitive* (1935).

13. Cf. W. Schmidt, in *Anthropos*, 7 (1912): 268–69; O. Leroy, *La Raison primitive* (Paris, 1927), pp. 47 ff.; Raoul Allier, *Le non-civilisé et nous* (1927); R. Thurnwald, in *Deutsche Literaturzeitung* (1928), pp. 486–94; Goldenweiser, *Early Civilization*, pp. 380–89; and Lowie, *History of Ethnological Theory*, pp. 216–21. See also E. E. Evans-Pritchard, *Theories of Primitive Religion* (Oxford, 1965), pp. 78–99.

as an elementary form of exchange are worth mentioning.[14] Unfortunately, he did not finish his *opus magnum*, a treatise on ethnology considered as the science of *le fait social total*. Mauss's teaching and example influenced a great number of French historians of religions. We may cite Georges Dumézil and Maurice Leenhardt. The latter's *Do Kamo* represents one of the most vivid and stimulating contributions to the understanding of myth and ritual among the primitives.[15]

No less important are the works of the French Africanists, especially M. Griaulle and his disciples.[16] In a fascinating book, *Dieu d'Eau* (1948), Griaulle presented the esoteric mythological traditions of the Dogon. The book has had considerable consequences for the reappraisal of "primitive religions": it revealed an amazing capacity for systematic speculations, not the childish lucubrations expected from a "prelogical mentality"; it also revealed the inadequacy of our information concerning the *real* religious thinking of the "primitives." For Griaulle was not introduced to the esoteric doctrine until he had made repeated sojourns among the Dogon, and only then thanks to a series of fortunate circumstances. One is entitled to suspect, therefore, that most of the writings on "primitive religions" present and interpret almost exclusively the exterior, and the least interesting, aspects.

Other French ethnologists and sociologists made significant contributions to the understanding of the religious life of nonliterate societies. We may cite Alfred Métraux's studies in South American and Haitian religions, G. Balandier's monographs on African sociology, and especially Claude Lévi-Strauss' writings on totemism, the structure of myth, and the operations of the "savage mind" in general, which enjoy a wide and growing popularity. As a matter of fact, Lévi-Strauss is the only one to have recaptured the interest of the cultivated public in the "primitives" enjoyed by Lévi-Bruhl fifty years before.[17]

14. Most of these studies have been reprinted in a posthumous work, *Sociologie et Anthropologie* (Paris, 1950), with an important introduction by Cl. Lévi-Strauss.

15. Maurice Leenhardt, *Do Kamo. La personne et le mythe dans le monde melanésien* (Paris, 1947).

16. See, *inter alia*, M. Griaulle, *Dieu d'eau. Entretiens avec Ogotemmeli* (Paris, 1948); G. Dieterlen, *Essai sur la religion bambara*, (1951); cf. also E. Michael Mendelson, "Some Present Trends of Social Anthropology in France," *The British Journal of Sociology*, 9 (1958): 251–70.

17. Alfred Métraux, *Le Vaudou haïtien* (Paris, 1958), and *Religions et*

18   HISTORY OF RELIGIONS IN RETROSPECT

Parallel to Durkheim's influence, but limited at the beginning to Germany and reaching the United States, South America, and Italy only after World War II, was the impact of the sociology of religion *sensu stricto*, such as was exemplified by Max Weber and Ernst Troeltsch. In France, the sociology of religion in this proper sense has been a late comer. But since World War II this new discipline has been developing rapidly. One need only refer to Gabriel le Bras and the group of young researchers who publish the *Archives de Sociologie des Religions*.[18] In the United States, important contributions have been made by Talcott Parsons,[19] J. Milton Yinger,[20] and Joachim Wach. Wach published an *Einführung in die Religionssoziologie* in 1931, and his masterwork, *Sociology of Religion*, thirteen years later.[21] Wach's methodological position is especially relevant to our topic. He was mainly a historian of religions, or, more precisely, a student of *Religionswissenschaft*, of which, to him, the sociology of religion was one of four branches (with the history of religions, phenomenology of religion, and psychology of religion). All through his life Wach wrestled with the problem of hermeneutics, and his *Das Verstehen* in three volumes (1926–33) remains the standard work on the subject. Wach felt the necessity of taking the sociological conditioning of religious life and the social contexts of religious expressions into serious consideration. He rejected, however, the extremist view

magies indiennes d'Amérique du Sud (1967); G. Balandier, *Sociologie actuelle de l'Afrique noire* (1955); Claude Lévi-Strauss, *Totemisme aujourd'hui* (1962), *La Pensée sauvage* (1962), and *Le Cru et le cuit* (1964).

18. Cf. Gabriel le Bras, *Etudes de Sociologie religieuse*, 2 vols. (Paris, 1955–56); *Archives de Sociologie des Religions*, no. 1 (January–June, 1956), and no. 13 (January–June, 1962); see also *Sociologie des Religions. Tendances actuelles de la Recherche et Bibliographies* (Paris, UNESCO, 1956); *Current Sociology*, vol. 5, p. 1.

19. Talcott Parsons, "The Theoretical Development of the Sociology of Religion," *Journal of the History of Ideas* (1944): 176–90; *Essays in Sociological Theory Pure and Applied* (Glencoe, Ill., 1949).

20. J. Milton Yinger, "Present Status of the Sociology of Religion," *Journal of Religion*, 31 (1951): 194–210; *Religion, Society and the Individual: An Introduction to the Sociology of Religion* (New York, 1957).

21. On Joachim Wach, see Joseph M. Kitagawa, "Joachim Wach et la Sociologie de la Religion," *Archives de Sociologie des Religions*, no. 1 (January–June, 1956): 25–40; Henri Desroche, "Sociologie et théologie dans la typologie religieuse de Joachim Wach," *ibid.*, pp. 41–63; Kitagawa's Introduction ("Life and Thought of Joachim Wach") to the posthumous book of Wach, *The Comparative Study of Religions* (New York, 1958), pp. xiii–xlvii. Cf. also a bibliography of Wach in *Archives de Sociologie des Religions*, 1 (1956): 64–69.

that religious life is an epiphenomenon of social structure. With little success he strove to interest the sociologists of religion in *Religionswissenschaft*. The majority of these men, especially in the English-speaking world, are inclined to think that the sociological approach and its tools are sufficient for the clarification of religious structures and events. Up to a certain point, this attitude is understandable, for each branch of knowledge tries to cover as much ground as it can. Moreover, the tremendous growth of the social sciences in the last fifty years rather encourages the self-sufficient attitude of the sociologist of religion. Somehow, the sociology of religion seems to be more "scientific" and more "useful," at least in the context of Western culture, than other branches of *Religionswissenschaft*.

Be this as it may, the sociology of religion has brought, and continues to bring, important contributions to the general science of religion. Sociological data help the scholar to understand the living context of his documents and protect him against the temptations of abstract interpretations of religion. Indeed, there is no such thing as a "pure" religious fact. Such a fact is always *also* a historical, sociological, cultural, and psychological fact, to name only the most important contexts. If the historian of religions does not always insist on this multiplicity of meanings, it is mainly because he is supposed to concentrate on the religious signification of his documents. The confusion starts when *only one* aspect of religious life is accepted as primary and meaningful, and the other aspects or functions are regarded as secondary or even illusory. Such a reductionist method was applied by Durkheim and other sociologists of religion. An even more drastic reductionism was brought forward by Freud in his *Totem und Tabu*.

Depth Psychology and the History of Religions

For Freud, religion as well as human society and culture in general started with a primordial murder. Freud accepted Atkinson's view that the earliest communities consisted of "an adult male and a number of females and immature individuals, the males among the latter being driven off by the head of the group as they became old enough to evoke his jealousy." [22] The expelled sons

22. A. L. Kroeber, "Totem and Taboo: An Ethnological Psycho-analysis," *American Anthropologist*, 22 (1920): 48–55, quoted by W. Schmidt in *Origin and Growth of Religion*, p. 110.

finally killed their father, ate him, and appropriated the females. Freud writes: "That they should also eat their victim is a matter of course among cannibal savages. . . . The totemic banquet, perhaps the first feast mankind ever celebrated, was the repetition, the festival of remembrance, of this noteworthy criminal deed, with which so much began — the organization of society, moral restrictions, and religion." [23] As Wilhelm Schmidt points out, Freud "holds that God is nothing more or less than the sublimated physical Father of human beings; hence in the totemic sacrifice it is God Himself who is killed and sacrificed. This slaying of the father-god is mankind's ancient original sin. This blood-guilt is atoned for by the bloody death of Christ." [24]

Freud's interpretation of religion has been repeatedly criticized and entirely rejected by ethnologists, from W. H. Rivers and F. Boas to A. L. Kroeber, B. Malinowski, and W. Schmidt.[25] Summarizing the most important ethnological objections to the extravagant reconstructions brought forward in *Totem und Tabu*, Schmidt observes that (1) totemism is not to be found at the beginnings of religion; (2) it is not universal, nor have all peoples passed through it; (3) Frazer had already proved that of the many hundred totemic tribes, only *four* know a rite approximating the ceremonial killing and eating of the "totem-god" (a rite assumed by Freud to be an invariable feature of totemism); furthermore, this rite has nothing to do with the origin of sacrifice, since totemism does not occur at all in the oldest cultures; (4) "the pre-totemic peoples know nothing of cannibalism, and patricide among them would be a sheer impossibility, psychologically, sociologically and ethically"; and (5) "the form of pre-totemic family, and therefore of the earliest human family we can hope to know anything about through ethnology, is neither general promiscuity nor group-marriage, neither of which, according to the verdict of the leading ethnologists, ever existed at all." [26]

23. S. Freud, *Totem und Tabu*, p. 110, quoted by Kroeber, "Totem and Taboo," cf. Schmidt, *Origin and Growth of Religions*, p. 111.
24. Schmidt, *Origin and Growth of Religions*, p. 112.
25. See W. H. Rivers, "The Symbolism of Rebirth," *Folk-Lore*, 33 (1922): 14–23; F. Boas, "The Methods of Ethnology," *American Anthropologist*, n. s 12 (1920): 311 ff.; B. Malinowski, *Sex, Repression and Savage Society* (London, 1927).
26. Schmidt, *Origin and Growth of Religion*, pp. 112–15. E. Vollhard ha

Freud did not take these objections into consideration, but from time to time a psychoanalyst would try to refute Kroeber or Malinowski, and psychoanalysts with anthropological training (such as Geza Róheim) proposed new sets of ethnological arguments.[27] We need not go into this discussion. In order to judge adequately Freud's contribution to the understanding of religion, one must distinguish between his main discovery, i.e., that of the unconscious and of the method of psychoanalysis, and his theoretical views on the origin and structure of religious life. With the exception of psychoanalysts and some enthusiastic dilettantes, the theory presented in *Totem und Tabu* was not accepted by the scientific world. But Freud's discovery of the unconscious encouraged the study of symbols and myths, and has been partially responsible for the modern interest in the archaic and oriental religions and mythologies (see below, p. 50). The historian of religions is especially grateful to Freud for proving that images and symbols communicate their "messages" even if the conscious mind remains unaware of this fact. The historian is now free to conduct his hermeneutical work upon a symbol without having to ask himself how many individuals in a certain society and at a given historical moment understood all the meanings and implications of that symbol.

Freud's reductionism constitutes another stimulating challenge to the contemporary student of religion. It forces him to delve into the depths of the psyche and to take into consideration the psychological presuppositions and contexts of religious manifestations. One can even say that Freud's reductionism has forced the historian of religions to distinguish more sharply between what may be called a "spiritual embryology" and a "spiritual morphology." Freud's discovery of the unconscious made such a tremendous impact on the modern world that for some time the enthusiastic converts thought about spiritual values and cultural forms exclusively in embryological terms. But it became obvious that the embryonic state does not account for the mode of being of the adult; the embryo acquires significance only in so far as it is related to, and compared with, the adult. It is not the fetus which explains man,

---

roved that cannibalism is a rather late phenomenon; cf. *Kannibalismus* Stuttgart, 1939).

27. Cf. Benjamin Nelson, "Social Science, Utopian Mythos, and the Oedipus Complex," *Psychoanalysis and the Psychoanalytic Review*, 45 (1958): 120–26; Meyer Fortes, "Malinowski and Freud," *ibid.*, pp. 127–45.

for the specific mode of being of man in the world emerges just when he no longer leads a fetal existence.[28]

C. G. Jung's *Wandlungen und Symbole der Libido* announced his separation from Freud. He was impressed, as Freud was not, by the presence of transpersonal, universal forces in the depth of the psyche. It was mainly the striking similarities between the myths, symbols, and mythological figures of widely separated peoples and civilizations that forced Jung to postulate the existence of a collective unconscious. He noticed that the contents of this collective unconscious manifest themselves through what he called "archetypes." Jung proposed many definitions of the archetypes, one of the last being "patterns of behavior" or propensities that are part of human nature. For him, the most important archetype is that of the Self, i.e., the wholeness of man. He believed that in every civilization man is working — through what Jung called the process of individuation — toward the realization of the Self. In Western civilization the symbol of the Self is Christ, and the realization of the Self is "redemption." Contrary to Freud, who despised religion, Jung was convinced that religious experience has a meaning and a goal, and, accordingly, that it must not be "explained away" by reductionism.[29] He insisted on the ambivalence of the religious figures in the unconscious. (One will recall Rudolf Otto's similar stress on ambivalence in his description of numinous phenomena.) Moreover, Jung made a careful study of archaic and oriental religions, and his contributions stimulated the researches of many historians of religion.[30]

28. M. Eliade, *Myths, Dreams and Mysteries*, trans. Philip Mairet (New York, 1960), pp. 120 ff.
29. Jung's most important writings related to religion have been recently translated by R. F. C. Hall and published in vol. 11 of Jung's collected works: *Psychology and Religion: West and East*, Bollingen Series (New York, 1958). See also his *Psychology and Alchemy* (New York, 1953); *Archetypes and the Collective Unconscious* (1959); and *Aion: An Historical Inquiry into the Symbolism of the Self* (1959). On Jung's interpretation of religion, cf. Ira Progoff, *Jung's Psychology and its Social Meaning* (New York, 1953), R. Hostie, *Analytische Psychologie en Godsdienst* (Utrecht-Antwerpen, 1955), (German translation: *C. G. Jung und die Religion* [Munich, 1957]), and Victor White, *Soul and Psyche* (London, 1960).
30. One may cite Heinrich Zimmer, Karl Kerényi, Joseph Campbell, and Henry Corbin. Cf. also Ernst Neumann, *The Origins and History of Consciousness*, trans. R. F. C. Hull (New York, 1957); and *The Great Mother*, trans. Ralph Manheim (New York, 1955).

Rudolph Otto

Though not the work of a psychologist, Rudolf Otto's famous book *Das Heilige* (1917) might be mentioned in this context. With great psychological subtlety, Otto describes and analyzes the different modalities of the numinous experience. His terminology — *mysterium tremendum, majestas, mysterium fascinans,* etc. — has become part of our language. In *Das Heilige,* Otto insists almost exclusively on the nonrational character of religious experience. Because of the great popularity of this book there is a tendency to regard him as an "emotionalist" — a direct descendant of Schleiermacher. But Otto's works are more complex, and it would be better to think of him as a philosopher of religion working first-hand with documents of the history of religions and of mysticism.

He made a more enduring impact on the Western, especially German, cultivated public than on historians of religions proper or theologians. He did not touch on the problem of myth and mythical thinking, which provoked tremendous interest after World War II. Perhaps it is for this reason that his otherwise admirable analyses of the different "religious Universes" seem incomplete. But Otto is important also for other reasons: he illustrates in what sense history of religions could play a role in the renewal of the contemporary Western culture. He compared the "mediation" between rational and irrational carried out by De Wette in his theology with the efforts of Clement of Alexandria and Origenes to reconcile the pagan philosophy with the Christian revelation. Most probably, Otto tacitly claimed for himself a similar role, that of mediator between *revelatio generalis* and *revelatio specialis,* between Indo-Aryan and Semitic religious thought, between Eastern and Western types of mysticism.[31]

From *Ursprung der Gottesidee* to Social Anthropology

When it was completed in 1955, one year after the death of its author, Wilhelm Schmidt's *Ursprung der Gottesidee* numbered more than 11,000 pages! No wonder few historians of religions

31. The amazing popular success of *Das Heilige* (translated under the title *The Idea of the Holy* [1923]) overshadowed his other two important books: *Mysticism East and West* (English translation, 1932) and *The Kingdom of God and the Son of Man* (English translation, 1938).

read all of this enormous treatise. Despite its polemical excesses (chiefly in the first volume) and apologetic tendencies, *Ursprung der Gottesidee* is a great work. Whatever one may think of Schmidt's theories on the origin and growth of religion, one must admire his stupendous learning and industry. Wilhelm Schmidt was certainly one of the greatest linguists and ethnologists of this century.

Schmidt was strongly impressed by Andrew Lang's discovery of the "High Gods" among the oldest primitive cultures, and no less by the methodological inconsistencies of that brilliant Scottish scholar (see below, p. 45). Schmidt understood that such a decisive question as the origin of the idea of God cannot be answered without first using a solid historical method which would enable one to distinguish and clarify the historical stratifications in the so-called primitive cultures. Schmidt reacted emphatically against the ahistorical approaches of Tylor, Frazer, Durkheim, and the majority of anthropologists. He was one of the first to realize the importance of Graebner's historical ethnology and especially of the concept of *Kulturkreis*. The historical stratification allowed him to separate the archaic, even "primordial," traditions from subsequent developments and influences. In the case of Australia, for instance, Schmidt tried to prove that the belief in a High God is attested in the oldest strata, while totemism characterizes only the culturally younger tribes. For historical ethnology, the Southeastern Australian tribes, the Pygmies, some North Asiatic and North American tribes, and the Fuegians are considered to be the living remnants of the oldest civilization. Schmidt thought that starting from such living fossils, one could reconstruct the primordial religion. To him, the *Urreligion* consisted in the belief in an eternal, creator, omniscient, and beneficent High God, supposed to live in the sky. He concluded that in the beginning a sort of *Urmonotheismus* existed everywhere, but that the later development of human societies degraded and in many cases almost obliterated the original beliefs.

Robert H. Lowie, Paul Radin, and other ethnologists acknowledged the belief in the existence of supreme beings among the most archaic peoples.[32] What cannot be accepted in Schmidt's

<hr/>

32. Cf. Lowie, *Primitive Religion*, pp. vi, 122 ff.; Paul Radin, *Monotheism Among Primitive People* (New York, 1924); and A. W. Nieuwenhuis, *Der Mensch in de Werkelijkheid, zijne Kenleer in den heidenschen Godsdiens* (Leiden, 1920).

reconstruction is his exclusively rationalistic approach. He asserts that primitive man discovered the idea of God through a logical quest for a cause. He neglects the obvious fact that religion is a very complex phenomenon — that it is, first of all, an experience *sui generis*, incited by man's encounter with the sacred. Schmidt was inclined to think that all the irrational elements represent a "degeneration" of the genuine, primordial religion. The truth is that we do not have any means to investigate this "primordial religion." Our oldest documents are relatively recent. They take us no further than the paleolithic age; we ignore everything of what prelithic man thought during many hundreds of thousands of years. It is true that the belief in High Gods seems to characterize the oldest cultures, but we also find there other religious elements. As far as we can reconstruct the most remote past, it is safer to assume that religious life was from the very beginning rather complex, and that "elevated" ideas coexisted with "lower" forms of worship and belief.

Wilhelm Schmidt's conceptions were corrected by his collaborators and pupils.[33] Important contributions to the knowledge of archaic religions were made by Paul Schebesta, M. Gusinde, and M. Vanoverbergh.[34] Among the younger generation of the Vienna School, Joseph Haekel, Chr. v. Fürer-Haimendorf, Alex. Slawik, and Karl Jettmar must be mentioned.[35]

Many other ethnologists of various orientations have tried to re-

33. Cf. Wilhelm Koppers, *Primitive Man and his World Picture* (New York, 1952); Josef Haekel, "Prof. Wilhelm Schmidts Bedeutung für die Religionsgeschichte des vorkolumbischen Amerika," *Saeculum*, 7 (1956): 1–39, "Zum heutigen Forschungsstand der historischen Ethnologie," in *Die Wiener Schule der Völkerkunde Festschrift* (Vienna, 1956), pp. 17–90, and "Zur gegenwärtigen Forschungssituation der Wiener Schule der Ethnologie," in *Beiträge Oesterreichs zur Erforschung der Vergangenheit und Kulturgeschichte der Menschheit* (Vienna, 1959), pp. 127–47. See also Rudolf Rahmann's critical observations on Haekel's appraisal of the "Wiener Schule" in *Anthropos*, 54 (1959): 1002–6, and Haekel's rejoinder and Rahmann's reply, *ibid.*, 56 (1961): 274–76, 277–78. On Schmidt's *Urmonotheismus*, see the strictures of W. E. Mühlmann, "Das Problem des Urmonotheismus," *Theologische Literaturzeitung*, 78 (1953): coll. 705 ff.; and Paul Schebesta's rejoinder in *Anthropos*, 49 (1954): 689 ff. Cf. also R. Pettazzoni, "Das Ende des Urmonotheismus," *Numen*, 5 (1958): 161–63.

34. Cf. especially P. Schebesta, *Die Negrito Asiens*, vol. 2, second half: *Religion und Mythologie* (Mödling, 1957); M. Gusinde, *Die Feuerland Indianer*, 2 vols. (Mödling, 1931, 1937).

35. See essential bibliographies in Haekel, "Zur gegenwärtigen Forschungssituation," pp. 141–45.

constitute the beginnings and growth of religion. K. Th. Preuss postulated a preanimistic phase from which evolved both magic and the idea of High Gods.[36] According to R. Thurnwald, there was a general belief in the sacredness of animals ("theriomism") during the food-gatherers' period; totemism corresponded to the hunters' cultures; the personification of divinities (through animism, demonism, etc.) characterized the earliest agriculturalists; and the belief in High Gods was specific to the pastoral people.[37] Ad. E. Jensen correlated the notions of a celestial creative God and a Lord of Animals with the primitive hunting cultures, and the appearance of deities of the *dema*-type and their dramatic mythologies to the paleocultivators. The transformations of the *dema* in the gods of different polytheisms was supposed to have taken place in the higher cultures. We must add that Jensen's works are most valuable especially for their illuminating analyses of the mythical world of the early cultivators.[38]

There are also important books by German and Austrian ethnologists on the religious life of different archaic peoples, but the authors do not enter into the debates on the origin and growth of primitive religion. We may allude to some of the writings of L. Frobenius and H. Baumann on African religions and mythologies, W. E. Mühlmann's monograph on the Polynesian Arioi, and Werner Müller's ingenious works on the religions of North American aborigines. A. Friedrich merits special mention; his pioneering study of the early hunters' religions opened the way to a new line of research.[39]

36. K. Th. Preuss, "Der Ursprung der Religion und Kunst," *Globus*, 1904, 1905; *Der geistige Kultur der Naturvölker* (Leipzig, 1914); and *Glauben und Mystik im Schatten des Höchsten Wesens* (Leipzig, 1926).
37. R. Thurnwald, *Des Menschengeistes Erwachen, Wachsen und Irren* (Berlin, 1951).
38. Ad. E. Jensen, *Das religiöse Weltbild einer frühen Kultur* (Stuttgart, 1948); *Mythus und Kult bei Naturvölkern* (Wiesbaden, 1951), (English translation: *Myth and Cult among Primitive Peoples* [Chicago, 1963]; cf. the discussion in *Current Anthropology*, 6 (1965); 199–214). See also Kunz Dittmer, *Allgemeine Völkerkunde* (Braunschweig, 1954), pp. 73–120; Josef Haekel, in Leonard Adam and Hermann Trimborn, *Lehrbuch der Völkerkunde* (Stuttgart, 1958), pp. 40–72.
39. H. Baumann, *Schöpfung und Urzeit des Menschen im Mythos afrikanischer Völker* (Berlin, 1936); W. E. Mühlmann, *Arioi und Mamaia* (Wiesbaden, 1955); Werner Müller, *Die Religionen der Waldindianer Nordamerikas* (Berlin, 1956); Adolf Friedrich, "Die Forschung über das frühzeitliche Jägertum," *Paideuma*, 2 (1941).

Among English-speaking anthropologists interested in religion, we must name first of all Robert H. Lowie and Paul Radin, for each of them published a general treatise on primitive religion.[40] Lowie's book is perhaps the best work on the subject available today. It is written without dogmatism and discusses all the significant facets of archaic religions, taking into consideration psychological and social contexts as well as historical stratifications. Radin wrote in a more personal, almost polemical, spirit. He insists on the social-economic factors, and also on what he calls the neurotic-epileptoid constitution of shamans and religious formulators. From the imposing list of F. Boas' publications, we may refer to his latest monographs on the religion and mythology of the Kwakiutl. A. L. Kroeber, F. G. Speck, E. M. Loeb, and other American ethnologists have presented elaborate studies on the religious life of different tribes, but none is written from a comparative and history-of-religions perspective. Exceptions here are some of the writings of R. Redfield and C. Kluckhohn, and Ruth Benedict's *Patterns of Culture*.[41]

In England after the death of Frazer no anthropologist tried to cover all the provinces of primitive religion. B. Malinowski concentrated on the Trobrianders, and his functionalist approach to myth and ritual is grounded on facts observed in that area. A. R. Radcliffe-Brown made an ingenious contribution to the understanding of primitive belief in his *Taboo* (Frazer Lecture, 1939). E. E. Evans-Pritchard's monograph, *Witchcraft, Oracles and Magic among the Azande* (1937) and *Nuer Religion* (1956), as well as Raymond Firth's *The Work of the Gods in Tikopia* (1940), J. Middleton's *Lugbara Religion* (1960), and G. Lienhardt's *The Religion of the Dinka* (1961), illustrate the actual orientation of British social anthropologists to the problems of primitive religion. The era of Tylor, Frazer, and Marett seems to be ended; anthropology is no longer considered the key to such "great and final problems" as the origin and growth of religion.

40. R. H. Lowie, *Primitive Religion* (New York, 1924); Paul Radin, *Primitive Religion* (New York, 1937).
41. For a survey of religious-historical studies in the United States, see J. M. Kitagawa, "The History of Religions in America," in *The History of Religions: Essays in Methodology*, ed. M. Eliade and J. M. Kitagawa (Chicago, 1959), pp. 1–30. See also Clifford Geertz, "Religion as a Cultural System," in *Anthropological Approaches to the Study of Religion*, ed. Michael Banton (London, 1966).

This is also the conclusion of a recent book by E. E. Evans-Pritchard, *Theories of Primitive Religion* (1965).

Pettazzoni and the *allgemeine Religionswissenschaft*

At the beginning of this article reference is made to Raffaele Pettazzoni's monograph on the primitive religion of Sardinia — not so much for the value of the work as for the subsequent importance of its author. Pettazzoni was one of the very few historians of religions who took seriously the dimensions of his discipline. As a matter of fact, he attempted to master the entire field of *allgemeine Religionswissenschaft*.[42] He regarded himself as a historian, meaning that his approach and method were not those of the sociologist or the psychologist of religion. But he wanted to be a historian of *religions*, and not a specialist in a single field. This is an important distinction. Many excellent scholars likewise consider themselves "historians of religions" because they accept exclusively historical methods and presuppositions. They are in fact, however, experts in just one religion, and sometimes in only one period or one aspect of that religion. Of course, their works are of great value — indeed, indispensable for the building of an *allgemeine Religionswissenschaft*. One need only recall as examples the treatises of O. Kern and Walter Otto on Greek religion; of L. Massignon and H. Corbin on Islam; of H. Oldenberg, H. Zimmer, and H. von Glasenapp on the Indian religions; as well as the monumental *Barabudur* of Paul Mus and the equally fabulous *Tibetan Painted Scrolls* of Giuseppe Tucci or the twelve volumes of Erwin Goodenough's *Jewish Symbols in the Greco-Roman Period*. Through these works one is made to realize the consequence of this type of historical research. Nevertheless, the historian of religions, in the broad sense of the term, cannot limit himself to a single area. He is bound by the very structure of his discipline to study at least a few other religions so as to be able to compare them and thereby understand the modalities of religious behaviors, institutions, and ideas (myth, ritual, prayer, magic, initiation, High Gods, etc.).

Fortunately, some of the greatest specialists are at the same time competent in many other areas. Nathan Soederblom and G. F

42. A bibliography of the writings of R. Pettazzoni was published by Mario Gandini in *Studi e Materiali di Storia delle Religioni*, 31 (1961): 3–31.

Moore published significant contributions in their particular fields of study (Iranian religions, Judaism), but they also became popular as "generalists"; the Nestor of the historians of Greek religion, M. P. Nilsson, was also a student of folklore and primitive beliefs; the great Germanist, Jan de Vries, was an authority on Celtic religion as well as folklore and mythology; Franz Altheim moves from the history of Roman and Hellenistic religions to Iranian, Turkish, and Central Asiatic traditions; Georges Dumézil masters all the Indo-European religions and mythologies; W. F. Albright is a specialist in Israelite religion but published important contributions on other ancient Near Eastern religions; and Theodor H. Gaster is an expert on folklore and the ancient Near East. The list could be continued.

Of course, other scholars of Pettazzoni's generation aimed at the same goal of covering the entire domain of *allgemeine Religionsgeschichte*. One may mention, for instance, Carl Clemen, E. O. James, and G. van der Leeuw. But while Clemen, though extremely erudite and rigorous, generally did not go beyond philological exegesis and van der Leeuw was sometimes satisfied with an impressionistic approach, Pettazzoni aimed always at a historico-religious interpretation; i.e., he articulated the results of the different investigations within a general perspective. He did not hesitate to handle central, though immense, problems — the origin of monotheism, the Sky Gods, the Mysteries, confessions of sin, Zarathustra and Iranian religion, Greek religion, etc. His learning was vast and exact, and he wrote with clarity, poise, and elegance. Brought up under the pervasive influence of Croce's historicism, Pettazzoni viewed religion as a purely historical phenomenon.

He rightly insists on the historicity of every religious creation. "Greek civilization," he writes, "did not come out from nothing. There is not an *atemporal* 'grecité' that was manifested in historical time. Before the tribunal of history, every *phenomenon* is a *genomenon*." [43] In this connection, Pettazzoni stresses the necessity of understanding Greek religion historically, in order to deepen our own historical consciousness. One cannot but agree on the urgency of understanding historically any given religion. But the exclusive concentration on "origin" and development of

---

43. R. Pettazzoni, *La Religion dans la Grèce antique, des Origines à Alexandre* (Paris, 1953), pp. 18–19.

a religion form — *"every phenomenon is a genomenon"* — might reduce the *hermeneutical* inquiry to a purely *historiographical* work. This means ultimately that the history of Greek religion, for example, would become one of the numberless branches of Greek scholarship — on the same level and close to Greek history or literature, numismatics, epigraphy, or archaeology. And because the same thing would happen in all areas of research, the history of religions would disappear as an autonomous discipline. Fortunately, Pettazzoni was fully aware of such a risk and at the end of his career he strongly emphasized the complementarity of "phenomenology" and "history" (see above, p. 9, n. 8). Moreover, as in the case of Freud or Frazer, Pettazzoni's personal example is more important than his theories. Thanks mainly to him, the discipline of history of religions is understood today in Italy in a more comprehensive way than it is in many other European countries. His younger colleagues and disciples have succeeded in maintaining, at least in part, what may be called the "Pettazzoni tradition," namely, an interest in the central problems of the history of religions and an effort to make this discipline meaningful and actual for modern culture.[44] With Pettazzoni died the last of the "encyclopedists," fashioners of a splendid tradition that had been initiated by Tylor and A. Lang and continued by Frazer, Soederblom, Clemen, Mauss, Coomaraswamy, and van der Leeuw.

Myth and Ritual School

A highly spirited methodological debate developed over the "Myth and Ritual School" or "patternism." The British contributors to the two volumes edited by S. H. Hooke, *Myth and Ritual* (1933) and *The Labyrinth* (1935), as well as the Scandinavian scholars S. Mowinckel, I. Engnell, and G. Widengren, insisted rather emphatically on the common elements in the cultures and religions of the ancient Near East. Hooke, for instance, pointed out that

44. See, among Italian scholars, Uberto Pestalozza, *Religione mediterranea. Vecchi e nuovi studi* (Milan, 1951) and *Nuovi saggi di religione mediterranea* (Firenze, 1964); Momolina Marconi, *Riflessi mediterranei nella più antica religione laziale* (Messina-Milan, 1939); Angelo Brelich, *Gli Eroi greci. Un problema storico-religioso* (Rome, 1958); E. de Martino, *Morte e pianto rituale nel mondo antico* (Turin, 1958), and *La Terra del rimorso* (Milan, 1961); V. Lanternari, *La Grande Festa* (Milan, 1951); Alessandro Bausani, *La Persia religiosa* (Milan, 1959); Ugo Bianchi, *Il Dualismo religioso* (Rome, 1958).

the king, representing the god, was the center of the cultus, and as such was responsible for the crops and the prosperity of the cities. In his six-volume series *King and Saviour* (1945–55), G. Widengren went even further: the king was responsible for the very well-being of the Cosmos. This conception, Widengren estimated, later gave rise to Iranian savior-ideology and Jewish messianism. But the Swedish scholar's publications are not limited to the problems of "patternism." Widengren is also the author of a phenomenology of religion, a history of Iranian religions, and a great number of monographs on different aspects of religious life.[45]

"Patternism" has been attacked from many sides, especially by H. Frankfort.[46] This eminent scholar has maintained that differences are more important than similarities. He draws attention, for example, to the fact that the pharaoh is considered a god or becomes a god, while in Mesopotamia the king is only the representative of a god. But, of course, differences and similarities are equally important whenever we have to do with *historically related cultures*. The fact that Portuguese is different from French and Romanian does not prevent philologists from considering all three Romance languages; genetically, they all descend from a common source, Latin. The passionate discussion which took place around the "Myth and Ritual School" reveals a somewhat confused methodology. The reference here is not to the wild exaggerations of some Scandinavian authors, nor to their philological imprudences and historical distortions. What is at stake is the legitimacy of comparing historically related and structurally analogous religious phenomena of the ancient Near East. Indeed, if there is one area in which comparisons can be rightfully applied, it is the ancient Near East. We know that agriculture, neolithic village culture, and finally urban civilization start from a Near Eastern center with many radii.

45. *Religionens värld*, 2d ed. (Stockholm, 1953); *Hochgottglaube im alten Iran* (Uppsala, 1938); *Die Religionen Irans* (Stuttgart, 1965); etc.
46. Cf. H. Frankfort, *The Problem of Similarity in Ancient Near Eastern Religions* (Frazer Lecture, 1951); and the contributions of S. H. Hooke, "Myth and Ritual: Past and Present," in *Myth, Ritual and Kingship*, ed. S. H. Hooke (Oxford, 1958), pp. 1–21; and S. G. F. Brandon, "The Myth and Ritual Position Critically Considered," in *ibid.*, pp. 261–91. See also Theodor H. Gaster, *Thespis: Ritual, Myth and Drama in the Ancient Near East* (New York, 1950), (rev. ed. 1961).

Georges Dumézil and the Indo-European Religions

A similar methodological uneasiness explains the resistance against Dumézil's brilliant studies on Indo-European religious institutions and mythologies.[47] It was objected, for example, that one could not compare Celtic or Italic with Iranian or Vedic socio-religious conceptions, despite the fact that in this case too we know for sure of a common Indo-European cultural tradition which is still recognizable beneath multiple and various extraneous influences.

The resistance to Dumézil's approach, fortunately now being overcome in many countries, originated probably for three main reasons: 1) the fact that the discipline of comparative Indo-European mythology has been hopelessly discredited by the improvisations of Max Müller and his followers; 2) the tendency, general in the first quarter of the century, to interpret the spiritual and cultural life of the protohistorical peoples in the light of what was considered characteristic of the "primitives"; thus, the well-articulated mythology, and especially the implied ideological system, attributed by Dumézil to the early Indo-Europeans seemed too coherent and too "profound" for a protohistorical society; 3) the conviction of the specialists in the particular Indo-Euopean philologies that it is impossible for a single scholar to master the entire area of Indo-European studies.[48]

All these reasons were based on as many misunderstandings: 1) Dumézil did not use Max Müller's philological, i.e., etymologi-

47. The most convenient introduction to Dumézil's work is *L'idéologie tripartie des Indo-Européens* (Brussels, 1958), (Collection Latomus, vol. XXX). A new edition of the three volume *Jupiter, Mars, Quirinus* (Paris, 1941–45) is in preparation. A bibliography of Dumézil was published in *Hommages à Georges Dumézil* (Brussels, 1960), (Collection Latomus, vol. XLV), pp. xi–xxiii. On Dumézil see M. Eliade, "La souveraineté et la religion indo-européenne," *Critique*, 1949, pp. 342–49, and "Pour une histoire générale des religions indo-européennes," *Annales*, 4 (1949): 183–91; Huguette Fugier, "Quarante ans de recherches sur l'idéologie indo-européenne: la méthode de M. Georges Dumézil," *Revue d'Histoire et de Philosophie Religieuses*, 45 (1965): 358–74; C. Scott Littleton, *The New Comparative Mythology. An Anthropological Assessment of the Theories of Georges Dumézil* (Berkeley and Los Angeles, 1966).

48. It is probable that skepticism was aroused more by Dumézil's systematic reconstructions than by his stupendous erudition. Indeed, other contemporary scholars of fantastic learning, such as B. Laufer and Paul Pelliot, were respectfully accepted by the academic milieux. But these encyclopedic savants did not try to go beyond the philological and historiographical erudition.

cal, method, but a historical one; he compared historically related socio-religious phenomena (i.e., the institutions, mythologies, and theologies of a number of peoples descended from the same ethnic, linguistic, and cultural matrix), and eventually he proved that the similarities point to an original *system* and not to a casual survival of heterogeneous elements. 2) Modern research has exploded the evolutionist fallacy of the inability of the "primitive" to think rationally and "systematically"; furthermore, the proto-Indo-European culture, far from being "primitive," was already enriched through continuous, though indirect, influences from the higher, urban civilizations of the ancient Near East. 3) The "impossibility" of mastering so many philologies is a false postulate grounded on personal experience or statistical information, but ultimately irrelevant; the only convincing argument would have been to prove that Dumézil's interpretation of, let us say, a Sanskrit, Celtic, or Caucasian text betrays his inadequate knowledge of the respective language.

In an impressive series of books and monographs brought out between 1940 and 1960, Georges Dumézil has investigated what he called the Indo-European tripartite conception of society, namely, its division into three superposed zones corresponding to three functions: sovereignty, warrior force, economic prosperity. Each function constitutes the responsibility of a socio-political category (kings, warriors, food producers), and is directly related to a specific type of divinity (in ancient Rome, for example, Jupiter, Mars, Quirinus). The first function is divided into two complementary parts or aspects, the magical and juridical sovereignty, illustrated in vedic India by Varuṇa and Mitra. This basic ideological configuration of the proto-Indo-Europeans has been differently developed and reinterpreted by the various Indo-European peoples in the course of their separate histories. For example, Dumézil has convincingly shown that the Indian mind elaborated the original scheme in cosmological terms while the Romans have "historicized" the mythological data, so that the most archaic, and the only genuine, Roman mythology is to be deciphered in the "historical" personages and events described by Titus Livius in the first book of his *Histories*.

Dumézil has completed his thorough study of the tripartite ideology in a number of monographs on Indo-European rituals and on vedic and Latin goddesses, and, quite recently (1966), in a large book on Roman religion.[49] More and more the specialists accept and conveniently utilize Dumézil's method and results. In addition to the importance of his work — and, for the moment, it is the only new and significant contribution to the understanding of Indo-European religions — the *example* of Dumézil is no less important to the discipline of history of religions. He has shown how to complement a meticulous philological and historical analysis of the texts with insights gained from sociology and philosophy. He has also shown that only by deciphering the basic ideological system underlying the social and religious institutions can a particular divine figure, myth, or ritual be correctly understood.

Van der Leeuw and the Phenomenology of Religion

The name of Gerardus van der Leeuw is currently related to the phenomenology of religion. He wrote, it is true, the first important treatise on the subject. But as with Rudolf Otto, the multilaterality of his work does not permit a too rigid classification. Although he studied oriental languages as a young man and obtained his doctorate with a thesis on Egyptian religion, van der Leeuw later published two excellent books on primitive religion and innumerable articles and monographs on various other religions, the problem of *Urmonotheismus*, and the psychology of religion. In addition, he was a poet, a musician, a man of the Church, and the author of an important book, *The Holy in Art*.[50] Ultimately, however, his inexhaustible curiosity and his many-sided interests did not serve van der Leeuw's work. He was also an extremely gifted writer. He wrote beautifully and always with crystalline clarity. His books are easily understood; they do not need elaborate commentaries. In an epoch when dry, difficult, enigmatic writing has become almost a fashion in philosophical circles, clarity and artistic excellence are in danger of being confused with superficiality, dilettantism, or lack of original thinking.

In van der Leeuw's *Phänomenologie der Religion* (1933),[5] one

---

49. *Rituels indo-européens à Rome* (Paris, 1954); *Aspects de la fonction guerrière chez les Indo-Européens* (Paris, 1955); *Déesses latines et mythes védiques* (Brussels, 1956); *La religion romaine archaïque* (Paris, 1966).
50. Recently published in English translation as *Sacred and Profane Beauty* (New York, 1963).
51. Translated under the title *Religion in Essence and Manifestation* (Lon-

finds few references to Husserl, but quite a number to Jaspers, Dilthey, and Eduard Spranger. Van der Leeuw was strongly influenced by the results of *Gestaltpsychologie* and *Strukturpsychologie*.[52] Nevertheless, he remained a phenomenologist insofar as in his descriptions he respected the religious data and their peculiar intentionality. He pointed out the irreducibility of religious representations to social, psychological, or rational functions, and he rejected those naturalistic prejudices which seek to explain religion by something other than itself. For van der Leeuw, the main task of the phenomenology of religion is to illumine the inner structures of religious phenomena. He thought, wrongly, that he could reduce the totality of all religious phenomena to three *Grundstrukturen*: dynamism, animism, and deism. However, he was not interested in the *history* of religious structures. Here lies the most serious inadequacy of his approach, for even the most elevated religious expression (a mystical ecstasy, for example) presents itself through specific structures and cultural expressions which are historically conditioned (see below, p. 51). As a matter of fact, van der Leeuw never attempted a religious morphology or a genetical phenomenology of religion. But, again, such lacunae do not lessen the significance of his work. Even though his versatile genius did not allow him to complete and systematize a new religious hermeneutics, he was an enthusiastic pioneer.

"Phenomenologists" and "Historicists"

The growing interest in phenomenology of religion has created a tension among the students of *Religionswissenschaft*. The different historical and historicistic schools have reacted strongly against the phenomenologists' claim that they can grasp the *essence* and the *structure* of religious phenomena. For the historicists, religion is exclusively a historical fact without any transhistorical meaning

don, 1938) and reprinted (New York, 1963), with the additions of the second German edition.

52. See F. Sierksma, *Phaenomenologie der Religie en Complexe Psychologie* (Assen, the Netherlands, 1951). No less important for the phenomenology of religion are the works of Friedrich Heiler, especially his classic monograph *Das Gebet* ("Prayer"), (Munich, 1918), and his recent book *Erscheinungsformen und Wesen der Religion* (Stuttgart, 1961). Other phenomenological contributions have been presented by G. Mensching, W. Brede Kristensen, and C. J. Bleeker. See also Eva Hirschmann, *Phänomenologie der Religion* (Wurzburg and Anmuhle, 1940).

or value, and to seek for "essences" is tantamount to falling back into the old Platonic error. (The historicists have, of course, neglected Husserl.)

We have already alluded to the irreducibility of this tension between "phenomenologists" and historians or "historicists" (p. 8). On the other hand, there are also signs that many scholars are searching for a broader perspective in which the two methodological approaches could be integrated. For the moment, the different methodological approaches and theoretical presuppositions prove their validity, or their usefulness, primarily by the hermeneutical advance they help to bring forth. One may or may not agree with Ananda Coomaraswamy's personal conviction with regard to *philosophia perennis* and the universal, primordial "Tradition" informing all premodern cultures; what ultimately matters is the unexpected light that Coomaraswamy throws on the vedic and Buddhist religious creation. Likewise, one may not share Henry Corbin's "anti-historicism," but one cannot deny that thanks to this conception, Corbin has succeeded in disclosing a significant dimension of Islamic mystical philosophy previously almost ignored by Western scholarship.

Ultimately, the work of an author is judged by its contribution to the understanding of a specific type of religious creation. It is only in so far as he succeeds, through hermeneutics, in transmuting his materials into spiritual messages that the historian of religions will fulfill his role in contemporary culture. Unfortunately, this is not always the case, for reasons, and with results, which will be discussed in chapter 4.

3

The Quest for the "Origins" of Religion

A Primordial Revelation

A French proverb says that "Only the details are really important" (*Il n'y a que les détails qui comptent*). I will not claim that this is always true, but there are instances in the history of culture when details are unexpectedly illuminating. Let us consider the beginnings of the Italian humanism in Florence. It is generally known that Marsilio Ficino founded the Platonic Academy and translated into Latin Plato's *Dialogues* as well as some neo-Platonic works and commentaries. But there is a detail which usually escapes our attention: Cosimo de'Medici had entrusted Ficino with the translation of manuscripts of Plato and Plotinus which the statesman had been collecting for many years. But about 1460 Cosimo bought the manuscript of what was later called *Corpus hermeticum* and asked Ficino to render it immediately into Latin. At that time Ficino had not yet begun his translation of Plato; nevertheless, he put aside the *Dialogues* and hurriedly applied himself to the translation of *Poimandres* and the other Hermetical treatises, so that he could finish them in a few months. In 1463, a year before Cosimo's death, these translations were complete. Thus *Corpus hermeticum* was the first Greek text to be

This chapter is a revised and expanded version of an article first published in *History of Religions*, 4 (1964): 154–69. (© 1964 by The University of Chicago.)

translated and published by Marsilio Ficino. Only afterward did
he start working on Plato.[1]

This detail is important. It sheds light on an aspect of the Italian
Renaissance ignored or at least neglected by the historians of a
generation ago. Both Cosimo and Ficino were thrilled by the discovery of a primordial revelation, that is, the one disclosed in the
Hermetical writings. And, of course, they had no reason to doubt
the Egyptian, that is, the oldest revelation accessible — one which
preceded that of Moses and which inspired Pythagoras and Plato
as well as the Persian Magi.

Though he exalted the holiness and the veracity of the hermetic
texts, Ficino did not — and could not — suspect himself of not being
a good Christian. Already in the second century the Christian
apologist Lactantius considered Hermes Trismegistos a divinely
inspired sage, and interpreted some Hermetic prophecies as fulfilled in the birth of Jesus Christ. Marsilio Ficino reasserted this
harmony between Hermetism and Hermetic magic on the one hand
and Christianity on the other. No less sincere was Pico della
Mirandola, who considered that *Magia* and *Cabbala* confirmed the
divinity of Christ. Pope Alexander VI had a fresco teeming with
Egyptian — that is, Hermetic — images and symbols painted in the
Vatican! This was done not for aesthetic or ornamental reasons;
rather, Alexander VI wanted to mark his protection of the exalted
and occult Egyptian tradition.

Such an extravagant interest in Hermetism is highly significant.
It discloses the Renaissance man's longing for a "primordial
revelation" which could include not only Moses and *Cabbala* but
also Plato and, first and foremost, the mysterious religions of
Egypt and Persia. It reveals also a profound dissatisfaction with
the medieval theology and medieval conceptions of man and the
universe; a reaction against what we may call "provincial," that
is, purely *Western* Christianity; a longing for a universalistic, transhistorical, "mythical" religion. For almost two centuries Egypt and
Hermetism, that is, the Egyptian magic, obsessed innumerable
theologians and philosophers — believers as well as unbelievers
or crypto-atheists. If Giordano Bruno acclaimed Copernicus' discoveries enthusiastically, it was because he thought that the heliocentrism had a profound religious and magical meaning. While

1. Frances A. Yates, *Giordano Bruno and the Hermetic Tradition* (Chicago
1964).

he was in England, Giordano Bruno prophesied the imminent return of the magical religion of the ancient Egyptians as it was described in *Asclepius*. Bruno felt superior to Copernicus, for whereas Copernicus understood his own theory only as a mathematician, Bruno could interpret the Copernican diagram as a hieroglyph of divine mysteries.

It would be a fascinating study to trace the history of this religious and cultural myth of the "primordial Hermetic revelation" to its destruction in 1614 by the learned Greek scholar Isaac Casaubon. A detailed history of this pre-modern myth would lead us away from our topic. It is enough to say that Isaac Casaubon proved, on purely philological grounds, that, far from representing a "primordial revelation," *Corpus hermeticum* is a collection of rather late texts — no earlier than the second or third centuries of our era — reflecting the Hellenistic-Christian syncretism.

The rise and fall of this extravagant belief in a primordial revelation literally transmitted in a few treatises is symptomatic. One even can say that it anticipates what will take place in the following three centuries. In fact, the quest for a pre-Mosaic revelation prefigured, and later accompanied, the series of crises that shook Western Christendom and ultimately made way for the naturalistic and positivistic ideologies of the nineteenth century. The intense and continuous interest in "Egyptianism" and other "Eastern mysteries" did not encourage, during the Renaissance, the growth of what is called today comparative religions. On the contrary, the direct consequence of Ficino's, Pico's, Bruno's, and Campanella's striving with the Hermetical lore were various naturalistic philosophies and the triumph of mathematical and physical sciences. In the perspective of these new sciences and philosophies Christianity was not considered to be the only revealed religion — if it was a "revealed" religion at all. Eventually, in the nineteenth century, Christianity and all the other known religions came to be considered not only groundless but culturally dangerous because they usually obstructed the progress of science. The consensus among the intelligentsia was that the philosophers had proven the impossibility of demonstrating the existence of God; furthermore, it was claimed that the sciences were proving that man was made from matter only, that is, that there is no such thing as the "soul," a spiritual entity independent of the body and surviving it.

The Beginnings of Comparative Religions

Now it is remarkable to note that the beginnings of comparative religions took place during the middle of the nineteenth century at the very height of the materialistic and positivistic propaganda. Auguste Comte published his *Catéchisme positiviste* in 1852 and his *Système de politique positive* between 1855 and 1858. In 1855 Ludwig Buchner brought out his *Kraft und Stoffe*. He tried to prove that Nature is devoid of finality, that life is produced by spontaneous generation, and that the soul and the mind are organic functions. Furthermore, Buchner asserted that the mind is the result of all the forces reunited in the brain and that most probably what we call soul or mind is the effect of "nervous electricity." The following year, in 1856, Max Müller published his *Essays in Comparative Mythology*, which can be considered the first important book in the field of comparative religions. Three years later appeared Darwin's *Origin of Species*, and in 1862 Herbert Spencer issued his *First Principles*. In the latter Spencer attempted to explain the evolution of the universe by a mysterious change in the state of the primordial matter from a state of undetermined homogeneity to a determined heterogeneity.

These new discoveries, hypotheses, and theories which passionately interested the learned world rapidly became very popular. One of the bestsellers of the epoch was Ernst Haeckel's book *Natürliche Schöpfungsgeschichte*. Issued in 1868, it went through more than twenty editions before the end of the century and was translated into a dozen languages. Haeckel was, it must be confessed, neither a competent philosopher nor an original thinker. Inspired by Darwin, he thought that the theory of evolution constitutes the royal road to a mechanistic conception of nature. According to Haeckel, the theory of evolution made theological and teleological explanations obsolete and, in the same stroke, made easily comprehensible the origin of organisms exclusively in terms of natural causes.

While Haeckel's book was furiously reprinted and translated, and Herbert Spencer was elaborating his *System of Synthetic Philosophy* (1860–96), the new discipline of "history of religions" was making rapid progress. In his *Lectures on the Science of Language* (2d ser., 1864), Max Müller introduced his theory concerning solar mythology among the Aryans — a theory grounded in his belief that the myths were born from a "disease of language." In 1871 Edward Burnett Tylor published his *Primitive Culture*, brilliantly trying to reconstruct the origin and evolution of religious experiences and religious beliefs. Tylor identified the first stage of religion with what he called animism: the belief that Nature is animated, that is, has a soul. From animism evolved polytheism, and polytheism finally gave way to monotheism.

I do not intend to recall all the important dates in the history of the scientific study of religion during the second half of the nineteenth century. But let us pause for a moment and examine the meaning of this synchronicity between the materialistic ideologies on the one hand and the growing interest in oriental and archaic forms of religion on the other. One could say that the anxious search for the origins of Life and Mind, the fascination in the "mysteries of Nature," the urge to penetrate and decipher the inner structures of Matter — all these longings and drives denote a sort of nostalgia for the primordial, for the original, universal *matrix*. Matter, Substance, represents the *absolute origin*, the beginning of all things: Cosmos, Life, Mind. There is an irresistible desire to pierce time and space deeply to reach the limits and the beginnings of the visible Universe, and especially to disclose the ultimate ground of Substance and the germinal state of living Matter.[2] From a certain point of view to say that the human soul is ultimately a product of matter is not necessarily a humiliating affirmation. True the human soul is no longer regarded as a creation of God from such a perspective; but taking into consideration the fact that God does not exist, it is rather consoling to discover that the soul is the result of a fantastically long and complicated evolution and has its origin in the oldest cosmical reality:

2. Let us add that the preoccupation with the *absolute origin*, the beginning of all things, is a characteristic of what may be called the archaic mind. As we have pointed out in many of our previous writings, the cosmogonic myth plays a central role in archaic religions essentially for this reason: while relating how the world came into being, it reveals how *reality* ("Being" itself) came into being (see Eliade, *Myth and Reality* [New York, 1963]; see also chap. 5 below). The first systematic cosmogonies and cosmologies were in a sense "ontogenies" (see *Myth and Reality*, pp. 111 ff.). From a certain point of view, there is no solution of continuity between the archaic mind and scientific ideologies of the nineteenth century. Freud also utilizes the notion of the "absolute beginning" for his understanding of the specificity of the human condition, but for Freud the "primordial" loses its cosmic dimension and is reduced to a "personal *primordium*," i.e., the earliest childhood (see *ibid.*, pp. 77 ff.; see also p. 49 below).

physicochemical matter. For the scientists and the scientifically minded intelligentsia of the second half of the nineteenth century, matter not only solved all the problems but almost reduced the future of mankind to a continuous, nondramatic, tiresome progress. Through science man will come to know matter ever more correctly and master it ever more completely. There will be no end to this progressive perfectibility. One can unravel from this enthusiastic confidence in science, scientific education, and industry a kind of religious messianic optimism: man, at last, will be free, happy, rich, and powerful.

Materialism, Spiritism, Theosophy

Optimism matched perfectly well with materialism, positivism, and the belief in an unlimited evolution. This is demonstrated not only in *L'Avenir de la science*, written by E. Renan in the middle of the century, but also in some important parareligious movements of the later 1800's; for instance, in the so-called spiritism (or spiritualism). This movement started in 1848 at Hydesville, New York. Members of the family of John D. Fox heard a series of mysterious knockings which seemed to have an intelligent cause.

One of the daughters suggested a code, three raps for *yes*, one for *no*, two for *doubtful*, and communication was established with what claimed to be a "spirit." The three Fox sisters became the first "mediums" and the practice of sitting in "circles" (holding *séances*) for the purpose of communicating with "spirits," who answered by raps, tilts of the table, or other signals, rapidly spread over the whole world.[3]

Spiritistic phenomena have been known from ancient times and have been differently interpreted by various cultures and religions. But the important new element in the modern spiritism is its materialistic outlook. First of all, there are now "positive proofs" of the existence of the soul, or rather of the postmortem existence of a soul: knockings, tilts of the table, and a little later the so-called materializations. The problem of the survival and the immortality of the soul had obsessed the Western world since Pythagoras, Empedocles, and Plato. But it was a philosophical or a theological problem. Now, in a scientific and positivistic era, the immortality

3. F. C. S. Schiller, "Spiritism," *Encyclopaedia of Religion and Ethics*, ed. James Hastings (New York, 1921), vol. 11, p. 806.

of the soul was related to the success of an experiment: to demonstrate it "scientifically," one must bring "real," that is, physical, proofs. Later on, complicated paraphernalia and laboratories were devised for the sake of examining the evidence of the soul's survival. One can recognize the positivistic optimism in almost all the parapsychological researches: there is always the hope that the postexistence of the soul will one day be scientifically demonstrated.

No less optimistic and positivistic is the other great parareligious movement, the Theosophical Society, founded in New York in November, 1875, by Helena Petrovna Blavatsky. In her *Isis Unveiled* (1877) and other voluminous writings, this fascinating and gifted adventuress presented the modern world with an occultistic revelation in terms which it could understand. The modern world believed in evolution and, consequently, in an infinite progress. Mme Blavatsky presented a theory of indefinite spiritual evolution through metempsychosis and progressive initiation. She claimed that during her purported sojourn in Tibet she had received the primordial, that is, Asiatic and even supraterrestrial, revelation. But I must interrupt at this point to observe that if there is anything characteristic of all Eastern traditions, it is precisely an antievolutionistic conception of the spiritual life. Moreover, Mme Blavatsky believed in the necessity of bringing positive, material "proofs" to substantiate the theosophical doctrine, and she regularly "materialized" messages from her mysterious Mahatmas in Tibet. These messages, though written in English and on ordinary paper, had nevertheless the prestige of a solid, material fact — and convinced a great number of apparently intelligent people of the authenticity of Mme Blavatsky's secret doctrine. And, of course, it was an optimistic secret doctrine, conveniently disclosed for a spiritually optimistic society: you had only to read the two volumes of *Isis Unveiled* and become a member of a theosophical group to be gradually initiated into the most profound mysteries of the Universe and of your own immortal and transmigrating soul. You knew finally that there is an unlimited progress and that not only you but all humanity one day will reach perfection.

One must not smile when listening to all these fantastic claims. The spiritistic movement, as well as the Theosophical Society, expresses the same *Zeitgeist* as the positivistic ideologies. The readers of *Origin of Species, Kraft und Stoffe, Essays in Comparative*

Mythology, and *Isis Unveiled* were not the same, but they shared something in common: all of them were dissatisfied with Christianity and a certain number were not even "religious." A vacuum had been produced by the syncope of historical Christianity among the intelligentsia and because of this vacuum some tried to reach the source of creative matter while others tried to communicate with the spirits or with invisible Mahatmas. The new discipline of history of religions developed rapidly in this cultural context. And, of course, it followed a like pattern: the positivistic approach to the facts and the search for the origins, for the very beginning of religion.

The Obsession with Origins

During that time, all Western historiography was obsessed with the quest of *origins.* "Origin and development" of something became almost a cliché. Great scholars wrote about the origin of language, of human societies, of art, of institutions, of the Indo-Aryan races, and so on. We touch here a fascinating though complex problem, but we cannot discuss it. Suffice it to say that this search for the origins of human institutions and cultural creations prolongs and completes the naturalist's quest for the origin of species, the biologist's dream of grasping the origin of life, the geologist's and the astronomer's endeavor to understand the origin of the Earth and the Universe. From a psychological point of view, one can decipher here the same nostalgia for the "primordial" and the "original."

Max Müller thought that the Rig Veda reflects a primordial phase of Aryan religion and consequently one of the most archaic stages of religious beliefs and mythological creations. But even in the early 1870's the French Sanskrit scholar Abel Bergaigne proved that the Vedic hymns, far from being the spontaneous and naïve expressions of a naturalistic religion, were the product of a highly learned and sophisticated class of ritualistic priests. Once again, the exhilarating confidence that a primordial form of religion had been grasped was dispelled by an exacting, meticulous philological analysis.

Scholarly discussion about the Vedas was only an episode in the long and dramatic battle to identify "the origin of religion." A brilliant and learned writer, Andrew Lang, contributed decisively to the demolition of the mythological reconstructions of Max Müller. Two of Lang's most successful works, *Custom and Myth* (1883) and *Modern Mythology* (1897) were drawn up from articles in which he discredited Max Müller's ideas with the aid of E. B. Tylor's theories. But a year after the publication of *Modern Mythology*, in 1898, Andrew Lang brought out another book, *Making of Religion*, in which he rejected Tylor's view that the origin of religion is to be found in animism. Lang based his arguments on the presence of a belief in High Gods among some very primitive peoples, such as the Australians and the Andamanese. Tylor held that such a belief could not possibly be original, that the idea of God developed from the belief in nature spirits and the cult of ancestor ghosts. But among the Australians and Andamanese, Andrew Lang found neither ancestor worship nor nature cults.

This unexpected and antievolutionistic claim, that a High God was not at the end of the religious history but at the beginnings, did not greatly impress the contemporary scholarly milieu. It is true that Andrew Lang did not master his documentation thoroughly, and in a discussion with Hartland he was compelled to surrender portions of his earlier thesis. Besides, he had the misfortune to be an excellent and versatile writer, and author, among other works, of a volume of poetry. And literary gifts usually arouse the scholar's suspicions.

However, Andrew Lang's conception of the primitive High God is significant for other reasons. In the last years of the nineteenth century and the first years of the twentieth, animism ceased to be considered the first stage of religion. Two new theories were proclaimed in that period. They might be called preanimistic, because both of them claimed that they identified a more archaic stage of religion than that described by animism. The first theory is that of Andrew Lang, postulating a belief in a High God at the beginnings of religion. Though almost ignored in England, this hypothesis, corrected and completed, was later accepted by Graebner and some Continental scholars. Unfortunately, one of the most learned ethnologists of our time, Wilhelm Schmidt, elaborated the hypothesis of the primitive belief in High Gods into a rigid theory of a primordial monotheism (*Urmonotheismus*). I say unfortunately because Schmidt, though a very able scholar, was also a Catholic priest, and the scientific world suspected him of apologetic intentions. Furthermore, as we have already noted (p. 24 above), Schmidt was a thorough rationalist, and tried to prove that the idea of God had been grasped by primitive men strictly through causalistic thinking. As Schmidt was publishing the monumental volumes of his *Ursprung der Gottesidee*, however, the Western world witnessed the irruption of quite a number of irrationalistic philosophies and ideologies. Bergson's *élan vital*, Freud's discovery of the unconscious, Lévy-Bruhl's investigations of what he called the prelogical, mystical mentality, R. Otto's *Das Heilige*, as well as the artistic revolutions of dadaism and surrealism, mark some of the important events in the history of modern irrationalism. Thus, very few ethnologists and historians of religions could accept Schmidt's rationalistic explanation of the discovery of the idea of God.

On the contrary, that epoch, roughly between 1900 and 1920, was dominated by the second preanimistic theory, that of *mana*, the belief in an indistinct and impersonal magico-religious force. It was especially the British anthropologist Marett who insisted on the preanimistic character of the belief in *mana*, showing that this magico-religious experience does not presuppose the concept of a soul and, consequently, represents a more archaic stage than Tylor's animism (see above, p. 13).

What interests us in this vivid opposition of hypotheses on the origin of religion is the preoccupation with the "primordial." We noticed a similar concern among the Italian humanists and philosophers after the rediscovery of the Hermetic texts. On quite another level and with a different purpose, the search for the "primordial" characterizes the activity of nineteenth-century scientific ideologists and historians. Both preanimistic theories — that of the primordial belief in a High God and that of an original experience of the sacred as an impersonal force — maintained that they had reached a deeper level of religious history than Tylor's animism. As a matter of fact, both theories claimed that they had disclosed the very beginnings of religion. Moreover, both theories rejected the unilinear evolution of religious life implied in Tylor's hypothesis. Marett and the *mana*-school were not interested in building up a general theory of the growth of religion. Schmidt, on the contrary, consecrated his life's work to this very problem, believing, we should note, that this was a historical problem and not a naturalistic one. According to Schmidt, at the beginning man believed in one powerful and creative God only. Later on, owing to historical circumstances, man neglected and even forgot this unique God, becoming involved in more and more complicated beliefs in a multitude of gods and goddesses, ghosts, mythical ancestors, and so on. Though this process of degeneration started tens of thousands of years ago, Schmidt claimed that it must be called a historical process because man is a historical being. Schmidt introduced historical ethnology on a large scale into the study of primitive religion. And we shall see later on the consequences of this important shift of perspective.

High Gods and the Death of God

For a moment, however, let us return to Andrew Lang's discovery of the primitive belief in a High God. I do not know if Lang ever read Nietzsche. Most probably he did not. But more than twenty years before Lang's discovery, Nietzsche proclaimed, through his mouthpiece Zarathustra, the death of God. Nietzsche's proclamation, though unobserved in his lifetime, had a tremendous impact on the following generations of Europeans. It announced the radical end of Christianity — of religion — and also prophesied that modern man must live henceforth in an exclusively immanent, godless world. Now, I find it interesting that Lang, detecting the existence of High Gods among the primitives, discovered their death also — though he did not realize this aspect of his discovery. Indeed, Lang notices that the belief in a High God is not too frequent, that the cult of such gods is rather poor, that is to say, their actual role in religious life is very modest. Lang even tried to find an explanation of the degeneration and final disappearance of the High Gods and their substitution by other religious figures. Among other causes he thought that the mythological imagination contributed drastically to the deterioration of the High God idea. He was wrong, but for our purpose it does not matter. The fact is that the primitive High God became a *deus otiosus* and is believed to have retired to the highest heaven, quite indifferent to human affairs. Ultimately he is forgotten. In other words, *he dies* — not that there are myths relating his death, but he completely vanishes from the religious life and subsequently even from myths.

This oblivion of the High God means also his death. Nietzsche's proclamation was new for the Western, Judeo-Christian world, but the death of God is an extremely old phenomenon in the history of religions — of course, with this difference: that the disappearance of the High God gives birth to a more vivid and more dramatic, though inferior, pantheon — whereas in Nietzsche's conception, after the death of the Judeo-Christian God, man has to live by himself — alone, in a radically desacralized world. But this radically desacralized and immanent world is the world of history. As a historical being, man killed God, and after this assassination — this "deicide" — he is forced to live exclusively in history. At this point it is interesting to recall that Schmidt, the promulgator of the *Urmonotheismus* theory, thought that the neglect of the High God, and finally his substitution by other religious figures, is the result not of a naturalistic process but of a historical one. The primitive man, merely because he was making material and cultural progress, passing from the stage of food collector to that of agriculture and pastoralism — in other words, by the simple fact that he was making history — lost his belief in one God and started worshiping a multitude of inferior gods.

In Nietzsche, as well as in Andrew Lang and Wilhelm Schmidt, a new idea confronts us: the responsibility of history in the degradation, the oblivion, and ultimately the "death" of God. The following generations of scholars will have to wrestle with this new meaning of history. Meanwhile, the discipline of comparative religions was progressing. More and more documents were published, more books were written, and more chairs of history of religions were founded all over the world.

There was a time, especially in the second half of the nineteenth century, when it was thought that one or two generations should devote themselves exclusively to the publication and analysis of the documents so that the succeeding scholars would be free to elaborate synthetic interpretations. But, of course, this was only a dream, though even Renan believed in it when he was writing his *L'Avenir de la science*. History of religions, as well as all other historical disciplines, followed the patterns of scientific activity, that is, concentrating more and more on collecting and classifying "facts." Yet this ascetic modesty of the historian of religions toward his materials is not without grandeur, and it has almost a spiritual significance. One can describe the situation of the scholar immersed in his documents, sometimes almost buried under their mass and weight, as a kind of *descensus ad inferos;* a descent into the deep, dark subterranean regions where he is confronted with the germinal modes of the living matter. In some cases, this total immersion in "materials" amounts to a spiritual death; for, sadly enough, the creativity of the scholar may be sterilized.

Such an urge to *descensus* corresponds to a general tendency of the Western mind at the beginning of the century. One cannot better describe the psychoanalytical technique elaborated by Freud than to say that it is a *decensus ad inferos,* a descent into the deepest and most dangerous zones of the human psyche. When Jung revealed the existence of the collective unconscious, the exploration of these immemorial treasures — the myths, symbols, and images of archaic humanity — began to resemble the techniques of oceanography and speleology. Just as descents into the depths of the sea or expeditions to the bottoms of the caves had revealed elementary organisms long vanished from the surface of the earth, so analysis retrieved forms of deep psychic life previously inaccessible to study. Speleology presented biologists with Tertiary and even Mesozoic organisms, primitive zoömorphic forms not susceptible of fossilization — in other words, forms that had vanished from the surface of the earth without leaving a trace. By discovering "living fossils," speleology markedly advanced our knowledge of archaic modes of life. Similarly, archaic modes of psychic life, "living fossils" buried in the darkness of the unconscious, now become accessible to study through the techniques developed by Freud and other depth psychologists.

Of course, one must distinguish Freud's great contribution to learning, that is, the discovery of the unconscious and of psychoanalysis, from the Freudian ideology, wich is just one more among the numberless positivistic ideologies. Freud also thought that, with the aid of psychoanalysis, he had reached the "primordial" phase of human culture and religion. As we have seen (p. 20), he identified the origin of religion and culture in a primeval murder, more exactly in the first parricide. For Freud, God was merely the sublimated physical father who was slain by his expelled sons. This astonishing explanation was universally criticized and and rejected by all responsible ethnologists. But Freud neither renounced nor modified his theory. Probably, he thought that he found proofs of the killing of God the Father among his Viennese patients. But this "discovery" was tantamount to saying that some modern men were beginning to feel the consequences of their "deicide." As Nietzsche had announced thirty years before the publication of *Totem und Tabu*, God was dead; or, more precisely, he had been killed by man. Perhaps Freud was unconsciously projecting the neurosis of some of his Viennese patients into a mythical past. A "death of God" was known also among the primitives, but that meant the occultation and remoteness of God and not his "murder" at the hands of man, as it was proclaimed by Nietzsche.

Two facets of Freud's achievement are relevant to our inquiry: first, exemplifying the well-known yearning of Western scientists for the "primordial," for the "origins," Freud tried to go further than any other man had dared to go into the history of mind. For him this meant penetrating into the unconscious. And, second, Freud thought that he found at the beginning of human culture and institutions not a biological fact but rather an historical event, namely, the murder of the Father at the hands of his elder sons. Whether such a primordial historical event did or did not actually take place is a matter of indifference in our discussion. What is significant is the fact that Freud — *naturalist* though he undoubtedly was — firmly believed that the origin of religion was related to an *event*: the first parricide. And this is additionally significant because thousands of psychoanalysts and hundreds of thousands of more or less cultivated Western men are convinced today that Freud's explanation is scientifically correct.

Historicity and Historicism

So it appears that the Western man's longing for "origins" and the "primordial" forced him finally into an encounter with history. The historian of religions knows by now that he is unable to reach the "origin" of religion. What happened in the beginning, *ab origine*, is no longer a problem for the historian of religions, though conceivably it might be one for the theologian or the philosopher. Almost without noticing it, the historian of religions found himself in a cultural milieu quite different from that of Max Müller and Tylor, or even that of Frazer and Marrett. It was a new environment nourished by Nietzsche and Marx, Dilthey, Croce, and Ortega; an environment in which the fashionable cliché was not *Nature* but *History*. In itself, the discovery of the irreducibility of history, that is to say, that man is always a historical being, was not a negative, sterilizing experience. But very soon this evident fact gave way to a series of relativistic and historicistic ideologies and philosophies, from Dilthey to Heidegger and Sartre. At the age of seventy, Dilthey himself recognized that "the relativity of all human concepts is the last word of the historical vision of the world."

The validity of historicism need not be discussed here. But to understand the actual situation of the historian of religions we must take into consideration the grave crisis brought on by the discovery of the historicity of man. This new dimension, the historicity, is susceptible of many interpretations. But it must be admitted that from a certain point of view the understanding of man as first and foremost a historical being implies a profound humiliation for the Western consciousness. Western man considered himself successively God's creature and the possessor of a unique Revelation, the master of the world, the author of the only universally valid culture, the creator of the only real and useful science, and so on. Now he discovered himself on the same level with every other man, that is to say, conditioned by the unconscious as well as by history — no longer the unique creator of a high culture, no longer the master of the world, and culturally menaced by extinction. When Valéry exclaimed: "Nous autres, civilisations, nous savons maintenant que nous sommes mortels," he echoed Dilthey's pessimistic historicism.

But this humiliation of Western man following his discovery of the universal historical conditioning has not been without positive results. First of all, the acceptance of man's historicity helped us to get rid of the last remnants of angelism and idealism. We now take more seriously the fact that man belongs to *this* world, that he is not a spirit imprisoned in matter. To know that man is always conditioned is to discover that he is equally a creative being. He responds creatively to the challenge of cosmic, psychological, or historical conditionings. For that reason we no longer accept the naturalistic explanations of human cultures and religions. To give only one example, we know now that primitive man did not — and, as a matter of fact, could not — have a naturistic religion. In the time of Max Müller and Tylor the scholars used to speak of naturistic cults and of fetishism, meaning that primitive man adored natural objects. But the veneration of cosmic

objects is not "fetishism." It is not the tree, the spring, or the stone
that is venerated, *but the sacred which is manifested through these
cosmic objects.* This understanding of archaic man's religious experience is the result of the broadening of our historical consciousness. Ultimately, one can say that in spite of the risks of relativism
the doctrine that man is exclusively a historical being gave way to
a new kind of universalism. If man makes himself through history
then everything man did in the past is important for every one of
us. This is tantamount to saying that Western consciousness
recognizes only one history, the Universal History, and that the
ethnocentric history is surpassed as being provincial. For the historian of religions this means that he cannot ignore any important form, though, of course, he is not expected to be an expert
on all of them.

So, after more than a century of untiring labor, scholars were
forced to renounce the old dream of grasping the origin of religion with the aid of historical tools, and they devoted themselves
to the study of different phases and aspects of religious life. Now
we may ask, is this the last word in the science of religion? Are
we condemned to work indefinitely with our religious materials,
considering them to be nothing more than historical documents,
that is to say, expressions of different existential situations during
the ages? Does the fact that we cannot reach the *origin* of religion
also mean that we cannot grasp the *essence* of religious phenomena? Is religion an exclusively historical phenomenon, in
the same way as, for instance, the fall of Jerusalem or of
Constantinople? For the student of religion "history" means
primarily that all religious phenomena are conditioned. A *pure*
religious phenomenon does not exist. A religious phenomenon
is always also a social, an economic, a psychological phenomenon, and, of course, a historical one, because it takes place in
historical time and it is conditioned by everything which had
happened before.

But the question is: Are the multiple systems of conditioning a
self-sufficient explanation of the religious phenomenon? When a
great discovery opens new perspectives to the human mind, there
is a tendency to explain everything in the light of that discovery
and on its plane of reference. The scientific acquisitions of the
nineteenth century compelled the contemporaries to explain everything through matter — not only life but also the mind and its

works. The discovery, at the beginning of the century, of the importance of history urged many of our contemporaries to reduce man to his historical dimension, that is to say, to the system of conditionings in which every human being is hopelessly "situated." But we must not confuse the historical circumstances which make a human existence what it actually is with the fact that there is such a thing as a human existence. For the historian of religions the fact that a myth or a ritual is always historically conditioned does not explain away the very existence of such a myth or ritual. In other words, the historicity of a religious experience does not tell us what a religious experience ultimately *is*. We know that we can grasp the sacred only through manifestations which are always historically conditioned. But the study of these historically conditioned expressions does not give us the answer to the questions: What is the sacred? What does a religious experience actually mean?

In conclusion, the historian of religions who does not accept the empiricism or the relativism of some fashionable sociological and historistic schools feels rather frustrated. He knows that he is condemned to work exclusively with historical documents, but at the same time he feels that these documents tell him something more than the simple fact that they reflect historical situations. He feels somehow that they reveal to him important truths about man and man's relation to the sacred. But how to grasp these truths? This is the question that obsesses many contemporary historians of religions. A few answers have been proposed already. But more important than any single answer is the fact that historians of religions asked *this* question. As so often in the past, a correct question may infuse new life into a wornout science.

4

Crisis and Renewal

Let us recognize it frankly. History of religions, or comparative religion,[1] plays a rather modest role in modern culture. When one recalls the passionate interest with which the informed public in the second half of the nineteenth century followed the speculations of Max Müller on the origin of myths and the evolution of religions and followed his polemics with Andrew Lang; when one recalls the considerable success of *The Golden Bough*, the vogue of *mana* or of the *mentalité prélogique* and *participation mystique*; and when one recalls that *Les Origines du Christianisme*, the *Prolegomena to the Study of Greek Religion*, and *Les Formes élémentaires de la vie religieuse* were the bedside books of our fathers and grandfathers, one cannot contemplate the present situation without melancholy.

Certainly, one could respond that in our day there is no Max Müller, Andrew Lang, or Frazer, which is perhaps true, not because today's historians of religions are inferior to them, but sim-

This chapter is a revised version of an article originally entitled "Crisi and Renewal in History of Religions," which was first published in *History o Religions*, 5 (1965): 1–17. (© 1965 by The University of Chicago.)
1. These terms are distressingly vague, but as they belong to current lan guage we are resigned to employing them. One generally understands "his tory of religions" or "comparative religion" to mean the integral study o the religious realities, that is to say, the historical manifestations of a par ticular type of "religion" (tribal, ethnic, supranational) as well as th specific structures of the religious life (divine forms, conceptions of th soul, myths, rituals, etc.; institutions, etc.; typology of religious experience etc.). These preliminary precisions are not at all intended to circumscribe th field or to define the methods of the history of religions.

ply because they are more modest, more withdrawn, indeed more timid. It is exactly this problem that intrigues me. Why have the historians of religions allowed themselves to become what they are today? A first response would be: Because they have learned the lesson of their illustrious predecessors; in other words, they have taken account of the caducity of any premature hypothesis, of the precariousness of any too ambitious generalization. But I doubt that, in whatever other discipline, a creative mind has ever given up the attempt to accomplish its work because of the fragility of the results obtained by its predecessors. The inhibition from which historians of religions suffer at present surely has more complex causes.

The "Second Renaissance"

Before discussing them I should like to recall an analogous example in the history of modern culture. The "discovery" of the Upanishads and Buddhism at the beginning of the nineteenth century had been acclaimed as a cultural event that presaged considerable consequences. Schopenhauer compared the discovery of Sanskrit and the Upanishads to the rediscovery of the "true" Greco-Latin culture during the Italian Renaissance. One expected a radical renewal of Western thought as a consequence of the confrontation with Indian philosophy. As is known, however, not only did this miracle of the "second Renaissance" not take place, but, with the exception of the mythologizing vogue launced by Max Müller, the discovery of the Indian spirituality did not give rise to any significant cultural creation. Two reasons especially are invoked today to explain this failure: (1) the eclipse of metaphysics and the triumph of the materialist and positivist ideologies in the second half of the nineteenth century; (2) the fact that the early generations of Indianists concentrated on the editing of texts, vocabularies, and philological and historical studies. In order to be able to advance the understanding of Indian thought, it was necessary at any cost to establish a philology.

Nevertheless, grand and audacious syntheses were not wanting during the first century of Indianism. Eugène Burnouf published his *Introduction à l'histoire du bouddhisme indien* in 1844; Albert Weber, Max Müller, and Abel Bergaigne would not flinch before projects that today, after more than a century of rigorous philology, seem enormous to us; toward the end of the nineteenth century Paul Deussen wrote the history of Indian philosophy; Sylvain Lévi made his debut with some works that an Indianist of our day would attempt only at the summit of his career (*La Doctrine du sacrifice dans les Brāhmanas*, 1898; *Le Théâtre Indien*, 2 vols., 1890) and, while still young, he published his sumptuous three-volume monograph, *Le Népal* (1905–8); and Hermann Oldenberg did not hesitate to present his grandiose surveys of the religions of the Vedas (1894) as well as of the Buddha and early Buddhism (1881).

Thus the insolvency of the "second Renaissance," expected as a consequence of the discovery of Sanskrit and Indian philosophy, is not due to the orientalists' excessive concentration on philology. But the "Renaissance" did not come about for the simple reason that the study of Sanskrit and other oriental languages did not succeed in passing beyond the circle of philologians and historians, while, during the Italian Renaissance, Greek and classical Latin were studied not only by the grammarians and humanists but also by the poets, artists, philosophers, theologians, and men of science. To be sure, Paul Deussen wrote some books on the Upanishads and the Vedānta in which he attempted to make Indian thought "respectable" by interpreting it in the light of German Idealism — by showing, for example, that certain ideas of Kant or Hegel were found in germ in the Upanishads. Deussen believed that he served the cause of Indianism by insisting on the analogies between Indian thought and Western metaphysics; he hoped thereby to arouse interest in Indian philosophy. Paul Deussen was an eminent scholar, but he was not an original thinker. One has only to imagine his colleague, Friedrich Nietzsche, devoting himself to the study of Sanskrit and Indian philosophy in order to realize what a true encounter between India and a creative Western mind would have been able to produce. As a concrete example, one considers the results of a creative confrontation between Western and Muslim philosophy and mysticism when he sees what a profoundly religious spirit like Louis Massignon learned from Al Hallaj, and how a philosopher who is also a theologian such as Henry Corbin, interprets the thought of Sohrawardi, Ibn Arabi, and Avicenna.

Indianism, like Orientalism in general, has long since become a "respectable" and useful discipline, one among numerous othe disciplines that constitute what is called the humanities — but the prestigious role that Schopenhauer had predicted for it has not been realized. If one dares to hope still for a stimulating encounter with the thought of India and Asia, it will be the result of history, of the fact that Asia is now present in the historical actuality; it will not be the work of Western Orientalism.[2]

And yet, Europe has shown several times that it is avid for dialogue and exchange with the extra-European spiritualities and cultures. Let us recall the effect the first exposition of Japanese painting had on the French impressionists, or the influence of African sculpture on Picasso, or the consequences of the discovery of "primitive art" for the first generation of surrealists. But in all these examples, the "creative encounter" was with artists, not with scholars.

A Total Hermeneutics

The history of religions constituted itself an autonomous discipline shortly after the beginnings of Orientalism, in some respects relying on the researches of the Orientalists, and it has profited enormously from the progress of anthropology. In other words, the two principal documentary sources for the history of religions have been, and still are, the cultures of Asia and the peoples whom one calls (for lack of a more adequate term) "primitive." In both cases it is a question of peoples and nations who, for a half-century and especially in the last ten or fifteen years, have divested themselves of Eurpean tutelage and have assumed their responsibilities in history. It is difficult to imagine another humanistic discipline that occupies a better position to contribute both to the widening of the Western cultural horizon and to the rapprochement with representatives of the oriental and archaic cultures. However exceptional their gifts, the greatest Indianist and the most eminent anthropologist find themselves forcibly contained within their domains, however immense. But if he is faithful to the aims of his discipline, a historian of religions ought to be able to know the essential aspects of the religions of Asia and of the vast "primitive" world, just as one expects that he is capable of understanding the fundamental ideas of the religions of the ancient Near East,

2. The contemporary vogue of Zen is largely due to the uninterrupted and intelligent activity of D. T. Suzuki.

the Mediterranean world, and of Judaism, Christianity, and Islam. Obviously, it is not a question of mastering all these domains as a philologist and a historian but of assimilating the researches of the specialists and of integrating them in the specific perspective of the history of religions. Frazer, Carl Clemen, Pettazzoni, and van der Leeuw endeavored to follow the progress in a multitude of fields, and their example has not lost its value, even if one no longer agrees with their interpretations.[3]

I have recalled these facts in order to deplore the small profit that the historians of religions have drawn from their privileged situation. Certainly, I do not forget the contributions made by the historians of religions during the past three-quarters of a century in all fields of research. It is thanks to these contributions that today one can speak of the history of religions as an independent discipline. But one deplores the fact that the majority of the historians of religions have done only this, worked with devotion and tenacity in order to constitute the solid foundations of their discipline. The history of religions is not merely a historical discipline, as, for example, are archeology or numismatics. It is equally a *total hermeneutics,* being called to decipher and explicate every kind of encounter of man with the sacred, from prehistory to our day. Now, by reason of modesty, or perhaps from an excessive timidity (provoked above all by the excesses of their eminent predecessors), historians of religions hesitate to valorize culturally the results of their researches. From Max Müller and Andrew Lang to Frazer and Marett, from Marett to Lévy-Bruhl, and from Lévy-Bruhl to historians of religions of our day one notices a progressive loss of creativity and an accompanying loss of interpretive cultural syntheses in favor of fragmented, analytical research.[4] If one still speaks of taboo and totemism, it is above all due to the popularity of Freud; if one is interested in the religions of the "primitives," it is thanks to Malinowski and some other anthro-

3. We have cited these authors because they envisage the history of religions as a "total science." But this does not at all imply that we share their methodological presuppositions or their personal valorizations of the history of religions.
4. It is true that a Rudolf Otto or a Gerardus van der Leeuw succeeded in awakening the interest of the informed public in religious problems. But their case is more complex in that they have not exercised an influence a historians of religions but, rather, through their prestige as theologians an philosophers of religion.

pologists; if the so-called myth and ritual school still attracts the attention of the public, it is because of the theologians and some literary critics.

This defeatist attitude of the historians of religions (rewarded by the progressive disinterest of the public in their work) was crystallized precisely in an epoch in which knowledge concerning man increased considerably due to psychoanalysis, phenomenology, and revolutionary artistic experiments and, above all, at the moment when the confrontation with Asia and the "primitive" world began. Personally we consider this fact both paradoxical and tragic, for this spiritual timidity became general exactly at a time when the history of religions should have been able to constitute the exemplary discipline for deciphering and interpreting the "unknown universes" that Western man confronted.[5]

However, we do not believe that it is impossible to reestablish the history of religions in the central position it merits. It requires, above all, that the historians of religions become aware of their unlimited possibilities. It is not necessary to let oneself become paralyzed by the immensity of the task; it is necessary above all to renounce the easy excuse that not all the documents have been conveniently collected and interpreted. All the other humanist disciplines, to say nothing of the natural sciences, find themselves in an analogous situation. But no man of science has waited until *all* the facts were assembled before trying to understand the facts already known. Besides, it is necessary to free oneself from the superstition that analysis represents the *true* scientific work and that one ought to propose a synthesis or a generalization only rather late in life. One does not know any example of a science or a humanist discipline whose representatives are devoted exclusively to analysis without attempting to advance a working hypothesis or to draft a generalization. The human mind works in this compartmented manner only at the price of its own creativity. There exist, perhaps, in the diverse scientific disciplines some scholars who have never gone beyond the stage of analysis — but they are victims of the modern organization of research. In any case, they ought not be considered models. Science does not owe any significant discovery to them.

5. We have discussed this problem a number of times, most recently in the preface to our book *Méphistophélès et l'Androgyne* (Paris, 1962), (English translation, 1965).

"Initiation" or Self-alienation

For the history of religions, as for many other humanist disciplines, "analysis" is equivalent to "philology." One does not consider a scholar responsible unless he has mastered a philology (understanding by this term knowledge of the language, history, and culture of the societies whose religion he studies). Justifiably, Nietzsche spoke of philology (in his case, classical philology) as an "initiation": one cannot participate in the "Mysteries" (i.e., in the sources of Greek spirituality) without first being initiated, in other words, without mastering the classical philology. But none of the great classicists of the nineteenth century, from Frederich Welcky to Erwin Rohde and Willamowitz-Moelendorff, remained within the bounds of philology *stricto sensu*. Each, in his own way, produced magnificent works of synthesis which have continued to nourish Western culture even when, from a strictly philological point of view, they have been surpassed. Certainly, a considerable number of scholars belonging to various humanist disciplines have not attempted to go beyond "philology." But their example ought not to preoccupy us, for the exclusive concentration on the *exterior* aspects of a spiritual universe is equivalent in the end to a process of self-alienation.

For the history of religions, as for every other humanist discipline, the road toward synthesis passes through hermeneutics. But in the case of the history of religions, hermeneutics shows itself to be a more complex operation, for it is not only a question of comprehending and interpreting the "religious facts." Because of their nature these religious facts constitute a material on which one can think — or even ought to think — and think in a creative manner, just as did Montesquieu, Voltaire, Herder, and Hegel when they applied themselves to the task of thinking about human institutions and their history.

Such a creative hermeneutics does not always seem to guide the work of the historians of religions because, perhaps, of the inhibition provoked by the triumph of "scientism" in certain humanist disciplines. In the measure that the social sciences and a certain anthropology have endeavored to become more "scientific," the historians of religions have become more prudent, indeed, more timid. But it involves a misunderstanding. Neither the history of religions nor any other humanist discipline ought to conform —

as they have already done too long — to models borrowed from the natural sciences, still more as these models are out of date (especially those borrowed from physics).

By reason of its own mode of being, the history of religions is constrained to produce *oeuvres*, not only erudite monographs. Contrary to the natural sciences and to a sociology that strives to follow their model, hermeneutics ranges itself among the living sources of a culture. For, in short, every culture is constituted by a series of interpretations and revalorizations of its "myths" or its specific ideologies. It is not only the creators *stricto sensu* who reassess the primordial visions and who reinterpret the fundamental ideas of a culture; it is also the "hermeneuts." In Greece, along with Homer, the tragic poets, and the philosophers from the pre-Socratics to Plotinus, there is a vast and complex category of mythographers, historians, and critics, from Herodotus to Lucian and Plutarch. The importance of Italian humanism in the history of thought is due more to its "hermeneuts" than to its writers. By his critical editions, philological erudition, commentaries, and correspondence, Erasmus renewed Western culture. From a certain point of view one could say that the Reformation and the Counter-Reformation constituted vast hermeneutics, intense and sustained efforts to revaluate the Judeo-Christian tradition by an audacious reinterpretation.

It is useless to multiply examples. Let us recall only the considerable repercussion of the *Kultur der Renaissance in Italien* (1860) of Jakob Burckhardt. The case of Burckhardt illustrates admirably what we understand by the expression "creative hermeneutics." Indeed, his work is more than a respectable work, one volume among others in the vast historiographic literature of the nineteenth century. This book helped to *form* the historiographic consciousness of the nineteenth century. It enriched Western culture with a new "value" by revealing a dimension of the Italian Renaissance that was not evident before Burckhardt.

Hermeneutics and the Changing of Man

The fact that a hermeneutics leads to the creation of new cultural values does not imply that it is not "objective." From a certain point of view, one can compare the hermeneutics to a scientific or technological "discovery." Before the discovery, the reality that one came to discover was there, only one did not see it, or did not understand it, or did not know how to use it. In the same way, a creative hermeneutics unveils significations that one did not grasp before, or puts them in relief with such vigor that after having assimilated this new interpretation the consciousness is no longer the same.

In the end, the creative hermeneutics *changes* man; it is more than instruction, it is also a spiritual technique susceptible of modifying the quality of existence itself. This is true above all for the historico-religious hermeneutics. A good history of religions book ought to produce in the reader an action of *awakening* — like that produced, for example, by *Das Heilige* or *Die Götter Griechlands*. But in principle every historico-religious hermeneutics ought to have similar results. For in presenting and analyzing the Australian, African, or Oceanian myths and rituals, in giving a commentary on the hymns of Zarathustra, Taoist texts, or the shamanistic mythologies and techniques, the historian of religions unveils some existential situations that are unknown or that are imaginable only with great difficulty by the modern reader; the encounter with these "foreign" worlds cannot continue without consequences.

Obviously, the historian of religions himself will feel the consequences of his own hermeneutical work. If these consequences are not always evident, it is because the majority of historians of religions defend themselves against the messages with which their documents are filled. This caution is understandable. One does not live with impunity in intimacy with "foreign" religious forms, which are sometimes extravagant and often terrible. But many historians of religions end by no longer taking seriously the spiritual worlds they study; they fall back on their personal religious faith, or they take refuge in a materialism or behaviorism impervious to every spiritual shock. Besides, excessive specialization allows a great number of historians of religions to station themselves for the rest of their days in the sectors they have learned to frequent since their youth. And every "specialization" ends by making the religious forms banal; in the last instance it effaces their meanings.

Despite all these failures, we do not doubt that the "creative hermeneutics" will finally be recognized as the royal road of the history of religions. Only then will its role in culture begin to show itself to be important. This will be due not only to the new values discovered by the effort to understand a primitive or exotic religion or a mode of being foreign to Western traditions — values susceptible of enriching a culture as have *La Cité antique* or the *Kultur des Renaissance Italien* — it will be due above all to the fact that the history of religions can open new perspectives to Western thought, to philosophy properly speaking as well as to artistic creation.

We have often repeated it: Western philosophy cannot contain itself indefinitely within its own tradition without the risk of becoming provincial. Now the history of religions is able to investigate and elucidate a considerable number of "significant situations" and modalities of existing in the world that are otherwise inaccessible. It is not just a matter of presenting "raw materials," for the philosophers would not know what to do with documents that reflect behavior and ideas too different from those familiar to them.[6] The hermeneutical work ought to be done by the historian of religions himself, for only he is prepared to understand and appreciate the semantic complexity of his documents.

But it is exactly at this point that certain grave misunderstandings have occurred. The rare historians of religions who have wanted to integrate the results of their researches and meditations in a philosophical context have contented themselves with imitating certain fashionable philosophers. In other words, they have compelled themselves to think according to the model of the professional philosophers. And that was a mistake. Neither philosophers nor men of culture are interested in second-hand replicas of their colleagues and favorite authors. In deciding to "think like X" about archaic or oriental thought the historian of religions mutilates and falsifies it. What one expects from him is that he will decipher and elucidate enigmatic behavior and situations, in brief, that he will advance the understanding of man by recovering, or reestablishing meanings that have been forgotten, discredited, or abolished. The originality and importance of such contributions reside precisely in the fact that they explore and illuminate spiritual universes that are submerged or that are ac-

6. It suffices to examine what some rare contemporary philosophers interested in the problems of myth and religious symbolism have done with the "materials" they have borrowed from ethnologists or historians of religions in order to renounce this (illusory) division of labor.

cessible only with great difficulty. It would be not only illegitimate but ineffectual to disguise archaic and exotic symbols, myths, and ideas in a form already familiar to contemporary philosophers.

History of Religion and Cultural Renewal

The example of Nietzsche ought to encourage and, at the same time, guide the historians of religions. Nietzsche succeeded in renewing Western philosophy precisely because he attempted to formulate his thought with the means that seemed adequate to it. Certainly that is not to say that the historian of religions ought to imitate the style or mannerisms of Nietzsche. It is rather the example of his freedom of expression that should be underlined. When one wants to analyze the mythical worlds of "primitives," or the techniques of the neo-Taoists, or shamanistic initiations, and so forth, one is not at all obliged to borrow either the methods of a contemporary philosopher or the perspective or language of psychology, cultural anthropology, or sociology.

This is the reason we have said that a historico-religious creative hermeneutics would be able to stimulate, nourish, and renew philosophical thought. From a certain point of view, one could say that a new *Phenomenology of the Mind* awaits elaboration by taking account of all that the history of religions is capable of revealing to us. There would be important books to write on modes of existing in the world or on the problems of time, death, and dream, based on documents that the historian of religions has at his disposal.[7] These problems have passionate interest for philosophers, poets, and art critics. Some of them have read the historians of religions and have utilized their documents and interpretations. It

---

7. There are, above all, urgent rectifications to bring to so many clichés still encumbering contemporary culture, for example, Feuerbach's and Marx's celebrated interpretations of religion as alienation. As one knows, Feuerbach and Marx proclaimed that religion estranges man from the earth, prevents him from becoming completely human, and so on. But, even if this were correct, such a critique of religion could be applied only to late forms of religiosity such as those of post-Vedic India or of Judeo-Christianity — that is, religions in which the element of "other-worldness" plays an important role. Alienation and estrangement of man from the earth are unknown, and, moreover, inconceivable, in all religions of the cosmic type, "primitive" as well as oriental; in this case (that is to say, in the overwhelming majority of religions known to history), the religious life consists exactly in exalting the solidarity of man with life and nature.

is not their fault if they have not profited from these readings as they expected.

We have alluded to the interest that the history of religions holds for artists, writers, and literary critics. Unhappily, historians of religions, like most scholars and erudites, have interested themselves in modern artistic experiments only sporadically and in a kind of clandestine manner. There is a preconceived idea that the arts are not "serious," for they do not constitute instruments of knowledge. One reads the poets and novelists and visits museums and expositions to find distraction or relaxation. This prejudice, which is fortunately beginning to disappear, has created a kind of inhibition whose principal results are the uneasiness, ignorance, or suspicion of the erudites and scientists vis-à-vis modern artistic experiments. It is naïvely believed that six months of "field work" among a tribe whose language one can scarcely speak haltingly constitutes "serious" work that can advance knowledge of man — and one ignores all that surrealism or James Joyce, Henry Michaux, and Picasso have contributed to the knowledge of man.

The contemporary artistic experiments are capable of aiding the historians of religions in their own research, and, conversely, a truly historico-religious exegesis is called to stimulate the artists, writers, and critics, not because one finds "the same thing" in both cases, but because one encounters situations which they can clarify reciprocally. It is not without interest to note, for example, that in their revolt against the traditional forms of art and their attacks on bourgeois society and morality the surrealists not only elaborated a revolutionary aesthetic but also formulated a technique by which they hoped to *change* the human condition. A number of these "exercises" (for examples, the effort to obtain a "mode of existence" that participates in both the waking and sleeping states or the effort to realize the "coexistence of the conscious and the unconscious") recall certain Yogic or Zen practices. Moreover, one deciphers in the early *élan* of surrealism, and notably in the poems and theoretical manifestos of André Breton, a nostalgia for the "primordial totality," the desire to effect *in concreto* the coincidence of opposites, the hope of being able to annul history in order to begin anew with the original power and purity — nostalgia and hopes rather familiar to historians of religions.

Moreover, all the modern artistic movements seek, consciously or unconsciously, the destruction of the traditional aesthetic uni-

verses, the reduction of "forms" to elementary, germinal, larval
states in the hope of re-creating "fresh worlds"; in other words,
these movements seek to abolish the history of art and to reintegrate the auroral moment when man saw the world "for the
first time." It is unnecessary to mention how all this should interest
the historian of religions familiar with the rather well-known
mythological system that involves the symbolic destruction and
re-creation of the universe in order to periodically begin anew a
"pure" existence in a fresh, strong, and fertile world.

It is not a question of developing close correspondences here
between the modern artistic experiments and certain behaviors,
symbolisms, and beliefs familiar to historians of religions. For a
generation already, especially in the United States, critics have
utilized historico-religious documents in the interpretation of literary works. We have stressed in another chapter (see below, p. 123)
the interest in symbolisms and rituals of initiation shown by literary critics; indeed, they have grasped the importance of this
religious complex for the elucidation of the secret message of certain works. To be sure, it is not a matter of homologous phenomena; the pattern of initiation survives in literature in relation to
the structure of an imaginary universe, while the historian of
religions has to do with lived experiences and traditional institutions. But the fact that the pattern of initiation persists in the imaginary universes of modern man — in literature, dreams, and
daydreams — invites the historian of religions to meditate more
attentively on the value of his own documents.

Resistances

In brief, the history of religions affirms itself as both a "peda-
gogy," in the strong sense of that term, for it is susceptible of changing man, and a source of creation of "cultural values," whatever
may be the expression of these values, historiographic, philo-
sophic, or artistic. It is to be expected that the assumption of this
function by the history of religions will be suspected, if not frankly
contested, by the scientists as well as by the theologians. The
former are suspicious of any effort to revalorize religion. Satisfied
with the vertiginous secularization of Western societies, the scientists are inclined to suspect obscurantism or nostalgia in authors who see in the different forms of religion something other

than superstition, ignorance, or, at the most, psychological behavior, social institutions, and rudimentary ideologies fortunately left behind by the progress of scientific thought and the triumph of technology. Such a suspicion does not belong exclusively to the scientists in the strict sense of the term; it is equally shared by a large number of sociologists, anthropologists, and social scientists who conduct themselves, not as humanists, but as naturalists with respect to their object of study. But it is necessary to accept such resistance gracefully; it is inevitable in any culture that can still develop in complete freedom.

As for the theologians, their hesitations are explained by various reasons. On the one hand, they are rather suspicious of historico-religious hermeneutics that might encourage syncretism or religious dilettantism or, worse yet, raise doubt about the uniqueness of the Judeo-Christian revelation. On the other hand, the history of religions envisages, in the end, cultural *creation* and the *modification* of man. The humanist culture poses an embarrassing problem for theologians and for Christians in general: What do Athens and Jerusalem have in common? We do not intend to discuss here this problem that still obsesses certain theologians. But it would be futile to ignore the fact that nearly all the contemporary philosophies and ideologies recognize that man's specific mode of being in the universe inevitably forces him to be a creator of culture. Whatever the point of departure for an analysis that seeks a definition of man, whether one utilizes the psychological, sociological, or existentialist approach, or some criterion borrowed from classical philosophies, one comes, explicitly or implicitly, to characterize man as a creator of culture (i.e., language, institutions, techniques, arts, etc.). And all the methods of liberation of man — economic, political, psychological — are justified by their final goal: to deliver man from his chains or his complexes in order to open him to the world of the spirit and to render him *culturally creative*. Moreover, for the unbelievers or the irreligious all that a theologian, indeed, simply a Christian, considers heterogeneous in the sphere of culture — the mystery of faith, the sacramental life, etc. — is included in the sphere of "cultural creations." And one cannot deny the character of "cultural facts," at least to the *historical expressions* of the Christian religious experience. Many contemporary theologians have already accepted the presuppositions of the sociology of religion and are ready to accept the inevitability

of technology. The fact that there are some theologies of culture
indicates the direction in which contemporary theological thought
is moving.[8]

But for the historian of religions the problem is posed differently, although not necessarily in contradiction with the theologies of culture. The historian of religions knows that what one
calls "profane culture" is a comparatively recent manifestation in
the history of the spirit. In the beginning, every cultural creation —
tools, institutions, arts, ideologies, etc. — was a religious expression or had a religious justification or source. This is not always
evident to a nonspecialist, particularly because he is used to con-
ceiving "religion" according to the forms familiar in Western
societies or in the great Asian religions. It is conceded that dance,
poetry, or wisdom were, in their beginning, religious; one has
difficulty in imagining that alimentation or sexuality, an essential
work (hunting, fishing, agriculture, etc.), the tools employed, or
a habitation, equally participate in the sacred. And yet one of
the embarrassing difficulties for the historian of religions is that
the nearer he approaches to "origins," the greater becomes the
number of "religious facts." This is so much so that in certain
cases (for example, in archaic or prehistoric societies) one asks
himself what is *not* or has not once been "sacred" or connected
with the sacred.

The Fallacy of Demystification

It would be useless, because ineffectual, to appeal to some reductionist principle and to demystify the behavior and ideologies of
homo religiosus by showing, for example, that it is a matter of
projections of the unconscious, or of screens raised for social, economic, political, or other reasons. Here we touch a rather thorny
problem that comes again to each generation with new force.
We shall not try to discuss it in a few lines, especially as we
have already discussed it in several earlier publications.[9] Let us

8. The recent "anticultural" crises should not impress us too much. Con-
tempt for or rejection of culture constitutes dialectical moments in the history
of the mind.

9. See, for example, *Images et symboles* (Paris, 1952), pp. 13 ff. (English
translation: *Images and Symbols* [New York, 1961], pp. 9 ff.); *Mythes,
rêves et mystères* (Paris, 1957), pp. 10 ff., 156 ff. (English translation: *Myths,
Dreams and Mysteries* [New York, 1960], pp. 13 ff., 106 ff.); *Méphistophélès
et l'Androgyne*, pp. 194 ff.

recall, however, a single example. In a number of traditional archaic cultures the village, temple, or house is considered to be located at the "Center of the World." There is no sense in trying to "demystify" such a belief by drawing the attention of the reader to the fact that there exists no Center of the World and that, in any case, the multiplicity of such centers is an absurd notion because it is self-contradictory. On the contrary, it is only by taking this belief seriously, by trying to clarify all its cosmological, ritual, and social implications, that one succeeds in comprehending the existential situation of a man who believes that he is at the Center of the World. All his behavior, his understanding of the world, the values he accords to life and to his own existence, arise and become articulated in a "system" on the basis of this belief that his house or his village is situated near the *axis mundi*.

We have cited this example in order to recall that demystification does not serve hermeneutics. Consequently, whatever may be the reason for which human activities in the most distant past were charged with a religious value, the important thing for the historian of religions remains the fact that these activities *have had* religious values. This is to say that the historian of religions recognizes a spiritual unity subjacent to the history of humanity; in other terms, in studying the Australians, Vedic Indians, or whatever other ethnic group or cultural system, the historian of religions does not have a sense of moving in a world radically "foreign" to him. Certainly, the unity of the human species is accepted *de facto* in other disciplines, for example, linguistics, anthropology, sociology. But the historian of religions has the privilege of grasping this unity at the highest levels — or the deepest — and such an experience is susceptible of enriching and changing him. Today history is becoming truly universal for the first time, and so culture is in the process of becoming "planetary." The history of man from paleolithic to present times is destined to occupy the center of humanist education, whatever the local or national interpretations. The history of religions can play an essential role in this effort toward a *planétisation* of culture; it can contribute to the elaboration of a universal type of culture.

Certainly, all this will not come tomorrow. But the history of religions will be able to play this role only if the historians of religions become conscious of their responsibility, in other words, if they break free of the inferiority complexes, timidity, and immobility of the last fifty years. To remind historians of religions that they are supposed to contribute creatively to culture, that they do not have the right to produce only *Beiträge* but also some *cultural values* does not mean to say that one invites them to make facile syntheses and hasty generalizations. It is on the example of an E. Rohde, a Pettazzoni, a van der Leeuw that one ought to meditate and not on that of some successful journalist. But it is the attitude of the historian of religions vis-à-vis his own discipline that ought to change if he wants to hope for an early renewal of this discipline. In the measure that historians of religions will not attempt to integrate their researches in the living stream of contemporary culture, the "generalizations" and "syntheses" will be made by dilettantes, amateurs, journalists. Or, what is no happier, instead of a creative hermeneutics in the perspective of the history of religions, we shall continue to submit to the audacious and irrelevant interpretations of religious realities made by psychologists, sociologists, or devotees of various reductionist ideologies. And for one or two generations yet we shall read books in which the religious realities will be explained in terms of infantile traumatisms, social organization, class conflict, and so on. Certainly such books, including those produced by dilettantes as well as those written by reductionists of various kinds, will continue to appear, and probably with the same success. But the cultural milieu will not be the same if, beside this production, appear some responsible books signed by historians of religions. (This on the condition, understandably, that these books of synthesis are not improvised, at the demand of a publisher, as happens sometimes even with very respectable scholars. Obviously, "synthesis," like "analysis," is not amenable to improvisation.)

It seems to me difficult to believe that, living in a historical moment like ours, the historians of religions will not take account of the creative possibilities of their discipline. How to assimilate *culturally* the spiritual universes that Africa, Oceania, Southeast Asia open to us? All these spiritual universes have a religious origin and structure. If one does not approach them in the perspective of the history of religions, they will disappear as spiritual universes; they will be reduced to *facts* about social organizations economic regimes, epochs of precolonial and colonial history etc. In other words, they will not be grasped as spiritual creations they will not enrich Western and world culture — they will serve to augment the number, already terrifying, of *documents* classified in archives, awaiting electronic computers to take them in charge.

It may be, of course, that this time also the historians of religions will sin through an excessive timidity and leave to other disciplines the task of interpreting these spiritual universes (alas! already changing vertiginously, perhaps even disappearing). It may also be that, for various reasons, the historians of religions will prefer to remain in the subordinate situation that they have previously accepted. In this case we must expect a slow but irrevocable process of decomposition, which will end in the disappearance of the history of religions as an autonomous discipline. Thus, in one or two generations, we shall have some Latinist "specialists" in the history of Roman religion, Indianist "specialists" in one of the Indian religions, and so on. In other words, the history of religions will be endlessly fragmented and the fragments reabsorbed in the different "philologies," which today still serve it as documentary sources nourishing its own hermeneutics.

As for the problems of more general interest — for example, myth, ritual, religious symbolism, conceptions of death, initiation, etc. — they will be treated by sociologists, anthropologists, philosophers (as was done, moreover, from the beginnings of our studies, although never exclusively). But this leads us to say that the problems that preoccupy the historians of religions today *will not in themselves disappear*; it is to say only that they will be studied in other perspectives, with different methods, and in the pursual of different objectives. The void left by the disappearance of the history of religions as an autonomous discipline will not be filled. But the gravity of our responsibility will remain the same.

5

Cosmogonic Myth
and "Sacred History"

The Living Myth and the Historian of Religions

It is not without fear and trembling that a historian of religion
approaches the problem of myth. This is not only because of that
preliminary embarrassing question: what is intended by myth? It
is also because the answers given depend for the most part on
the documents selected by the scholar. From Plato and Fontenelle
to Schelling and Bultmann, philosophers and theologians have proposed innumerable definitions of myth. But all of these have one
thing in common: they are based on the analysis of Greek mythology. Now, for a historian of religions this choice is not a very happy
one. It is true that only in Greece did myth inspire and guide
epic poetry, tragedy, and comedy, as well as the plastic arts; but
it is no less true that it is especially in Greek culture that myth
was submitted to a long and penetrating analysis, from which it
emerged radically "demythicized." If in every European language
the word "myth" denotes a "fiction," it is because the Greeks proclaimed it to be such twenty-five centuries ago. What is even more
serious for an historian of religion: we do not know a single Greek
myth within its ritual context. Of course this is not the case with
the paleo-oriental and Asiatic religions; it is especially not the case

This chapter is a revised and expanded version of an article first published in *Religious Studies*, 2 (1967): 171–83.

The article in *Religious Studies* represents a slightly modified translation
of a public lecture given at the XIII Congress of the "Sociétés de Philosophie
de Langue Française," Geneva, September 2–6, 1966. Hence the style of
the spoken word.

with the so-called primitive religions. As is well known, a *living myth* is always connected with a cult, inspiring and justifying a religious behavior. None of this of course means that Greek myth should not figure in an investigation of the mythical phenomenon. But it would seem unwise to begin our kind of inquiry by the study of Greek documents, and even more so to restrict it to such documents. The mythology which informs Homer, Hesiod, and the tragic poets represents already a selection and an interpretation of archaic materials, some of which had become almost unintelligible. In short, our best chance of understanding the structure of mythical thought is to study cultures where myth is a "living thing," where it constitutes the very ground of the religious life; in other words, where myth, far from indicating a *fiction*, is considered to reveal the *truth par excellence*.

This is what anthropologists have done, for more than half a century, concentrating on "primitive" societies. We cannot here review the contributions of Andrew Lang, Frazer, Lévy-Bruhl, Malinowski, Leenhard, or Lévi-Strauss. Some results of ethnological research will have our attention later on. We have to add, however, that the historian of religions is not always happy with the approach of the anthropologists nor with their general conclusions. Reacting against an excessive concern with comparison, most of the authors have neglected to supplement their anthropological research with a rigorous study of other mythologies, for example those of the ancient Near East, in the first place of Mesopotamia and Egypt, those of the Indo-Europeans — especially the grandiose, exuberant mythologies of ancient and medieval India — and those, finally, of the Turco-Mongols, the Tibetans, and the peoples of Southeast Asia. A restriction of the inquiry to "primitive" mythologies risks giving the impression that there is no continuity between archaic thought and the thought of the peoples who played an important role in ancient history. Now, such a solution of continuity does not exist. Moreover, by limiting the research to primitive societies, we are left with no measure of the role of myths in complex and highly developed religions, like those of the ancient Near East and India, To give only one example, it is impossible to understand the religion and, in general, the style of Mesopotamian culture if we ignore the cosmogonic myth and the origin myths preserved in *Enuma elish* and in the Gilgamesh Epic. At every New Year the fabulous events related in *Enuma elish* were ritually reenacted; every New Year the world needed to be re-created — and this necessity reveals a profound dimension of Mesopotamian thought. Moreover, the myth of the origin of man illuminates, at least in part, the tragic world-view and pessimism characteristic of Mesopotamian culture: for man has been molded by Marduk from clay, that is, from the very body of the primordial monster Tiamat, and from the blood of the arch-demon Kingu. And the myth clearly indicates that man has been created by Marduk in order that the gods may be nourished by human labor. Finally, the Gilgamesh Epic presents an equally pessimistic vision by explaining why man did not, and could not, obtain immortality.

This is the reason why the historians of religions prefer the approach of their colleagues — a Raffaelle Pettazzoni or a Gerardus van der Leeuw — or even the approach of certain scholars in the field of comparative anthropology, like Adolf Jensen or H. Baumann, who deal with all categories of mythological creativity, those of the "primitives" as well as of the peoples of high cultures. While one may not always agree with the results of their researches, one is at least certain that their documentation is sufficiently broad to permit valid generalizations.

But the divergences resulting from an incomplete documentation do not constitute the only difficulty in the dialogue between the historian of religions and his colleagues from other disciplines. It is his very approach which separates him, for instance, from the anthropologist or the psychologist. The historian of religions is too conscious of the axiological difference of his documents to marshal them on the same level. Aware of nuances and distinctions, he cannot ignore the fact that there exist great myths and myths of less importance; myths which dominate and characterize a religion, and secondary myths, repetitious and parasitical. *Enuma elish*, for example, cannot figure on the same plane with the mythology of the female demon Lamashtu; the Polynesian cosmogonic myth has not the same weight as the myth of the origin of a plant, for it precedes it and serves as a model for it. Such differences may not be important for an anthropologist or a psychologist. For instance, a sociologist concerned to study the French novel in the nineteenth century or a psychologist interested in literary imagination might discuss Balzac and Eugène Sue, Stendhal or Jules Sandeau indifferently, irrespective of the quality of their art. But for a literary critic such conflation is simply unthinkable, for it annihilates his own hermeneutical principles.

When, in one or two generations, perhaps even earlier, we have historians of religions who are descended from Australian, African, or Melanesian tribal societies, I do not doubt that, among other things, they will reproach Western scholars for their indifference to the scale of values *indigenous* to these societies. Let us imagine a history of Greek culture in which Homer, the tragic poets, and Plato are passed by silently while the *Book of Dreams* of Artemidorus and the novel of Heliodorus from Emessa are laboriously commented on, under the pretext that such works better illuminate the specific traits of the Greek genius and help us to understand its destiny. To come back to our theme, I do not think that we can grasp the structure and function of mythical thought in a society which has myth as its foundation if we do not take into account the *mythology in its totality* and, at the same time, the *scale of values* which such mythology implicitly or explicitly proclaims.

Now in every case where we have access to a still living tradition, and not to an acculturated one, one thing strikes us from the very beginning: the mythology not only constitutes, as it were, the "sacred history" of the tribe, not only does it explain the total reality and justify its contradictions, but it equally reveals a hierarchy in the series of fabulous events that it reports. In general, one can say that any myth tells how something came into being, the world, or man, or an animal species, or a social institution, and so on. But by the very fact that the creation of the world precedes everything else, the cosmogony enjoys a special prestige. In fact, as I have tried to show elsewhere,[1] the cosmogonic myth furnishes the model for all myths of origin. The creation of animals, plants, or man presupposes the existence of a world.

Certainly, the myth of the creation of the world does not always look like a cosmogonic myth *stricto sensu*, like the Indian or Polynesian myth, or the one narrated in *Enuma elish*. In a great part of Australia, for example, such cosmogonic myths are unknown. But there is always a central myth which describes the beginnings of the world, that is, what happened before the world became as

1. See especially *The Myth of the Eternal Return* (translated from the French by Willard R. Trask), (New York and London, 1954); *Myth and Reality* (New York and London, 1963).

it is today. Thus, there is always a *primordial history* and this history has a *beginning*: a cosmogonic myth proper, or a myth that describes the first, germinal stage of the world. This beginning is always implied in the sequence of myths which recounts the fabulous events that took place after the creation or the coming into being of the universe, namely, the myths of the origin of plants, animals, and man, or of the origin of marriage, family, and death, etc. Taken all together, these myths of origin constitute a fairly coherent history. They reveal how the cosmos was shaped and changed, how man became mortal, sexually diversified, and compelled to work in order to live; they equally reveal what the supernatural beings and the mythical ancestors did, and how and why they abandoned the earth and disappeared. We can also say that any mythology that is still accessible in an appropriate form contains not only a beginning but also an end, determined by the last manifestation of the supernatural beings, the cultural heroes, or the ancestors.

Now this primordial, sacred history, brought together by the totality of significant myths, is fundamental because it explains, and by the same token justifies, the existence of the world, of man and of society. This is the reason that a mythology is considered at once a *true history*: it relates how things came into being, providing the exemplary model and also the justifications of man's activities. One understands what one is — mortal and of a certain sex — and how that came about, because the myths tell how death and sexuality made their appearance. One engages in a certain type of hunting or agriculture because the myths report how the cultural heroes taught these techniques to the ancestors. I have insisted on this paradigmatic function of myth in other publications, and consequently I do not need to repeat the point again.

I would like, however, to amplify and complete what I have said, having regard mainly to what I called the sacred history preserved in the great myths. This is easier said than done. The first difficulty which confronts us is a material one. To analyze and interpret a mythology or a mythological theme conveniently, one has to take into consideration all the available documents. But this is impossible in a lecture, or even in a short monograph. Claude Lévi-Strauss has devoted more than 300 pages to the analysis of a group of South American myths, and he had to leave aside the mythologies of the Fuegians and other neighboring peoples in order to concentrate primarily on the origin myths of the Amazonians. I must therefore limit myself to one or two characteristic examples. I will examine primarily those elements that seem essential to the myths of aborigines. Of course even such résumés might appear too long. But since I am dealing with rather unfamiliar mythologies, I cannot be content with mere allusions to them, as I could in the case of *Enuma elish* or the Greek, and even Indian, myths. Moreover, any exegesis is grounded in a philology. It would be pointless to propose an interpretation of the myths I have in mind without providing at least a minimum of documentation.

Meaning and Function of a Cosmogonic Myth

My first example is the mythology of the Ngadju Dayak of Borneo. I have chosen it because there is available a work about it which deserves to become a classic: *Die Gottesidee der Ngadju Dajak in Süd-Borneo* (Leiden, 1946) by Hans Schärer.[2] The author, who unfortunately died prematurely, studied these people for many years. The mythological documents which he collected, if ever printed, would cover 12,000 pages. Hans Schärer not only mastered the language of these people and thoroughly knew their customs, but he also understood the structure of mythology and its role in the life of the Dayak. As for many other archaic peoples, for the Dayak the cosmogonic myth discloses the eventful creation of the world and of man and, at the same time, the principles which govern the cosmic process and human existence. One must read this book to realize how much everything attains consistency in the life of an archaic people, how the myths succeed each other and articulate themselves into a sacred history which is continuously recovered in the life of the community as well as in the existence of each individual. Through the cosmogonic myth and its sequel, the Dayak progressively unveils the structures of reality and of his own proper mode of being. What happened in the beginning describes at once both the original perfection and the destiny of each individual.

At the beginning, so the myth goes, the cosmic totality was still

2. The book has recently been translated into English by Rodney Needham, *Ngaju Religion. The Conception of God among a South Borneo People* (The Hague, 1963).

undivided in the mouth of the coiled watersnake. Eventually two
mountains arise and from their repeated clashes the cosmic reality
comes progressively into existence: the clouds, the hills, the sun
and the moon, and so on. The mountains are the seats of the two
supreme deities, and they are also these deities themselves. They
reveal their human forms, however, only at the end of the first
part of the creation. In their anthropomorphic form, the two supreme deities, Mahatala and his wife Putir, pursue the cosmogonic work and create the upperworld and the underworld. But
there is still lacking an intermediary world, and mankind to inhabit it. The third phase of the creation is carried out by two hornbills, male and female, who are actually identical with the two
supreme deities. Mahatala raises the tree of life in the "Center,"
the two hornbills fly over toward it, and eventually meet each
other in its branches. A furious fight breaks out between the two
birds, and as a result the tree of life is extensively damaged. From
the knotty excrescences of the tree and from the moss falling out
from the throat of the female hornbill, a maiden and a young
man come forth, the ancestors of the Dayak. The tree of life is
finally destroyed and the two birds end by killing each other.

   In sum, during the work of creation the deities reveal themselves under three different forms: cosmic (the two mountains),
anthropomorphic (Mahatala and Putir), theriomorphic (the two
hornbills). But these polar manifestations represent only one aspect of the divinity. Not less important are the godhead's manifestations as a *totality*: the primordial watersnake, for instance, or
the tree of life. This totality — which Schärer calls divine/ambiv-
alent totality — constitutes the fundamental principle of the religious life of the Dayak, and it is proclaimed again and again
in different contexts. One can say that, for the Dayaks, every divine form contains its opposite in the same measure as itself:
Mahatala is also his own wife and *vice versa*, and the watersnake
is also the hornbill and *vice versa*.

   The cosmogonic myth enables us to understand the religious life
of the Dayaks as well as their culture and their social organization. The world is the result of a combat between two polar principles, during which the tree of life — i.e. their own embodi-
ment — is annihilated. "But from destruction and death spring the
cosmos and a new life. The new creation originates in the death

of the total godhead."[3] In the most important religious ceremonies — birth, initiation, marriage, death — this creative clash is
tirelessly reiterated. As a matter of fact, everything which is significant in the eyes of a Dayak is an imitation of exemplary
models and a repetition of the events narrated in the cosmogonic
myth. The village as well as the house represent the universe and
are supposed to be situated at the Center of the World. The exemplary house is an *imago mundi*: it is erected on the back of
the watersnake, its steep roof symbolizes the primeval mountain
on which Mahatala is enthroned, and an umbrella represents the
tree of life on whose branches one can see the two birds.

During the ceremonies of marriage, the couple return to the
mythical primeval time. Such a return is indicated by a replica of
the tree of life that is clasped by the bridal pair. Schärer was told
that clasping the tree of life means to form a unity with it. "The
wedding is the reenactment of the creation, and the reenactment
of the creation is the creation of the first human couple from
the Tree of Life."[4] Birth also is related to the original time. The
room in which the child is born is symbolically situated in the
primeval waters. Likewise, the room where the young girls are
enclosed during initiation ceremonies is imagined to be located in
the primordial ocean. The young girl descends to the underworld
and after some time assumes the form of a watersnake. She comes
back to earth as a new person and begins a new life, both socially
and religiously.[5] Death is equally conceived as a passage to a
new and richer life. The deceased person returns to the primeval
era, his mystical voyage indicated by the form and decorations
of his coffin. In fact, the coffin has the shape of a boat, and on its
sides are painted the watersnake, the tree of life, the primordial
mountains, that is to say the cosmic/divine totality. In other words,
the dead man returns to the divine totality which existed at the
beginning.

On the occasion of each decisive crisis and each *rite de passage*,
man takes up again *ab initio* the world's drama. The operation is
carried out in two times: (1) the return to the primordial totality,
and (2) the repetition of the cosmogony, that is to say, the breaking
up of the primitive unity. The same operation takes place again

3. Hans Schärer, *Ngaju Religion*, p. 34.
4. *Ibid.*, p. 85.
5. *Ibid.*, p. 87.

during the collective annual ceremonies. Schärer points out that
the end of the year signifies the end of an era and also of a world; [6]
the ceremonies clearly indicate that there is a return to the precosmic time, the time of the sacred totality embodied in the watersnake and in the tree of life. In fact, during this period, sacred
par excellence, which is called *helat nyelo,* "the time between
the years," a replica of the tree of life is erected in the village and
all the population returns to the primeval (i.e., precosmogonic)
age. Rules and interdictions are suspended since the world has
ceased to exist. While waiting for a new creation the community
lives near the godhead, more exactly lives *in* the total primeval
godhead. The orgiastic character of the interval between the years
ought not to obscure its sacrality. As Schärer puts it, "there is no
question of disorder (even if it may appear so to us) but of another order." [7] The orgy takes place in accordance with the divine
commandments, and those who participate in it recover in themselves the total godhead. As is well known, in many other religions, primitive as well as historical, the periodical orgy is
considered to be the instrument *par excellence* to achieve the perfect totality. It is from such a totality that a new creation will take
place — for the Dayaks as well as for the Mesopotamians.

Primordiality and Totality

Even this imperfect résumé of an immense amount of material has
enabled us to grasp the considerable role that the cosmogonic
myth plays in an archaic society. The myth unveils the religious
thought of the Dayaks in all its depth and complexity. As we have
just seen it, the individual and collective life has a cosmological
structure: every life constitutes a cycle, whose model is the sem-
piternal creation, destruction, and re-creation of the world. Such
a conception is not restricted to the Dayak, or even to peoples having their type of culture. In other words, the Dayak myth reveals
to us a meaning which transcends its ethnographic frontiers. Now,
what is striking in this mythology is the great importance bestowed upon the *primordial totality.* One may almost say that the
Dayaks are obsessed by two aspects of the sacred: the *primordiality* and the *totality.* This does not mean that they belittle the work

6. Hans Schärer, *Ngaju Religion,* pp. 94 ff.
7. *Ibid.,* p. 97.

of creation. There is nothing of the Indian or gnostic pessimism in the Dayak conception of the cosmos and of life. The world is good and significant because it is sacred, since it came out from the tree of life, that is to say from the total godhead. But only the primordial total godhead is perfect. If the cosmos must be periodically abolished and re-created, it is not because the first creation did not succeed, but because it is only that stage which precedes the creation which represents a plenitude and a beatitude otherwise inaccessible in the created world. On the other hand, the myth points out the necessity of creation, that is, of the breaking up of the primeval unity. The original perfection is periodically reintegrated, but such perfection is always transitory. The Dayak myth proclaims that the creation — with all that it made possible: human existence, society, culture — cannot be definitively abolished. In other words, a "sacred history" has taken place, and this history must be perpetuated by periodical reiteration. It is impossible to freeze the reality in its germinal modality, such as it was in the beginning, immersed as it were in the primordial divine totality.

Now, it is this exceptional value conferred upon the "sacred history," ground and model of all human history, that is significant. Such attribution of value is recognizable in many other primitive mythologies, but it becomes particularly important in the mythologies of the ancient Near East and of Asia. If we examine a mythology in its totality we learn the judgment of the particular people upon its own sacred history. Every mythology presents a successive and coherent series of primordial events, but different peoples judge these fabulous acts in different ways, underlining the importance of some of them, casting aside, or even completely neglecting, others. If we analyze the context of what may be called the myth of the estrangement of the creator god and his progressive transformation into a *deus otiosus*, we notice a similar process, involving an analogous choice and judgment: out of a series of primordial creative events, only some of them are exalted, those in particular which are of consequence for human life. In other words, the coherent series of events which constitute the *sacred history* is incessantly remembered and extolled, while the previous stage, everything which existed *before* that sacred history — first and above all, the majestic and solitary presence of the creator God — fades away. If the High God is still remembered, he is known to have created the world and man, but this is almost all. Such a Supreme God seems to have ended his role by achieving the work of creation. He plays almost no role in the cult, his myths are few and rather banal, and, when he is not completely forgotten, he is invoked only in cases of extreme distress, when all other divine beings have proved utterly ineffectual.

The "Great Father" and the Mythical Ancestors

This lesson of the primitive myths is particularly revealing. It not only shows us that man, turning toward the divinities of life and fecundity, became as it were more and more incarnated. It also shows that early man assumes already, in his way, a history of which he is at once both the center and the victim. What happened to his mythical ancestors became, for him, more important than what happened *before* their appearance. One can illustrate this process with innumerable examples. I have discussed a number of such myths in previous works.[8] But I would like to examine now the mythical traditions of a people who for more than half a century have enjoyed a considerable vogue among anthropologists, sociologists, and psychologists, namely the Aranda tribes of Central Australia. I will draw exclusively from the materials collected by T. G. H. Strehlow,[9] the son of the famous missionary Carl Strehlow, whose writings gave rise to heated controversies in Durkheim's time. I think I choose the best living authority, for Aranda was the first language spoken by T. G. H. Strehlow, and he studied these tribes intensely for more than thirty years.

According to the Aranda, the sky and the earth have always existed and have always been inhabited by supernatural beings. In the sky there is an emu-footed personage, having emu-footed wives and children: it is the Great Father (*knaritja*), called also the Eternal Youth (*altjira nditja*). All these supernatural beings live in a perpetually green land, rich in flowers and fruits, trav-

8. See particularly *Myth and Reality,* pp. 92 ff.
9. Especially his *Aranda Traditions* (Melbourne, 1947) and his recent article "Personal Monototemism in a Polytotemic Community" in *Festschrift für Ad. E. Jensen* (Munich, 1964), pp. 723–54; cf. also "La gémellité de l'âme humaine" in *La Tour Saint-Jacques* (Paris, 1957), nos. 11–12, pp. 14–23. See also Mircea Eliade, "Australian Religion: An Introduction. Part II,' *History of Religions,* 6 (1967): 208–35, especially pp. 209 ff.

ersed by the Milky Way. All of them are eternally young, the
Great Father being in appearance as young as his children. And
all of them are as immortal as the stars themselves, for death cannot
enter their home.

Strehlow thinks that it would be impossible to regard this emu-
footed Great Father as a supernatural being analogous to certain celestial gods of Southeast Australia. Indeed, he did not create
or shape the earth, nor did he bring into existence either plants,
animals, man, or the totemic ancestors, nor did he inspire or control
the ancestors' activities. The Great Father and the other inhabitants of heaven were never interested in what happened on the
earth. Evil-doers had to fear not the celestial Great Father but the
wrath of the totemic ancestors and the punishment of the tribal
authorities. For, as we shall see in a moment, all the creative and
meaningful acts were effected by the earth-born totemic ancestors.
In sum, one can see here a drastic transformation of a celestial
being into a *deus otiosus*. The next step could only be his falling
into total oblivion. This probably did happen outside of the western Aranda territory, where Strehlow could not find any comparable beliefs in sky beings.

Nevertheless, there are some characteristic traits which allow
this otiose and transcendent Great Father and Eternal Youth a
place in the category of supreme beings. There is, first, his immortality, his youth, and his beatific existence; there is then his
ontological anteriority with regard to the totemic heroes; indeed,
he had been up there, in the sky, for a long time before the
emergence of the totemic ancestors from under the earth. Finally,
the religious importance of the sky is repeatedly proclaimed: for
example, in the myths of certain heroes who conquered immortality by ascending to heaven, in the mythical traditions of trees or
ladders connecting heaven and earth, and especially in the widespread Aranda beliefs that death came into being because the communications with heaven had been violently interrupted. Strehlow
recalls the traditions concerning a ladder joining the earth to
heaven, and describes the sites where, according to the legend,
there grew gigantic trees which certain mythical ancestors were
able to climb to heaven. Similar beliefs are to be found in many
other archaic traditions, particularly in myths relating that after
the interruption of the communications between heaven and earth,
the gods retired to the highest sky and became more or less *dii*

otiosi. From that moment on, only a few privileged personages – heroes, shamans, medicine men — have been able to ascend to heaven. We do not know how much of this mythical theme was familiar to the Aranda. But the fact is that, despite the reciprocal indifference between the Aranda and the celestial beings, the religious prestige of heaven continues to survive along with the haunting memory of a conquest of immortality by an ascension to heaven. One is tempted to read in these mythical fragments a certain nostalgia for a primordial situation irretrievably lost.

In any case the *primordium* represented by the celestial Great Father does not have any immediate significance for the Aranda. On the contrary, the Aranda seem to be interested exclusively in what happened at a certain moment *on the earth*. Such happenings are supremely significant; that is to say, in our terminology they have a religious value. Indeed, the events that took place in the mythical times, in the "Dream Time," are religious in the sense that they constitute a paradigmatic history which man has to follow and repeat in order to assure the continuity of the world of life and society.

While the Great Father and his family lived a sort of paradisiacal existence in the sky, without any responsibility, on the surface of earth there existed even from time immemorial amorphous semiembryonic masses of half-developed infants. They could not develop into individual men and women, but neither could they grow old or die. Indeed, neither life nor death was known on earth. Life existed fully *below* the surface of the earth, in the form of thousands of slumbering supernatural beings. They also were uncreated (as a matter of fact they are called "born out of their own eternity," *altijirana nambakala*). Finally they awoke from their sleep and broke through the surface of the earth. Their birthplaces are impregnated with their life and power. One of these supernatural beings is the sun, and when he emerged out of the ground the earth was flooded with light.

The forms of these chthonian beings were varied; some emerged in animal forms, others as men and women. But all of them had something in common: the theriomorphic ones acted and thought like humans, and those in human forms could change at will into a particular species of animal. These chthonian beings, commonly designated totemic ancestors, began to wander on the surface of the earth and to modify the land, giving the Central Australian landscape its actual physical features. Such works constitute properly speaking a cosmogony; the ancestors did not create the earth, but they gave form to a preexistent *materia prima*. And the anthropogony repeats the cosmogony. Some of the totemic ancestors took on the roles of culture heroes, slicing apart the semiembryonic aggregate, then shaping each individual infant by slitting the webs between his fingers and toes and cutting open his ears, eyes, and mouth. Other culture heroes taught men how to make tools and fire and to cook food, and they also revealed social and religious institutions to them.

As a result of all these labors, an extreme fatigue overpowered the ancestors, and they sank into the ground or turned into rocks, trees, or ritual objects (*tjurunga*). The sites which marked their final resting places are, like their birth places, regarded as important sacred centers, and are called by the same name, *pmara kutata*. But the disappearance of the ancestors, which put an end to the primordial age, is not final. Though reimmersed in their initial slumber under the surface of the earth, they watch over the behavior of men. Moreover, the ancestors reincarnate themselves perpetually; as Strehlow has shown,[10] the immortal soul of each individual represents a particle of an ancestor's life.

This fabulous epoch when the ancestors were roaming about the land is for the Aranda tantamount to a paradisiacal age. Not only do they imagine the freshly formed earth as a paradise, where the different animals allowed themselves to be easily captured and water and fruits were in abundance, but the ancestors were free from the multitude of inhibitions and frustrations that inevitably obstruct all human beings who are living together in organized communities.[11] This primordial paradise still haunts the Aranda. In a certain sense, one can interpret the brief intervals of ritual orgy, when all the interdictions are suspended, as ephemeral returns to the freedom and beatitude of the ancestors.

Such a terrestrial and paradisiacal primordiality — which constitutes both a history and a propaedeutic — is the one that interests the Aranda. In this mythical time man became what he is today, not only because he was then shaped and instructed by the ancestors, but also because he has to repeat continuously every-

10. Cf. "Personal Monototemism in a Polytotemic Community," p. 730.
11. *Ibid.*, p. 729. Cf. also *Aranda Traditions*, pp. 36 ff., on the "Golden Age" of the totemic ancestors.

thing that the ancestors did *in illo tempore*. The myths disclos
this sacred and creative history. Moreover, through initiatio
every young Aranda not only learns what happened *in principi*
but ultimately discovers *that he was already there*, that someho
he participated in those glorious events. The initiation brings abou
an *anamnesis*. At the end of the ceremony, the novice finds ou
that the hero of the myths just communicated to him is himself. H
is shown a sacred and well-guarded ritual object, a *tjurunga*, an
one old man tells him: This is your own body! — for that *tjurung*
represents the body of one of the ancestors. This dramatic revel;
tion of the identity between the eternal ancestor and the individu;
in which he is reincarnated can be compared with *tat tvam asi* o
the Upanishads. These beliefs are not exclusively Aranda. In Nortl
east Australia, for instance, when an Unambal proceeds to repaii
the image of a Wondjina on the rock wall (the Wondjina ai
the equivalent of the Central Australian totemic ancestors), h
says: "I am going now to refresh and invigorate myself; I pair
myself anew, so that the rain can come." [12]

To the irrevocability of death, as a result of the brutal interrup
tion of the communications between earth and heaven, the Arand
replied with a theory of transmigration thanks to which the ar
cestors — that is to say, they themselves — are supposed to re
turn perpetually to life. One can distinguish, then, two sorts o
primordiality, to which two types of nostalgia correspond: (1
the *primordium* represented by the celestial Great Father and b
the celestial immortality that is inaccessible to ordinary huma
beings; (2) the fabulous epoch of the ancestors, when life in gei
eral and human life in particular was brought about. The Arand
yearn above all for the terrestrial paradise represented by th
second *primordium*.

Two Types of Primordiality

Such a process is also known in other religions, even in the mo;
complex ones. We may refer, for example, to the primordiality o
Tiamat and the passage to the creative primordial epoch repr
sented by the victory of Marduk, along with the cosmogony, ar
thropogony, and the founding of a new divine hierarchy. Or w

12. See Eliade, "Australian Religions: An Introduction. Part II," p. 227

might compare the primordiality of Ouranos with the establishment of Zeus's supremacy, or point the passage from the almost forgotten Dyaus to Varuṇa, and later still to the consecutive supremacies of Indra, Shiva, and Vishnu. In all these cases one may say that the creation of a new world is implied, even when there is no question of a cosmogony properly speaking. But it is always the emergence of a new religious world that appears to be in a more direct relation with the human condition.

What is significant in this substitution of an existential primordiality for a rather speculative one is that this process represents a more radical incarnation of the *sacred* in *life* and in *human existence* as such. Of course, this process is fairly common in the history of religions, and it is not completely foreign to the Judeo-Christian tradition. One may say that we have in Bonhoeffer the most recent example of the incarnation of the sacred in the profane existence of historical man; one may also identify in the most recent American theology, the god-is-dead theology, yet another variant, drastically secularized, of the myth of *deus otiosus*.

Thus, we can distinguish two types of primordialities: (1) a precosmic, unhistorical primordiality, and (2) a cosmogonic or historical one. In effect, the cosmogonic myth opens the *sacred history;* it is an *historical myth*, though not in the Judeo-Christian sense of the word, for the cosmogonic myth has the function of an exemplary model and as such it is periodically reactualized. We can distinguish also two species of *religious nostalgias*: (1) the longing to reintegrate the primordial totality that existed before the creation (the Dayak type of religious nostalgia); and (2) the longing to recover the primordial epoch that began immediately *after* the creation (the Aranda type). In this latter case the nostalgia yearns for the *sacred history* of the tribe. It is with such *myths of the sacred history* — still alive in many traditional societies — that the Judeo-Christian idea of history has to vie.

6

Paradise and Utopia: Mythical Geography and Eschatology

The "Fashion" of Messianism

Over the past ten years works on the various millenarianisms and different forms of utopia have increased considerably. And this is true not only of studies on the primitive messianic and prophetic movements — the most well-known being the "cargo cults" — but also of research on the messianisms of Judeo-Christian origin, from the beginning of our era to the Renaissance and the Reformation, and of works on the religious implications of geographic discoveries and colonization, principally the colonization of the two Americas. Finally, in recent years several efforts at synthesis have been published: historians, sociologists, and philosophers have tried to compare the different forms of utopias and millenarianisms, and to articulate them with a view to a final synthesis

This enormous recent bibliography will not be presented here Suffice it to recall the several efforts at synthesis: the work of Norman Cohn on the pursuit of the millennium, the works of Lanternari, Guariglia, and Mühlmann on primitive millenarianisms, the research of Alphonse Dupront on the spirit of the crusades, and

This chapter is a revised and expanded version of a paper first published in English as a contribution to *Utopia and Utopian Thought*, ed. Frank E Manuel (Boston: Houghton Mifflin Co., 1966), pp. 260–80. Reprinted by permission of *Daedalus*, Journal of the American Academy of Arts and Science
The original version, "Paradis et Utopie: Géographie Mythique et Eschatologie," was published in *Vom Sinn der Utopie, Eranos Jahrbuch 196* (Zurich: Rhein-Verlag, 1964).

the monographs of several American scholars on the eschatological implications of colonization.[1]

The interest of Western scholars in millenarist movements and utopias is significant; it could even be said that this interest constitutes one of the characteristic traits of contemporary Western thought. The reasons for this interest are manifold. First of all, there is the curiosity aroused by the messianic cults that buffeted "primitive" societies in the last decades of the colonial period. Then there is the recent research on the importance of prophetic movements in medieval Europe, especially the movement of Gioacchino da Fiore and the Gioacchinists in Transalpine Europe. And, finally, there is the rigorous analysis of the religious implications of the colonization of America; for, as we shall see later, the discovery and colonization of the New World took place under the sign of eschatology.

The undertaking of such research and the posing of such problems betray an orientation of thought which tells us a great deal about the spiritual situation of contemporary Western man. Let us point out, to begin with, that contrary to systems of deterministic explanation of history, today we recognize the importance of the religious factor, especially the importance of movements of tension and frenzy — the prophetic, eschatological, millenarist movements. But there is something, in my opinion, still more significant: the interest in the *origins* of the *recent* Western world — that is, in the origins of the United States and the nations of Latin America — reveals among the intellectuals of that continent the desire to turn back and to find their *primordial history*, their "absolute beginnings." This desire to return to one's beginnings, to recover a primordial situation, also denotes the desire to start out again, the nostalgia for the earthly paradise that the ancestors

1. Cf. Norman Cohn, *The Pursuit of the Millennium*, 2d ed. (New York, 1961); Vittorio Lanternari, *Movimenti religiosi di libertà e di salvezza dei popoli oppressi* (Milan, 1960); Guglielmo Guariglia, *Prophetismus und Heilsrwartungsbewegungen als völkerkundliches und religionsgeschichtliches Problem* (Horn, 1959); Wilhelm E. Mühlmann, *Chiliasmus und Nativismus* (Berlin, 1961). Cf. also Sylvia L. Thrupp, ed., *Millenial Dreams in Action* (The Hague, 1962); Alphonse Dupront, "Croisades et eschatologie," in *manesimo e Esoterismo*, ed. Enrico Castelli (Padova, 1960), pp. 175–98. On the eschatological implications of the colonization of America, see the works of H. Richard Niebuhr, Charles L. Sanford, and George H. Williams cited below.

of the American nations had crossed the Atlantic to find. (Indeed there have rarely been published more books with titles containing the word "paradise" than on the colonization of the Americas. Among works published in recent years, let us point out: *Visão do Paraiso: os motivos edênicos no descobrimento e colonização do Brasil* [Rio de Janiero, 1959] by Sergio Buarque de Hollanda; *The Quest for Paradise* [1961], by Charles L. Sanford; *Wilderness and Paradise in Christian Thought* [1962], by George H. Williams, subtitled "From the Garden of Eden and the Sinai desert to the American frontier.")

All this betrays the desire to recover the religious origins, and thus a primordial history, of the recent transatlantic states. But the significance of this phenomenon is still more complex. One may also detect the desire for a renewal of old values and structures, the hope of a radical *renovatio* — just as one might interpret in the most recent experiments in art the will to destroy all means of expression already time-worn by history, but also the hope of beginning the artistic experience *ab initio*.

To return to our subject — Paradise and Utopia — I have chosen two sorts of illustrations. First of all I shall point out the eschatological and paradisiacal elements in the colonization of North America by the pioneers, and the progressive transformation of the "American Paradise," giving rise to the myth of indefinite progress, to American optimism, and to the cult of youth and novelty. Then I shall consider a Brazilian tribe, the Tupi-Guaranis, who, at the time of the discovery of South America, had already set forth across the Atlantic Ocean in search of a paradise — certain groups still continue the search today.

The Quest for the Earthly Paradise

Christopher Columbus did not doubt that he had come near the Earthly Paradise. He believed that the fresh water currents he encountered in the Gulf of Paria originated in the four rivers of the Garden of Eden. For Columbus, the search for the Earthly Paradise was not a chimera. The great navigator accorded an eschatological significance to this geographic discovery. The New World represented more than a new continent open to the propagation of the Gospel. The very fact of its discovery had an eschatological implication.

Indeed, Columbus was persuaded that the prophecy concerning the diffusion of the Gospel throughout the whole world had to be realized before the end of the world — which was not far off. In his *Book of Prophecies*, Columbus affirmed that this event, namely, the end of the world, would be preceded by the conquest of the new continent, the conversion of the heathen, and the destruction of the Antichrist. And he assumed a capital role in this grandiose drama, at once historical and cosmic. In addressing Prince John he exclaimed: "God made me the messenger of the new heaven and the new earth of which He spoke in the Apocalypse by Saint John, after having spoken of it by the mouth of Isaiah; and He showed me the spot where to find it." [2]

It was in this messianic and apocalyptic atmosphere that the transoceanic expeditions and the geographic discoveries that radically shook and transformed Western Europe took place. Throughout Europe people believed in an imminent regeneration of the world, even though the causes and reasons for this regeneration were multiple and often contradictory.

The colonization of the two Americas began under an eschatological sign: people believed that the time had come to renew the Christian world, and the true renewal was the return to the Earthly Paradise or, at the very least, the beginning again of sacred history, the reiteration of the prodigious events spoken of in the Bible. It is for this reason that the literature of the period, as well as sermons, memoirs, and correspondence, abounds in paradisiacal and eschatological allusions. In the eyes of the English, for instance, the colonization of America merely prolonged and perfected a sacred history begun at the outset of the Reformation. Indeed, the push of the pioneers toward the West continued the triumphal march of wisdom and the true religion from East to West. For some time already, Protestant theologians had been inclined to identify the West with spiritual and moral progress. Certain theologians had transferred the Ark of the Covenant of Abraham to the English. As the Anglican theologian William Crashaw wrote, "The God of Israel is . . . the God of England." In 1583, Sir Humphrey Gilbert asserted that if England had taken possession "of vast and pleasant territories," it was doubtless thanks

2. Charles L. Sanford, *The Quest for Paradise* (Urbana, Ill., 1961), p. 40.

to the fact that the word of God, that is, religion, which had begun in the East, had gradually advanced toward the West, where, he added, "it is very likely that it will stop."

Solar symbolism

This is a rather frequent motif in English literature of the period. The theologian Thomas Burnet, in his *Archaeologiae* (1692), wrote: "Learning, like the sun, began to take its Course from the *East*, then turned *Westward*, where we have long rejoiced in its light." And Bishop Berkeley, in his famous poem which opens with these lines, "Westward the course of empire takes its way . . . ," makes use of the solar analogy in order to exalt the spiritual role of England.[3]

Moreover, Berkeley was merely conforming to a European tradition already more than two centuries old. Indeed, Egyptian hermetism and solar symbolism, revived by Marsilio Ficino and the Italian humanists, had known an extraordinary vogue after the discoveries of Copernicus and Galileo, discoveries that for contemporaries illustrated above all the triumph of the sun and heliocentrism. Recent research has uncovered the religious implications most often hidden or camouflaged, in the astronomy and the cosmography of the Renaissance. For contemporaries of Copernicus and Galileo, heliocentrism was more than a scientific theory: it marked the victory of solar symbolism over the Middle Ages, that is, the revenge of the hermetic tradition — considered as venerable and primordial, preceding Moses, Orpheus, Zoroaster, Pythagoras and Plato — over the provincialism of the medieval Church.

The theme of solar symbolism in the Renaissance is too complex for consideration here, but this brief allusion is necessary in order to understand the emphasis placed on solar analogies by authors exalting the religious significance of the colonization of the New World. The first English colonists in America considered themselves chosen by Providence to establish a "City on a Mountain" that would serve as an example of the true Reformation for a Europe. They had followed the path of the sun toward the Fa

3. See the texts cited by Sanford, *ibid.,* pp. 52 ff. See also George F. Williams, *Wilderness and Paradise in Christian Thought* (New York, 196: pp. 65 ff.

West, continuing and prolonging in a prodigious fashion the traditional passing of religion and culture from East to West. They
saw a sign of divine Providence in the fact that America had been
hidden to the Europeans until the time of Reformation. The
first pioneers did not doubt that the final drama of moral regeneration and universal salvation would begin with them, since they
were the first to follow the sun in its course toward the paradisiacal
gardens of the West. As the Anglican poet George Herbert wrote
in his *Church Militant:*

> Religion stands tip-toe in our land
> Ready to pass to the American strand.[4]

And this "American strand," as we have seen and shall continually
note in what follows, was loaded with paradisiacal qualities. Ulrich
Hugwald had prophesized that following the discovery of America
humanity would return "to Christ, to Nature, to Paradise."

More than any other modern nation the United States was the
product of the Protestant Reformation seeking an Earthly Paradise in which the reform of the Church was to be perfected.[5] The
relationship between the Reformation and the recovery of the
Earthly Paradise has struck a very great number of authors, from
Heinrich Bullinger to Charles Dumoulin. For these theologians,
the Reformation hastened the coming of the great age of paradisiacal beatitude. It is significant that the millenarist theme enjoyed
its greatest popularity just prior to the colonization of America
and Cromwell's revolution. Hence, it is not surprising to note that
the most popular religious doctrine in the colonies was that America had been chosen among all the nations of the earth as the
place of the Second Coming of Christ, and the millennium, though
essentially of a spiritual nature, would be accompanied by a paradisiacal transformation of the earth, as an outer sign of inner perfection. As the eminent Puritan, Increase Mather, President of
Harvard University from 1685 to 1701, wrote: "when this Kingdom of Christ has filled all the earth, *this Earth will be restored
to its Paradise state.*" [6]

---

4. Quoted by Sanford, *Quest for Paradise,* p. 53.
5. *Ibid.,* p. 74. See also Williams, *Wilderness and Paradise,* pp. 99 ff.; H.
Richard Niebuhr, *The Kingdom of God in America* (New York, 1937).
6. Increase Mather, *Discourse on Prayer,* quoted in Sanford, *Quest for
Paradise,* pp. 82–83.

The American Paradise

Moreover, certain pioneers already saw Paradise in the various regions of America. Traveling along the coast of New England in 1614, John Smith compared it to Eden: "heaven and earth never agreed better to frame a place for man's habitation . . . we chanced in a lande, even as God made it." George Alsop presents Maryland as the only place seeming to be the "Earthly Paradise." Its trees, its plants, its fruits, its flowers, he wrote, speak in "Hieroglyphicks of our Adamitical or Primitive situation." Another writer discovered the "future Eden" in Georgia — a region located on the same latitude as Palestine: "That promis'd *Canaan*, which was pointed out by God's own choice, to bless the Labours of a favorite People." For Edward Johnson, Massachusetts was the place "where the Lord will create a new Heaven and a new Earth." Likewise, the Boston Puritan, John Cotton, informed those preparing to set sail from England for Massachusetts that they were granted a privilege of Heaven, thanks to "the grand charter given to *Adam* and his posterity in Paradise." [7]

But this reflects just one aspect of the millenarist experience of the pioneers. For many new immigrants, the New World represented a desert haunted by demonic beings. This, however, did not diminish their eschatological exaltation, for they were told in sermons that the present miseries were but a moral and spiritual trial before arriving at the Earthly Paradise that had been promised to them. [8] The pioneers considered themselves in the situation of the Israelites after the crossing of the Red Sea, just as, in their eyes, their condition in England and Europe had been a sort of Egyptian bondage. After the terrible trial of the desert, they would enter Canaan. As Cotton Mather wrote, "The Wilderness through which we are passing to the Promised Land is all over filled with Fiery flying serpents." [9]

But, later on, a new idea was born; the New Jerusalem would be in part produced by work. Jonathan Edwards (1703–58) thought that through work New England would be transformed into a sort of "Paradise on Earth." We see how the millenarianism of the pioneers gradually ends in the idea of progress. In the first

---

7. Texts quoted in *ibid.*, pp. 83–85.
8. Cf. Williams, *Wilderness and Paradise*, pp. 101 ff., 108 ff.
9. Sanford, *Quest for Paradise*, p. 87. Cf. also Williams, *Wilderness and Paradise*, p. 108.

stage, a relationship was established between paradise and the earthly possibilities presenting themselves in the New World. During the next stage, the eschatological tension was reduced by the omission of the period of decadence and misery that was supposed to precede the "Last Days," and by arriving finally at the idea of a progressive and uninterrupted amelioration.[10]

But before the American idea of progress crystallized, the millenarianism of the pioneers underwent other transformations. The first important crisis in this Puritan eschatology was provoked by the struggle among the European powers for the colonial empire. Rome and the Catholic nations were identified with the Antichrist, on whose destruction the coming of the future Kingdom depended.

At one particular time, English colonial literature was dominated by a single theme: the invasion of America by the Antichrist, who threatened to ruin the hope for the glorious triumph of Christ. For John Winthrop, the first duty of New England was to "raise a rampart against the kingdom of the Antichrist that the Jesuits are in the process of establishing in these regions." Other authors affirmed that the New World was a true Paradise before the arrival of the Catholics.

Obviously, the rivalry among the European powers for the domination of the transatlantic empires was in large measure economic in character, but it was exacerbated by an almost Manichean eschatology: everything seemed to be reduced to a conflict between Good and Evil. Colonial authors spoke of the threat that the French and the Spanish posed for the English colonies as a "new Babylonian captivity" or "an Egyptian bondage." The French and the Spanish were tyrants, slaves of the Antichrist. Catholic Europe was presented as a fallen world, a Hell, by contrast with the Paradise of the New World. The saying was "Heaven or Europe," meaning "Heaven or Hell." The trials of the pioneers in the desert of America had as their principal goal the redemption of man from the carnal sins of the pagan Old World.[11]

The Return to Primitive Christianity

As long as the conflict between Good and Evil took concrete form, in the eyes of the colonists, in the struggle between Protestantism and Catholicism, England remained immune from attack. But

10. Sanford, *Quest for Paradise*, p. 86.   11. *Ibid.*, pp. 89 ff.

after 1640, tension began to arise between the colonists and the mother country. For the perfectionists in the colonies, the English Reformation was an imperfect reformation. Worse yet, the religious practices of England were considered as the work of the Antichrist. In the colonial apocalyptic imagery, England replaced Rome. The immediate consequence of this substitution was that the colonists — as the chosen people — began to judge their mission in the desert not only as the continuation of a traditional religious activity, but also as something altogether new. Hopeful of being reborn far from the European Hell, the colonists considered that they were about to initiate the final stage of History. In 1647, John Eliot, the apostle to the Indians, announced "The Daybreaking, if not the Sunrising of the Gospel . . . in New England." [12]

Such language indicates the profound break with the European past. And it must be made clear that this break had already been consummated long before the American Revolution and independence. In 1646, New England considered itself as a free state and not as a "colony or corporation of England." The reasons for this *prise de conscience* of autonomy were in the first place religious. Cotton Mather expected in New England the return to the early days of Christianity. "In short," he wrote, "the *first* age was the *golden Age*; to return unto that, will make a man a *protestant*, and I may add, a *Puritan*." This return to the Golden Age of Christianity was to bring about a transfiguration of the earth. As Increase Mather declared, the restoration of the Early Church would transform the earth into paradise. [13]

The break with England and the European past was accentuated to the extent to which the pioneers prepared for the millennium by returning to the virtue of the Early Church. For the Puritans, the major Christian virtue was simplicity. On the other hand, intelligence, culture, learning, manners, luxury were of the Devil's creation. John Cotton wrote: "The more cultured and intelligent you are, the more ready you are to work for Satan." The superiority complex of the pioneers and the missionaries of the Frontier was already forming. This return to Early Christianity that was supposed to restore paradise to earth also implied a disdain

12. Cf. *ibid.*, pp. 96 ff.
13. Texts quoted in *ibid.*, p. 104.

for the erudition of the Jesuits, as well as a criticism of English
aristocracy — cultured, elegant, sophisticated, accustomed to power
and authority. Extravagance or luxury in clothing became the sin
par excellence of the "gentleman." In his book *Simple Cobbler of
Aggawam* (1647), Nathanael Ward contrasted the simple life
and moral superiority of the colonists to the corrupt mores of
England and drew from this contrast proof of the progress toward
the paradisiacal state of the Early Church.[14]

The colonists proclaimed their moral superiority over the English while recognizing their own inferiority in clothes and culture.
According to Charles L. Sanford, the origin of the American superiority complex — manifest in foreign policy as well as in the
enthusiastic effort to spread the "American way of life" across the
whole planet — must be sought in the activity of the Frontier missionaries.[15] A whole religious symbolism flowered about the Frontier, prolonging well into the nineteenth century the eschatology
of the pioneers. The vast forests, the solitude of the infinite plains,
the beatitude of the rural life are set in contrast to the sins and
vices of the city. A new idea now arises: the American paradise
has been infested with demonic forces coming from urban Europe. The critique of the aristocracy, luxury, and culture is now
subsumed to the critique of cities and urban life. The great "re-
vivalist" religious movements began on the Frontier and reached
the cities only later. And even in the cities, "revivalism" was more
popular among the poor than among the rich and educated
population. The fundamental idea was that the decline of religion
had been caused by urban vices, especially intoxication and luxury,
common to the aristocracy of European origin. For, obviously,
Hell was — and long remained — "the way of Europe."[16]

The Religious Origins of the "American Way of Life"

But, as we have already pointed out, eschatological millenarianism
and the expectation of the Earthly Paradise were subjected in the
end to a radical secularization. The myth of progress and the
cult of novelty and youth are among the most noteworthy consequences. However, even in drastically secularized form, one de-

14. *Ibid.*, pp. 105 ff.
15. *Ibid.*, pp. 93 ff.
16. *Ibid.*, pp. 109 ff.

tects the religious enthusiasm and the eschatological expectations inspiring the ancestors. For, in short, both the first colonists and the later European immigrants journeyed to America as *the country where they might be born anew*, that is, begin a new life. The "novelty" which still fascinates Americans today is a desire with religious underpinnings. In "novelty" one hopes for a "re-naissance"; one seeks a new life.

New England, *New* York, *New* Haven — all these names express not only the nostalgia for the native land left behind, but above all the hope that in these lands and these new cities life will know new dimensions. And not only life: everything in this continent that was considered an earthly paradise must be greater, more beautiful, stronger. In New England, described as resembling the Garden of Eden, partridges were supposedly so big that they could no longer fly, and the turkeys as fat as lambs.[17] This American flair for the grandiose, likewise religious in origin, is shared even more by the most lucid minds.

The hope of being born again to a new life — and the expectation of a future not only better, but beatific — may also be seen in the American cult of youth. According to Charles L. Sanford, since the era of industrialization, Americans have more and more sought their lost innocence in their children. The same author believes that the exaltation of things new, which followed the pioneers to the Far West, fortified individualism over authority, but also contributed to the American irreverence toward history and tradition.[18]

We shall end here these few considerations of the metamorphosis of the millenarist eschatology of the pioneers. We have seen how, in setting out in search of the Earthly Paradise across the ocean, the first explorers were conscious of playing an important role in the history of salvation; how America, after being identified with the Earthly Paradise, became the privileged place where the Puritans were to perfect the Reformation, which supposedly had failed in Europe; and how the immigrants believed that they had escaped from the Hell of Europe and expected a new birth in the New World. We have likewise seen to what extent modern America is the result of these messianic hopes, this confidence in

17. Texts quoted in *ibid.*, p. 111.
18. Cf. *ibid.*, pp. 112 ff.

the possibility of reaching paradise here on earth, this faith in youth and in the simplicity of the mind and soul.

One might continue the analysis and show how the long resistance of American elites to the industrialization of the country, and their exaltation of the virtues of agriculture, may be explained by the same nostalgia for the Earthly Paradise. Even when urbanization and industrialization had triumphed everywhere, the favorite images and clichés used by the pioneers retained their prestige. In order to prove that urbanization and industrialization did not necessarily imply (as in Europe!) vice, poverty, and the dissolution of mores, owners of factories multiplied their philanthropic activities, constructing churches, schools, and hospitals. At all costs, it had to be made plain that, far from threatening spiritual and religious values, science, technology and industry guaranteed their triumph. A book appearing in 1842 was entitled *The Paradise within the Reach of All Men, by Power of Nature and Machinery.* And one might detect the nostalgia for Paradise, the desire to find again that "Nature" of their ancestors, in the contemporary tendency to leave the metropolis and seek refuge in suburbia — luxurious and peaceful neighborhoods arranged with utmost care in paradisiacal landscapes.

But our concern here is not to present an analysis of the metamorphosis of the American millenarist ideal. What must be emphasized, as other authors have, is that the certainty of the eschatological mission, and especially of attaining once again the perfection of early Christianity and restoring Paradise to earth, is not likely to be forgotten easily. It is very probable that the behavior of the average American today, as well as the political and cultural ideology of the United States, still reflects the consequences of the Puritan certitude of having been called to restore the Earthly Paradise.

The Adamic Nostalgias of the American Writers

One can detect a similar eschatology in what may be called the revolt against the historical past, a revolt that is abundantly illustrated by almost all the important American writers of the first two-thirds of the nineteenth century. The paradisiacal elements — at least those of Judeo-Christian origin — are now more or less repressed, but we find the yearning for, and the exaltation of, a new beginning, an "Adamic" innocence, a beatific plenitude which precedes history. In his book *The American Adam* (1955), R. W. B. Lewis has brought together a great number of illuminating quotations from which one has, if anything, too much to choose from. In "Earth's Holocaust," a fantasy composed in 1844, Nathaniel Hawthorne presents the vision of a cosmic bonfire which destroys the heraldry of ancient aristocratic families, the robes and scepters of royalty and other symbols of old institutions, and finally the total body of European literature and philosophy. "Now," declares the chief celebrant, "we shall get rid of the weight of dead men's thoughts." [19] And in *The House of the Seven Gables* (1850), one of the characters, Holgrave, exclaims: "Shall we never, never get rid of this Past? It lies upon the present like a giant's dead body!" He complains that "we read in dead men's books! We laugh at dead men's jokes, and cry at dead men's pathos!" Hawthorne regrets, through his mouthpiece Holgrave, that the public edifices — "our capitals, statehouses, courthouses, city-halls and churches" — are built "of such permanent materials as stone or brick. It were better that they should crumble to ruin once in twenty years or thereabouts, as a hint to people to examine and reform the institutions which they symbolize" (Lewis, *American Adam*, pp. 18–19).

One finds the same angry rejection of the historical past in Thoreau. All the objects, values, and symbols associated with the past should be burned away. "I look on England today," writes Thoreau, "as an old gentleman who is traveling with a great deal of baggage, trumpery which has accumulated from long housekeeping, which he has not the courage to burn" (*ibid.*, pp. 21–22). Lewis shows how persistent the image of an American Adam was, how profound the belief that in America mankind has the unique chance to begin history anew.

The Adamic nostalgia also survives, in a camouflaged form, among many writers of the period. Thoreau admirably illustrates what an "Adamic life" can mean. He considered his morning bath in the pond "a religious exercise, and one of the best things which I did" (*ibid.*, p. 22). It was, for him, a rite of rebirth. Thoreau's love for children has equally an "Adamic" character: "every child

19. Quoted by R. W. B. Lewis, *The American Adam* (Cicago, 1955), p. 14. As early as 1789, in a letter written from Paris, Thomas Jefferson solemnly asserted that "the earth belongs in usufruct to the living, that the dead have neither power nor rights over it" (*ibid.*, p. 16).

begins the world again," he writes, unaware, perhaps, of the great discovery he was making.

Such yearning for the "Adamic," for the primordial, reflects an "archaic" type of mentality, resisting history and exalting the "sacrality" of life and body. Whitman, who calls himself "Chanter of Adamic songs," declares that the aroma of his body is "finer than prayer" and his head is "more than churches, bibles and all creeds" (*ibid.*, p. 43). Lewis judiciously recognizes an "Adamic narcissism" in such almost ecstatic proclamations: "If I worship one thing more than another, it shall be the spread of my own body"; or, "Divine am I, inside and out, and I make myself holy whatever I touch" — ecstatic proclamations that remind one of some tantric texts. Lewis detects in Whitman too the paradigmatic motif — the past is dead, it is a corpse — but "in Whitman's view the past had been so effectively burned away that it had, for every practical purpose, been forgotten altogether" (*ibid.*, p. 44). There was for Whitman and his contemporaries a general hope that man was born anew in a new society, that, as Lewis puts it, "the race was off to a fresh start in America" (*ibid.*, p. 45). Whitman expresses with force and glamour the contemporary obsession with the primordial, the absolute beginning. He enjoyed "reciting Homer while walking beside the Ocean" (*ibid.*, p. 44) because Homer belonged to the *primordium*; he was not a product of history — he had *founded* European poetry.

But the reaction against this new version of the paradisiacal myth was bound to come. The old Henry James, the father of William and Henry, boldly affirmed that "the first and highest service which Eve renders Adam is to throw him out of Paradise" (*ibid.*, p. 58). In other words, only after losing Paradise did man begin to become himself: open to culture, perfectible, creatively giving sense and value to human existence, to life, and to the world. But the history of this demythologizing of the American paradisiacal and Adamic nostalgia would take us to far beyond the theme of our discussion.

The Guaranis in Search of the Lost Paradise

In 1912, the Brazilian ethnologist Curt Nimuendaju encountered along the coast near São Paulo a group of Guarani Indians who had stopped there in their search for the Lost Paradise.

They danced tirelessly for several days in the hope that their bodies would become light through continual movement and would be able to fly off to heaven to the home of "Our Grandmother" who awaits her children in the East. Disappointed, but their faith intact, they returned, convinced that, attired in European clothing and nourished with European food, they had grown too heavy for the celestial adventure.[20]

This search for the Lost Paradise was the most recent in a series of migrations undertaken by the Guaranis over many centuries. The first attempt to find the "Beloved Country" dates back to 1515.[21] But it was especially between 1539 and 1549 that a great migration of the Tupinamba group toward the land of the "Great Ancestor" took place. Having set out from the region of Pernambuco, writes Alfred Métraux, these Indians arrived in Peru,

where they met up with certain Spanish conquistadors. These Indians had crossed practically the whole South American continent at its widest point in search of the "Land of Immortality and Eternal Rest." To the Spaniards, they related strange stories of half-imaginary cities filled with gold; and their stories, probably tinged with their personal dreams, inflamed the imagination of the Spaniards and determined to a great extent the unfortunate expedition of Pedro de Ursua, the alleged conqueror of the Eldorado. The Spaniards and the Indians sought after the same chimera, the main difference being that the Indians aspired to an eternal felicity, while the Spaniards sought to acquire, at the cost of great suffering, the means to a transient happiness.[22]

Nimuendaju gathered a very rich documentation on these fabled peregrinations of the Guarani tribes searching for the "Land-without-Evil." Alfred Métraux and Egon Schaden subsequently completed and provided more detailed information.[23] This collective

20. Alfred Métraux, "Les Messies de L'Amérique du Sud," *Archives de Sociologie des Religions*, 4 (1957): 108–12. See p. 151 for text reference.

21. Egon Schaden, "Der Paradiesmythos im Leben der Guarani-Indianer," *Staden-Jahrbuch*, 3 (São Paolo, 1955): 151–62. See p. 151 for text reference.

22. Alfred Métraux, *"Les Messies,"* p. 109.

23. Curt Nimuendaju, "Die Sagen von der Erschaffung und Vernichtung der Welt als Grundlagen der Religion der Apapocuva-Guarani," *Zeitschrift für Ethnologie*, 46 (1914): 284–403; Alfred Métraux, "Migrations historiques des Tupi-Guaranis," *Journal de la Société des Américanistes*, n. s. 19 (1927): 1–45; Alfred Métraux, "The Guarani," Bureau of American Ethnology, Bulletin 143: *Handbook of South American Indians*, 3 (1948): 69–94; Alfred Métraux, "The Tupinamba," *ibid.*, pp. 95–133; Alfred Métraux, *Religions et magies d'Amérique du Sud* (Paris, 1967), pp. 11–41; Egon Schaden, "Der Paradiesmythos im Leben der Guarani-Indianer" (cf. note 21); Egon Schaden, *Aspectos fundamentais da cultura guarani*, University

search for Paradise lasted over four centuries, and may doubtless be classified among the most singular religious phenomena of the New World. Indeed, the movements described by Nimuendaju in 1912 still continue today, but only one Guarani tribe, the Mbüás, still seeks Paradise to the East; the others believe that Paradise is found at the center of the earth and at the zenith.[24] We shall have occasion to return to the different locations and topographies of Paradise. For the moment, let us single out one characteristic of the religion of all the Tupi-Guarani tribes: the considerable role played by shamans and prophets. It was they who, following certain dreams or visions, set in motion and led the expeditions to the Land-without-Evil. Even in the tribes that were not consumed by the passion of the quest for Paradise, the shamans succeeded in stirring up the whole population by using certain typically paradisiacal images in recounting their dreams and ecstasies. A sixteenth-century Jesuit wrote concerning the Tupinambas:

> The shamans persuade the Indians not to work, not to go to the fields, promising them that the harvests will grow by themselves, that food instead of being scarce will fill their huts, and that spades will turn over the soil all alone, arrows will hunt for their owners, and will capture numerous enemies. They predict that the old will become young again.[25]

We recognize here the paradisiacal syndrome of the Golden Age. In order to hasten its coming, the Indians renounced all profane activities and danced night and day, stimulated by their prophets. As we shall see subsequently, dancing is the most effective means of arriving at ecstasy or, at least, of coming closer to divinity.

More than other archaic populations, the Tupi-Guaranis were avid to receive revelations from supernatural beings through the

of São Paulo, Faculty of Philosophy, Sciences, and Letters, Bulletin No. 188 (São Paulo, 1954), pp. 185–204; Egon Schaden, "Der Paradiesmythos im Leben der Guarani-Indianer," *XXXth International Congress of Americanists* (Cambridge, 1952), pp. 179–86. Cf. also Maria Isaura Pereira de Queiroz, "L'influence du milieu social interne sur les mouvements messianiques brésiliens," *Archives de Sociologie des Religions*, 5 (1958): 3–30; Wolfgang H. Lindig, "Wanderungen der Tupi-Guarani und Eschatologie der Apapocuva-Guarani," in Wilhelm E. Mühlmann, *Chiliasmus und Nativismus* (Berlin, 1961), pp. 19–40; Rene Ribeiro, "Brazilian Messianic Movements," in *Millenial Dreams*, ed. Thrupp, pp. 55–69.

24. Schaden, "Der Paradiesmythos," p. 152, and *Aspectos fundamentais*, p. 186.

25. Quoted by Métraux, "Les Messies," p. 108.

dreams of the shamans. More than their neighboring tribes, the Tupi-Guaranis did their utmost to maintain permanent contact with the supernatural world, in order to receive in time the instructions indispensable to reaching Paradise. Where does this singular religious sensitivity come from — this obsession with Paradise, this fear of not understanding the divine messages in time and consequently facing the risk of perishing in the imminent cosmic catastrophe?

The End of the World

The reply to this question may be found in myths. In the mythology of all the Guarani tribes still surviving in Brazil, there exists the tradition that a fire or a flood completely destroyed a former world — and that the catastrophe will be repeated in a more or less near future. The belief in a future catastrophe is, however, rare among the other Tupi groups.[26] Should this be considered as a Christian influence? Not necessarily. Similar ideas have been attested among many other archaic peoples. And, more important, in certain cases it is difficult to tell if the cosmic catastrophe has taken place in the past or if it will be repeated in the future as well; this is because the grammar of the respective languages does not make a distinction between past and future.[27] Finally, we must recall a Tukuma myth according to which the future catastrophe will be the work of the civilizing hero Dyoí. The latter is supposedly offended by the changing of tribal traditions as a result of the contact with white Christians. This belief is partially comparable to that of the Guaranis. Now, it is difficult to conceive that a myth announcing the imminent end of the world because of the cultural influences of the whites should be of Christian origin.

Whatever the case may be, the end of the world is not imagined in the same fashion by the various Guarani tribes. The Mbüás expect an imminent flood, or a fire of cosmic proportions, or a darkness indefinitely prolonged over the earth. For the Nandevas,

26. Schaden, *Aspectos fundamentais,* p. 187. The belief in a future catastrophe is attested among the Txiriguano (Métraux); Mundurukú (R. P. Albert Kruse, *Anthropos* [1951], p. 922); Tukuna (Nimuendaju, *The Tukuna* [Berkeley and Los Angeles, 1952], pp. 137–39).
27. Cf. Mircea Eliade, *Myth and Reality* (New York, 1963), pp. 55 ff.

the catastrophe will be provoked by the explosion of the earth, the latter being conceived as a disk. Finally, the Kaiovás imagine that the end of the world will be brought about by monsters — flying horses and monkeys hunting with flaming arrows.[28] It is important to emphasize that the portrayal of and the quest for Paradise are directly related to the fear of the impending catastrophe. The migrations were set in motion by the desire and the hope of reaching the Land-without-Evil before the apocalypse. Even the names given by the various Guarani tribes to Paradise convey the notion that the latter is the sole place where one is safe from universal destruction. The Nandevas call it *yvý-nomi-mybré*, "the land where one hides"; that is, the place where one can find refuge during the cataclysm. Paradise is also called *yvý-mará-ey*, the "Land-without-Evil," or simply *yváy*, "Heaven." Paradise is the place where one does not fear — and its inhabitants know neither hunger nor sickness nor death.[29]

We shall return shortly to the structure of Paradise and the means to arrive there. But first, we must consider the reasons which, according to the Guaranis, lead inevitably to the end of the world. Contrary to a widespread belief, shared by both Judaism and Christianity, the end of the world is not the consequence of the sins of mankind. For the Guaranis, mankind, as well as the earth itself, is tired of living and aspires to rest. Nimuendaju believes that the ideas of the Apapocuvas on the annihilation of the world are the product of what he calls "Indian pessimism." [30] One of his informers told him: "Today the earth is old, and our race will no longer multiply. We are going to see the dead again, darkness will fall, bats will touch us, all of us who still remain on earth will meet the end." [31] The idea is one of a cosmic fatigue, a universal exhaustion. Nimuendaju also reports the ecstatic experiences of a certain shaman: in a moment of ecstasy in the presence of the supreme God, Nanderuvuvu, he had heard the Earth beg the Lord to put an end to its creations. "I am exhausted," sighed the Earth. "I am stuffed with the cadavers that I have devoured. Let me rest,

28. Schaden, *Aspectos fundamentais*, p. 187; "Der Paradiesmythos," pp. 152–53 (cf. n. 21); *XXXth International Congress of Americanists*, p. 180 cf. n. 23).
29. Schaden, *Aspectos fundamentais*, p. 189.
30. Nimuendaju, "Die Sagen," p. 335.
31. *Ibid.*, p. 339.

Father. The waters also implored the Creator to grant them rest, and the trees . . . and thus all of Nature." [32]

One rarely encounters in ethnographic literature such a moving expression of cosmic fatigue and nostalgia for the final rest. It is true that the Indians encountered by Nimuendaju in 1912 were exhausted after three or four centuries of vagabond life and continual dances in search of Paradise. Nimuendaju believes that the notion of the end of the world is a native one, and denies the possibility of a potential Christian influence. He considers the pessimism of the Guaranis as one of the results of the Portuguese conquest — the consequence, especially, of the terror unleashed by the slave hunters. Certain scholars have recently questioned the interpretation of Nimuendaju.[33] It might indeed be questioned whether what Nimuendaju calls "Indian pessimism" does not have roots originating in a widespread belief among primitive peoples, which might be summarized as follows: the world is degenerating by virtue of the simple fact that it exists, and it must be periodically regenerated, that is, created again; the end of the world is thus necessary in order that a new creation may take place.[34]

It is probable that a similar belief was shared by the Apapocuva-Guaranis before the Portuguese conquest and the Christian propaganda. The shock of the conquerors must certainly have aggravated and intensified the desire to escape from a world of misery and suffering — but it was not the shock of the Portuguese conquest that created this desire. Like many other archaic populations, the Guaranis longed to live in a pure, fresh, rich, and blessed cosmos. The Paradise that they sought is the world restored to its primeval beauty and glory. The "Land-without-Evil," or the house of Nande ("Our Grandmother") exists here on earth: it is situated on the other side of the ocean or in the center of the earth. It is difficult to reach, but it is located in this world. Although it seems to some extent supernatural — since it entails paradisiacal dimensions (for instance, immortality) — the Land-without-Evil does not belong to the Beyond. It cannot even be said to be invisible; it is simply very well hidden. One arrives there not — or, more accurately, not only — in soul or spirit, but in flesh and bones. The collective expeditions undertaken in search of Paradise had precisely that

32. *Ibid.*, p. 335.
33. See, for instance, Lindig, "Wanderungen der Tupi-Guarani," p. 37.
34. Cf. Eliade, *Myth and Reality*, pp. 54 ff.

goal: to reach the Land-without-Evil before the destruction of the world, to settle down in Paradise and enjoy a beatific existence while the exhausted and unregenerate cosmos awaited its violent end.

The Land-without-Evil

The Paradise of the Guaranis is thus a world at once real and transfigured, where life continues according to the same familiar model, but outside of Time and History, that is, without misery or sickness, without sins or injustice, and without age. This Paradise is not of a "spiritual" domain: if today, according to the belief of some tribes, one can get there only after death, that is, as "spirit," in former times men were to arrive there *in concreto*. Paradise thus has a paradoxical character: on the one hand, it stands for the contrary of this world — purity, freedom, beatitude, immortality, and the like; on the other hand, it is concrete, that is, not "spiritual," and is included in this world, since it has a geographic reality and identity. In other words, Paradise for the Tupi-Guarani Indians stands for the perfect and pure world of the "beginning," when it had just been finished by the Creator and when the ancestors of the present tribes lived among the gods and heroes. Indeed, the original myth of Paradise spoke only of a sort of Island of the Blessed, in the middle of the ocean, where death was unknown, and which one reached by a rope or other such means. (Let us note in passing that images of rope, or liana, or steps are frequently used to represent the passing from one mode of being to another — from the profane to the sacred world.) In the beginning, one sought the fabulous Island in order to attain immortality by striving to live in spiritual communion with the gods; it was not sought as a refuge from an imminent cosmic catastrophe.[35] The apocalyptic transformation of the myth of Paradise took place later, perhaps as a result of Jesuit influence,[36] or simply because the Guaranis, like so many other primitive peoples, found that the world had grown too old and that it must be destroyed and created again.

35. Schaden, *Aspectos fundamentais*, p. 188.
36. In his most recent publications ("Der Paradiesmythos," p. 153, and *XXth International Congress of Americanists*, p. 181), Egon Schaden estimates that the apocalyptic transformation of the myth of paradise is probably due to Jesuit influence.

The fundamental conception of the religion of the Guaranis — the conception from which the certitude that one may reach paradise *in concreto* is derived — is summed up in the term *aguydjé*. This word may be translated as "supreme happiness," "perfection," and "victory." For the Guaranis, *aguydjé* constitutes the goal and the objective of all human existence. To attain *aguydjé* means to know concretely paradisiacal beatitude in a supernatural world. But this supernatural world is accessible before death, and it is accessible to any member of the tribe, provided that he follows the traditional moral and religious code.

Thanks to the recent work of Schaden, we now have fairly detailed information concerning the portrayal of Paradise among the various Guarani populations.[37] Thus, for instance, the Nandevas hold two distinct conceptions: one is peculiar to the Nandevas who began migrations long ago and did not reach the Land-without-Evil; the other belongs exclusively to the Nandevas who did not set out on such journeys. Those who sought after the Paradise without finding it — and who ended their wanderings some ten years ago when they arrived at the coast — no longer believe that Paradise lies on the other side of the ocean. They situate it at the zenith and believe that it cannot be reached before death.

The other Nandeva populations, who did not set out on such journeys to the ocean, believe that the world is doomed to destruction by fire, but the catastrophe is not considered imminent. The place of refuge is Paradise, conceived as a sort of Island of the Blessed in the middle of the ocean. Provided that he practice certain rituals, especially dances and songs, man can reach the island in flesh and bones, that is, before dying. But one must know the route — and this knowledge is almost completely lost today. In ancient times, one could find the way because people had confidence in Nanderykey, the civilizing hero: the latter came to meet humans and guided them toward the paradisiacal Island. Today Paradise can be reached only "in spirit," after death.

According to information given by a shaman (*nanderu*) to Egon Schaden, the paradisiacal Island "resembles heaven more than earth." There is a great lake in the center and, in the middle of the lake, a high cross. (The cross very probably represents a Christian influence — but the Island and the lake belong to native mytho-

37. Schaden, *Aspectos fundamentais*, pp. 189 ff., "Der Paradiesmythos," pp. 154 ff. (cf. n. 21).

ogy.) The Island is rich in fruits and the inhabitants do not work, but spend their time dancing. They never die. The island is not the land of the dead. The souls of the deceased arrive there, but do not settle down there; they continue their journey. In ancient times, it was easy to reach the Island. According to other information, likewise gathered by Schaden, the sea supposedly receded before those who had faith and formed a bridge over which they could pass. On the Island no one died. It was indeed a "holy land."[38]

Still more interesting is the portrayal of Paradise among the Mbüás, the only Guarani group that continues today to look to the coast in search of the Land-without-Evil. Of all the Guarani populations, the myth of Paradise plays the most important role among the Mbüás. This fact is highly significant in that the Mbüás were not at all subject to the influence of the Jesuit missions.[39] The Paradise of the Mbüás is not conceived of as a safe shelter from a future cataclysm. It is a fabulous garden, rich in fruits and game, where men continue their earthly existence. One attains Paradise by leading a just and pious life in conformity with traditional prescriptions.

The "Road" to the Gods

Among the third Guarani group, the Kaiovás, who, some decades ago, were still journeying to the Atlantic, there exists this peculiarity: the importance of Paradise increases in periods of crisis. Then, the Kaiovás dance night and day, without stopping, in order to accelerate the destruction of the world and to obtain the revelation of the route that leads to the Land-without-Evil. Dance, revelation, road to Paradise — these three religious realities stand together; they are characteristic, moreover, of all the Guarani tribes, and not only of the Kaiovás. The image and the myth of the "road" — that is, the passage from this world to the holy world — plays a considerable role. The shaman (*nanderu*) is a specialist of the "road": it is he who receives supernatural instructions which enable him to guide the tribe in its prodigious wanderings. In the tribal myth of the Nandevas, the Primordial Mother had personally covered the same path when she departed in search of

38. Schaden, *Aspectos fundamentais*, p. 192.
39. *Ibid.*, p. 195.

the Father of the Twins. During prayer, or after death, when crossing celestial regions, the soul follows the same mysterious and paradoxical "road," for it is both natural and supernatural.

When asked by Egon Schaden to trace this prestigious "road," the Kaiovás drew the road taken by the shaman in his frequent journeys to heaven.[40] All the Guarani peoples speak of themselves as *tapédja*, that is, "people of pilgrams and travelers." The nocturnal dances are accompanied by prayers, and all these prayers are none other than "roads" leading to the gods. "Without a road," confided one of Schaden's informants, "one cannot reach the place he desires." [41] Thus, for the Kaiovás, the "road" to the world of the gods symbolizes their whole religious life. Man needs a "road" to communicate with the gods and to reach his destiny. It is only at times of crisis that the quest for this "road" is charged with apocalyptic elements. Then they dance night and day to seek urgently the "road" leading to Paradise. They dance frenetically, for the end of the world is near and it is only in Paradise that one can be saved. But the rest of the time, in less dramatic periods, the "road" continues to play the central role in the life of the Guaranis. It is only in seeking and following the road that leads to the neighborhood of the gods that a Guarani believes he had fulfilled his mission on earth.

The Originality of Guarani Messianism

Let us conclude this brief presentation of Guarani messianism by some more general observations. We note, in the first place, that, in contrast to the prophetic movements of the North American tribes, Guarani messianism is not the consequence of the cultural shock of the European conquerors and the disorganization of social structures.[42] The myth of and the quest for the Land-without-Evil existed among the Tupi-Guaranis well before the arrival of the Portuguese and the first Christian missionaries. Contact with the conquerors exacerbated the search for Paradise, gave it an urgent and tragic — or even pessimistic — character of a despondent flight from an imminent cosmic catastrophe, but it was not the contact with the conquerors that inspired the quest. Moreover, we

40. *Ibid.*, p. 199.
41. *Ibid.*
42. Cf. de Queiroz, "L'Influence du milieu social interne," pp. 22 ff.

are not dealing here with tribes in the midst of a crisis of accultu-
ration, like the aborigines of North America, who for two centuries
had been periodically buffeted by prophetic and messianic movements. The culture and society of the Guaranis were neither dis-
organized nor hybridized.

This fact is not unimportant for an understanding of prophetic
and messianic phenomena in general. The importance of the historical, social, and economic context in the birth and spread of
messianic movements has been widely emphasized, and rightly so.
People await the end of the world, or a cosmic renewal, or the
Golden Age, especially in times of profound crisis; they herald
the imminence of an earthly Paradise to defend themselves against
the despair provoked by extreme misery, the loss of liberty, and the
collapse of all traditional values. But the example of the Tupi-
Guaranis demonstrates that entire collectivities have been brought
to seek Paradise, and to search for centuries, without social crises
as a stimulus. As we have already indicated, this Paradise is not
always conceived of as a purely "spiritual" Beyond; it belongs to
this world, to a real world transformed by faith. The Guaranis de-
sired to live as their mythical ancestors lived in the beginning of
the world — in Judeo-Christian terms, to live as Adam, before the
Fall, lived in Paradise. This is not an absurd and peculiar idea.
At a certain time in their history, many other primitive peoples
believed that it was possible to return periodically to the first days
of Creation — that it was possible to live in a dawning and perfect
world, such as it had been before it had been consumed by Time
and vilified by History.

7

Initiation and the Modern World

Toward a Definition

The term initiation in the most general sense denotes a body of rites and oral teachings whose purpose is to produce a radical modification of the religious and social status of the person to be initiated. In philosophical terms, initiation is equivalent to an ontological mutation of the existential condition. The novice emerges from his ordeal a totally different being: he has become *another*. Generally speaking, there are three categories, or types, of initiation.[1]

The first category comprises the collective rituals whose function is to effect the transition from childhood or adolescence to adulthood, and which are obligatory for all members of a particular society. Ethnological literature terms these rituals "puberty rites," "tribal initiation," or "initiation into an age group."

This chapter is a translation and revision of a paper originally entitled "L'Initiation et le monde moderne" (© 1965 by Mircea Eliade), which appeared in *Initiation*, ed. C. J. Bleeker (Leiden, 1965), pp. 1–14. This volume is a collection of papers presented at a symposium on initiation which was held in Strasbourg, France, in September, 1964.

I was invited to give the introductory lecture on the theme of initiation, and I decided to present first the function and meaning of initiation in archaic and traditional societies and then to examine the progress marked by recent research, reviewing especially the contributions of psychologists, historians of culture, and literary critics. It is my conviction that the study of the complex phenomenon designated by the term initiation illustrates in an exemplary way the benefits of the collaboration between scholars belonging to different disciplines.

1. See Mircea Eliade, *Birth and Rebirth* (New York, 1958), (French translation: *Naissances Mystiques* [Paris, 1959]).

The second category includes all types of rites of entering a secret society, a *Bund*, or a confraternity. These closed societies are limited to one sex and are extremely jealous of their secrets. Most of them are male, constituting secret fraternities (*Männerbünde*), but there are also some female societies. However, in the ancient Mediterranean and Near Eastern world, the Mysteries were open to both sexes. Although they differ somewhat in type, we can still classify the Greco-Oriental Mysteries in the category of secret confraternities.

Finally, there is a third category of initiation, the type that occurs in connection with a mystical vocation. On the level of primitive religions, the vocation would be that of the medicine man or shaman. A specific characteristic of this third category is the importance of the personal experience. I may add that initiation in secret societies and those of a shamanic type have a good deal in common. What distinguishes them in principle is the ecstatic element, which is of greatest importance in shamanic initiation. I may add too that there is a sort of common denominator among all these categories of initiation, with the result that, from a certain point of view, all initiations are much alike.

Puberty Rites

The tribal initiation introduces the novice into the world of spiritual and cultural values and makes him a responsible member of the society. The young man learns not only the behavior patterns, the techniques, and the institutions of adults, but also the myths and the sacred traditions of the tribe, the names of the gods and the history of their works; above all, he learns the mystical relations between the tribe and supernatural beings as those relations were established at the beginning of time. In a great many cases puberty rites, in one way or another, imply the revelation of sexuality. In short, through initiation, the candidate passes beyond the "natural" mode of being — that of the child — and gains access to the cultural mode; that is, he is introduced to spiritual values. In many cases, on the occasion of the puberty rites the entire community is religiously regenerated, for the rites are the repetitions of operations and actions performed by supernatual beings in mythical time.

Any age-grading initiation requires a certain number of more

or less dramatic tests and trials: separation from the mother, isola-
tion in the bush under the supervision of an instructor, interdiction
against eating certain vegetable and animal foods, knocking out
of an incisor, circumcision (followed in some cases by subinci-
sion), scarification, etc. The sudden revelation of sacred objects
(bull-roarers, images of supernatural beings, etc.) also constitutes
an initiatory test. In many cases, the puberty initiation implies a
ritual death followed by a "resurrection" or a "rebirth." Already
among certain Australian tribes the extraction of the incisor is interpreted as the neophyte's "death," and the same significance is
even more evident in the case of circumcision. The novices isolated
in the bush are assimilated to ghosts: they cannot use their fingers and must take food directly with their mouths, as the dead
are supposed to do. Sometimes they are painted white, a sign
that they have become ghosts. The huts in which they are isolated
represent the body of a monster or a water animal: the neophytes
are considered to have been swallowed by the monster and they
remain in its belly until they are "reborn" or "resuscitated." For
the initiatory death is interpreted either as a *descensus ad inferos*
or as a *regressus ad uterum,* and the "resurrection" is sometimes
understood as a "rebirth." In a number of cases, the novices are
symbolically buried, or they pretend to have forgotten their past
lives, their family relations, their names, and their language, and
must learn everything again. Sometimes the initiatory trials reach
a high degree of cruelty.

Secret Societies

Even on the archaic levels of culture (for example, in Australia),
the puberty initiation may entail a series of stages. In such cases
the sacred history can be only gradually revealed. The deepening
of the religious experience and knowledge demands a special vocation or an outstanding intelligence and will power. This fact
explains the emergence of both the secret societies and the confraternities of shamans and medicine men. The rites of entrance
into a secret society correspond in every respect to those of tribal
initiations: seclusion, initiatory tests and tortures, "death" and "resurrection," imposition of a new name, revelation of a secret doctrine, learning of a new language, etc. We may point out, however,
a few innovations characteristic of the secret societies: the great

importance of secrecy, the cruelty of initiatory trials, the predomi-
nance of the ancestor cult (the ancestors being personified by
masks), and the absence of a supreme being in the ceremonial
life of the group. As to the *Weiberbünde*, the initiation consists of
a series of specific tests followed by revelations concerning fertility, conception, and birth.

Initiatory death signifies both the end of the "natural," acultural
man, and the passage to a new mode of existence, that of a being
"born to the spirit," i.e., one who does not live exclusively in an
"immediate" reality. Thus the initiatory "death" and "resurrection"
represent a religious process through which the initiate becomes
another, patterned on the model revealed by gods or mythical ancestors. In other words, one becomes a *real man* to the extent that
one resembles a superhuman being. The interest of initiation for
the understanding of the archaic mind centers essentially in the
fact that it shows that the *real man* — the spiritual one — is not
given, is not the result of a natural process. He is "made" by the
old masters, in accordance with the models revealed by divine
beings in mythical times. These old masters form the spiritual
elites of archaic societies. Their main role is to transmit to the new
generations the deep meaning of existence and to help them to
assume the responsibility of "real men," and hence to participate
actively in the cultural life. But because culture means, for the
archaic and traditional societies, the sum of the values received
from supernatural beings, the function of initiation may be thus
summarized: it reveals to every new generation a world open to
the transhuman, a world, one may say, that is "transcendental."

Shamans and Medicine Men

As for the shamanic initiations, they consist in ecstatic experiences
(e.g., dreams, visions, trances) and in an instruction imparted by
the spirits or the old master shamans (e.g., shamanic techniques,
names and functions of the spirits, mythology and genealogy of
the clan, secret language). Sometimes initiation is public and includes a rich and varied ritual; this is the case, for example, among
the Buryat. But the lack of a ritual of this sort in no way implies
the absence of an initiation; it is perfectly possible for the initiation to be performed entirely in the candidate's dreams or ecstatic
experiences. In Siberia and Central Asia the youth who is called

to be a shaman goes through a psychopathic crisis during which he is considered to be tortured by demons and ghosts who play the role of masters of initiation. These "initiatory sicknesses" generally present the following elements: (1) torture and dismemberment of the body, (2) scraping of the flesh and reduction to a skeleton, (3) replacement of organs and renewal of blood, (4) a sojourn in the underworld and instruction by demons and the souls of dead shamans, (5) an ascent to heaven, (6) "resurrection," i.e., access to a new mode of being, that of a consecrated individual capable of communicating personally with gods, demons, and souls of the dead. A somewhat analogous pattern is to be found in the initiations of Australian medicine men.[2]

The little we know about Eleusis and the initiations in the Hellenistic Mysteries indicates that the mystes' central experience depended on a revelation concerning the death and resurrection of the divine founder of the cult. Thanks to this revelation the mystes acceded to another, superior mode of being, and concurrently secured for himself a better fate after death.

Recent Works on Initiations among the "Primitives"

It will be interesting to review briefly the results obtained in the last thirty to forty years in the study of the different categories of initiation. We will not try to evaluate every important contribution published in this period, nor shall we discuss their implicit methodologies. We will only mention certain authors and a few titles in order to illustrate the orientation of the research. From the outset, we must point out that although a number of studies have been published on specific types of initiation, there are only few works in which the initiatory complex is presented in the totality of its manifestations. One can cite the works of O. E. Briem, *Les Sociétés secrètes des Mystères* (French translation, 1941); W. E. Peuckert, *Geheimkulte* (1951); M. Eliade, *Birth and Rebirth* (1958); *Naissances mystiques* (1959); and now Frank W. Young, *Initiation Ceremonies* (1965), and the remarks of Geo Widengren at the Strasbourg symposium (in *Initiation*, ed. C. J. Bleeker, pp. 287–309).

The same qualification applies to the study of "primitive" initia-

2. See Mircea Eliade, *Shamanism: Archaic Techniques of Ecstasy* (New York, 1964), pp. 33 ff., 110 ff., 508 ff.

tions in general. Ad. E. Jensen brought out a suggestive and controversial work, *Beschneidung und Reifezeremonien bei Naturvölkern* (1933), R. Thurnwald an important article on the rebirth rites, and more recently some American anthropologists reex· amined the functions of puberty ceremonies.[3] On the other hand, there are a great number of regional monographs. Since we cannot cite all of these, we may mention, for Australia and Oceania, A. P. Elkin, *Aboriginal Men of High Degree* (1946); and R. M. Berndt, *Kunapipi* (1951); the studies of F. Speiser,[4] R. Piddington,[5] and D. F. Thomas;[6] the books and articles of J. Layard,[7] W. E. Mühlmann,[8] E. Schlesier, and C. A. Schmitz.[9] For the Americas we shall cite the works of M. Gusinde,[10] De Goeje,[11]

3. R. Thurnwald, "Primitive Initiation -und Wiedergeburtsriten," *Eranos Jahrbuch*, 7 (1946): 321–28; see also E. M. Loeb, *Tribal Initiation and Secret Societies*, University of California Publications in American Archaeology and Ethnology, vol. XXV (Berkeley and Los Angeles, 1929), pp. 249–88; J. W. M. Whiting, R. Kluckhohn, and A. Anthony, "The Functions of Male Initiation Ceremonies at Puberty," in *Readings in Social Psychology*, ed. E. E. Maccoby, Theodore Newcomb, and C. Hartley (New York, 1958), pp. 359–70; Edward Norbeck, D. Walker, and M. Cohn, "The Interpretation of Data: Puberty Rites," *American Anthropologist*, 64 (1964): 463–85.
4. F. Speiser, "Uber Initiationen in Australien und Neuguinea," in *Verhandlungen der Naturforschenden Gesellschaft in Basel* (1929), pp. 56–258; "Kulturgeschichtliche Betrachtungen über die Initiationen in der Südsee," *Bulletin der Schweizerischen Gesellschaft für Anthropologie und Ethnologie*, 22 (1945–46): 28–61.
5. Ralph Piddington, "Karadjeri Initiation," *Oceania*, 3 (1932–33): 46–87.
6. Donald F. Thomson, "The Hero-Cult, Initiation and Totemism on Cape York," *The Journal of the Royal Anthropological Institute*, 63 (1933): 453–537. See also E. A. Worms, "Initiationsfeiern einiger Küsten -und Binnenlandstämme in Nord-Westaustralien," *Annali Lateranensi*, 2 (1938): 147–74.
7. John W. Layard, *Stone Men of Malekula* (London, 1942); "The Making of Man in Malekula," *Eranos Jahrbuch*, 16 (1948): 209 ff.
8. W. E. Mühlmann, *Arioi und Mamaia* (Wiesbaden, 1955).
9. Erhard Schlesier, *Die melanesische Geheimkulte* (Göttingen, 1956). See also C. A. Schmitz, "Die Initiation bei den Pasum am Oberen Rumu, Nordost-Neuguinea," *Zeitschrift für Ethnologie*, 81 (1956): 236–46; "Zum Problem des Balumkultes," *Paideuma*, 6 (1957): 257–80. Dr. P. Hermann Bader, *Die Reifefeiern bei den Ngadha* (Mödling, n.d.); C. Laufer, "Jugendinitiation und Sakraltänze der Baining," *Anthropos*, 54 (1959): 905–38; P. Alphons Schaefer, "Zur Initiation im Wagi-Tal," *Anthropos*, 33 (1938): 101–23; Hubert Kroll, "Der Iniet. Das Wesen eines melanesischen Geheimbundes," *Zeitschrift für Ethnologie*, 70 (1937): 180–220.
10. M. Gusinde, *Die Yamana* (Mödling, 1937), pp. 940 ff.
11. C. H. de Goeje, "Philosophy, Initiation and Myths of the Indian Guiana and Adjacent Countries," *Internationales Archiv für Ethnographie*, 44 (1943). See also A. Metraux, "Les rites d'initiation dans le vaudou haïtien,"

J. Haeckel,[12] W. Müller,[13] and some others. For Africa we shall note the monographs of E. Johanssen, *Mysterien eines Bantu-Volkes* (1925), L. Bittremieux, *La Société secrète des Bakhimba* (1934), and A. M. Vergiat, *Les Rites secrets des primitifs de l'Oubangui* (1936); the work of Audrey I. Richards on the girls' initiation among the Bemba, *Chisungu* (1956), and especially the volumes of D. Zahan on the Bambara initiation.[14]

Thanks to recent research, we now have precise and sometimes abundant information concerning the initiation ceremonies among some primitive peoples, as, for example, the works of M. Gusinde on the Fuegians, of Zahan and Audrey Richards on certain African tribes, of Carl Laufer on the Baining rites, and of Piddington, Elkin, and Berndt on the Australian initiatory scenarios. On the other hand, the understanding of the various forms of initiation has been notably improved as a result of the illuminating analyses of Werner Müller, Mühlmann, Zahan, and other scholars.

Mystery Religions; Indo-European Secret Societies

Concerning the Mystery religions, however, the works published in recent times are characterized by a certain skepticism. A. D. Nock emphasized in 1952 that our information with regard to Hellenistic Mysteries is late and sometimes even reflects Christian influences.[15] In 1961, G. F. Mylonas declared in his book *Eleusis and the Eleusinian Mysteries* that we know almost nothing about the secret rites, that is to say, about the real initiation into the Mys-

Tribus, 4–5 (1953–55): 177–98; *Le vaudou haïtien* (Paris, 1958), pp. 171 ff.

12. Josef Haeckel, "Jugendweihe und Männerfest auf Feuerland," *Mitteilungen der Oesterreichischen Gesellschaft für Anthropologie, Ethnologie und Prähistorie,* 74–77 (1947): 84–114; "Schutzgeistsuche und Jugendweihe im westlichen Nordamerika," *Ethnos,* 12 (1947): 106–22; "Initiationen und Geheimbünde an der Nordwestküste Nordamerikas," *Mitteilungen der Anthropologische Gesellschaft in Wien,* 83 (1954): 176–90.

13. Werner Müller, *Die blaue Hütte* (Wiesbaden, 1954); *Weltbild und Kult der Kwakiutl-Indianer* (1955).

14. Dominique Zahan, *Sociétés d'initiation bambara* (Paris, 1960). See also Leopold Walk, "Initiationszeremonien und Pubertätriten der Südafrikanischen Stämme," *Anthropos,* 23 (1928): 861–966; M. Planquaert, *Les sociétés secrètes chez les Bayaka* (Louvain, 1930); E. Hildebrand, *Die Geheimbünde Westafrikas als Problem der Religionswissenschaft* (Leipzig 1937); H. Rehwald, *Geheimbünde in Afrika* (Munich, 1941).

15. A. D. Nock, "Hellenistic Mysteries and Christian Sacraments," *Mnemosyne,* 1952, pp. 117–213. See the bibliographies in Eliade, *Birth and Rebirth,* pp. 162 n. 15, 163 n. 16, 164 n. 33.

teries. Some new contributions to the understanding of Greek and
Hellenistic initiations were brought out in the Strasbourg symposium, and recently Carl Kerényi published a more constructive
book on the Eleusinian Mysteries.[16]

In contrast, the research marked important progress in an area
somehow neglected before the thirties, namely, the puberty rites
and the secret societies among the different Indo-European peoples. One has only to mention the works of Lily Weiser (1927)
and Otto Höfler (1934) on the Germanic initiations, the monographs of G. Widengren and Stig Wikander on the Indo-Iranian
initiatory rituals and mythologies, and the contributions of Georges
Dumézil on the initiatory scenarios of the Germans, Romans, and
Celts to appreciate the progress realized.[17] We should add that the
classicist W. F. Jackson Knight published a small monograph,
Cumaean Gates (Oxford, 1936), in which he tried to identify and
articulate the initiatory elements in the sixth book of the *Aeneid*.
Recently J. Gagé has studied the traces of feminine initiations in
ancient Rome.[18] The brilliant work of H. Jeanmaire, *Couroï et
Courètes* (1939), merits special mention: the lamented Hellenist
convincingly reconstructed the initiatory scenarios in the Theseus
saga, in the Tesmophories, and in the Spartan discipline of Ly-
curgus. Jeanmaire's enterprise did not remain alone. A. Brelich has
elucidated the initiatory significance of the curious Greek custom
of putting on a single sandal.[19] Moreover, in his book *Gli Eroi Greci*

16. Cf. Bleeker, *Initiation*, pp. 154–71, 222–31; C. Kerényi, *Eleusis: Archetypal Image of Mother and Daughter* (New York, 1967).

17. Lily Weiser, *Altgermanische Junglingsweihen und Männerbünde* (Baden,
1922); Otto Höfler, *Kultische Geheimbünde der Germanen* (Frankfurt am
Main, 1934); Geo Widengren, *Hochgottglaube im alten Iran* (Uppsala, 1938),
pp. 311 ff., and "Stand und Aufgaben der iranischen Religionsgeschichte,"
Numen, 1 (1955): 16–83, especially pp. 65 ff.; Stig Wikander, *Der arische
Männerbund* (Lund, 1938); Georges Dumézil, *Mythes et Dieux des Ger-
mains* (Paris, 1939), pp. 79 ff., and *Horace et les Curiaces* (Paris, 1942). See
also Alwyn Rees and Brinley Rees, *Celtic Heritage* (New York, 1961), pp.
246 ff., as well as the bibliographies in Eliade, *Birth and Rebirth*, pp. 15–
16, nn. 2, 4, 7–11. Marijan Molé was inclined to think that, at least in ancient times, the crossing of Cinvat Bridge was considered an initiatory test;
see "Daena, le pont Cinvat et l'Initiation dans le Mazdéisme," *Revue de
l'Histoire des Religions*, 157 (1960): 155–85, especially p. 182.

18. J. Gagé, *Matronalia. Essai sur les dévotions et les organisations cul-
tuelles de femmes dans l'ancienne Rome* (Brussels, 1963); cf. Brelich, *Studi e
Materiali di Storia delle Religioni*, 34 (1963): 355 ff.

19. A. Brelich, "Les monosandales," *La Nouvelle Clio*, 7–9 (1955–57); 469–
84; see also Brelich's article in *Initiation*, ed. Bleeker, pp. 222–31.

(Rome, 1955), Brelich has taken up again and developed the views of Jeanmaire on the feminine initiations and on the ritual significance of Theseus entering the labyrinth.[20] Likewise, Marie Delcourt has succeeded in deciphering some initiatory elements in the myths and legends of Hephaistos.[21]

More recently, R. Merkelback has brought out an important work, *Roman und Mysterium in der Antike* (Munich and Berlin, 1962), in which he attempted to show that the Greco-Roman novels — *Amor and Psyche* as well as *Ephesiaca* or *Aethiopica* — are "*Mysterientexte*," that is to say, narrative transpositions of an initiation. In his long review article, R. Turcan[22] does not dispute the religious significance, or even the allusions to the Mysteries, which are to be found in certain Alexandrinian novels. But he refuses to see in these literary texts, overcharged with clichés and reminiscences, concrete indications concerning the Mysteries. We shall not discuss here the validity of these two methodological approaches.[23] But it is significant that a classicist of such stature as R. Merkelbach thought that he could find in Hellenistic literary texts evidence of a secret religious experience with an initiatory structure.

Patterns of Initiation in Oral Literature

To envisage oral and written literature in such a perspective seems to be an approach characteristic of our epoch, and it is consequently relevant for the understanding of modern man. As a matter of fact, we have witnessed for some time now a concerted effort on the part of historians, critics, and psychologists to discover in the literary *oeuvres* values and intentions which go beyond the artistic sphere properly speaking. We may refer, for example, to the medieval romances giving a leading role to Arthur, the Fisher King, Percival, and the other heroes engaged in the Grail quest. The

20. On the initiatory symbolism of the labyrinth, see Clara Gallini, "Pontinjia Dapuritois," *Acme*, 12 (1959): 149 ff.
21. Marie Delcourt, *Héphaistos ou la légende du magicien* (Liège and Paris 1957).
22. Robert Turcan, "Le roman 'initiatique': A propos d'un livre récent,' *Revue de l'Histoire des Religions*, 1963, pp. 149–99.
23. See also *Beiträge zur Klassischen Philologie*, ed. Reinhold Merkelbach (Meisenheim am Glan): Ingrid Löffler, *Die Melampodie. Versuch eine Rekonstrucktion des Inhalts* (1962); Udo Hetzner, *Andromeda und Tarpei* (1962); Gerhard Binder, *Die Aussetzung des Königkindes* (1962).

medievalists have pointed out the continuity between the themes and figures of Celtic mythology and the scenarios and personages of the Arthurian cycle. The majority of these scenarios have an initiatory structure: there is always a long and dramatic "Quest" for marvelous objects involving, among other things, the hero's entering the other world. These enigmatic romances have sometimes occasioned daring interpretations. Thus, for example, a learned scholar like Jessie L. Weston did not hesitate to affirm that the Grail legend preserved traces of an ancient initiation ritual.[24]

This thesis has not been accepted by specialists. But it is the cultural resonance of Weston's book that is important and significant. This is so not only because T. S. Eliot could write *The Waste Land* after reading it, but especially because the success of this book has directed the attention of the general public to the proliferation of initiatory symbols and motifs in the Arthurian romances. One has only to read the competent synthesis of Jean Marx, *La légende arthurienne et le Graal* (1952), or the monograph by Antoinette Fierz-Monnier,[25] to realize that these initiatory motifs and symbols play an essential role by their very presence, independent of any possible genetic solidarity with actual initiatory scenarios. In other words, they partake of an *imaginary* universe, and this universe is no less important for human existence than the world of everyday life.

Similar interpretations have lately been put forward in regard to other oral literatures. Studying the neo-Greek epic *Digenis Akritas*, J. Lindsay writes:

But if we look deeper into the meaning of *Digenis* we recognize in it the initiation-term *Twiceborn* used of the second birth of the young man who has successfully passed the tests and ordeals. And we can call our hero the representative of the initiation-ritual, the youth who supremely defeats the dark forces of the crisis-moment and who therefore symbolizes his people in their death and renewal. Such an inter-

---

24. Jessie L. Weston, *From Ritual to Romance* (Cambridge, 1920).
25. *Initiation und Wandlung: zur Geschichte des altfranzösischen Romans in XII Jahrhundert* (Bern, 1951). Recently Henry and Renée Kahane have elucidated the hermetic sources of the *Parzifal*; cf. *The Krater and the Grail: Hermetic Sources of the Parzifal*, (Urbana, 1965), in which they point out some initiatory motifs (the test, pp. 40 ff.; rebirth, pp. 74 ff.; apotheosis, pp. 105 ff.).

pretation harmonizes with the many elements of fertility-ritual that surround Digenis in the ballads and the lay, and that show up in the folk-beliefs about his tomb and his Heraclean club.[26]

In his important book on Tibetan epic poetry and the Tibetan bard, R. A. Stein has clarified the relations between shamans and folk poets; he has shown, moreover, that the bard receives his songs from a god, and that in order to receive such revelations, the bard must undergo an initiation.[27] As for the initiatory elements present in the esoteric poems of the *Fedeli d'Amore*, they have been emphasized (perhaps too strongly) by L. Valli in 1928 and (in a more consistent way) by R. Ricolfi in 1933.[28] Henry Corbin has masterfully interpreted a text of Avicenna as an "initiatory recital." The same author has further elucidated in many of his writings the relation between philosophy, gnosis, and initiation.[29]

As could be expected, folk tales have been studied in a similar perspective. As early as 1923, P. Saintyves interpreted certain folk tales as the "texts" accompanying secret puberty rites. In 1946, the Soviet folklorist Vl. I. Propp went even further: he discerned in popular tales the traces of certain rites of "totemic initiations."[30] We have indicated elsewhere why this hypothesis does not seem plausible,[31] but it is significant that it was formulated. We must add that the Dutch scholar Jan de Vries has proved the persistence of initiatory themes in the heroic saga and even in certain children's games.[32] In a voluminous work on the symbolism of folk

26. J. Lindsay, *Byzantium into Europe* (London, 1952), p. 370.

27. R. A. Stein, *Recherches sur l'épopée et le barde au Tibet* (Paris, 1959), especially pp. 325 ff., 332, etc.

28. See Eliade, *Birth and Rebirth*, pp. 126 ff.

29. Henry Corbin, *Avicenne et le récit visionnaire* (Tehran and Paris, 1954), (English translation: *Avicenna and the Visionary Recital* [New York, 1960]); see also "Le Récit d'Initiation et l'Hermétisme en Iran," *Eranos Jahrbuch*, 17 (1949): 149 ff.

30. P. Saintyves, *Les contes de Perrault et les récits parallèles* (Paris, 1923); V. Ia. Propp, *Istoritcheskie korni volshebnoi skazki* (Leningrad, 1946).

31. Mircea Eliade, "Les savants et les contes de fées," *La Nouvelle Revue Française*, May, 1956, pp. 884–91; cf. Mircea Eliade, *Myth and Reality* (New York, 1963), pp. 195–202.

32. Jan de Vries, *Betrachtungen zum Märchen, besonders in seine Verhältnis zu Heldensage und Mythos*, FF Comm. no. 150 (Helsinki, 1954) *Heldenlied en heldensage* (Utrecht, 1959), especially pp. 194 ff.; *Untersuchung über das Hüpfspiel, Kinderspiel-Kulttanz*, FF Comm. no. 173 (Helsinki, 1957).

tales, a Swiss author, Hedwig von Beit, examined the initiatory motifs in the light of Jung's psychology.[33]

The Contribution of Psychoanalysts and Literary Critics

There was every likelihood that the psychoanalysts would be attracted by our subject. Freud had avidly encouraged the research of Otto Rank on the myths of the heroes. From then on, the psychoanalytical literature on the rites and symbols of initiation continued to increase. We may cite one of the most recent contributions to the analytical interpretation of puberty rites, which is also the most original: *Symbolic Wounds* (1954; new edition, 1962) by Bruno Bettelheim. But it is especially the analytical interpretation of literary works that is instructive. In 1934 Maud Bodkins published her book *Archetypal Patterns in Poetry*; applying Jung's ideas of the "archetype of the new birth," the author explained Coleridge's *Ancient Mariner* and Eliot's *Waste Land* as poetical projections of an (unconscious) process of initiation.

More recently, in his *Nerval: Expérience et Création* (1963), Jean Richer has analyzed with great acumen the initiatory structure of *Aurélie*. As a matter of fact, Gerard de Nerval was aware of the ritual significance of his experience. "As soon as I was sure that I was subject to the trials of the secret initiation," writes Nerval, "an invincible force entered my spirit. I considered myself a living hero under the glance of the gods." [34] According to Richer, the theme of Orpheus' descent into Hell dominates the entire literary creation of Nerval. As is well known, the *descensus ad inferos* constitutes the initiatory ordeal *par excellence*. Certainly, Nerval had read a great number of occult and hermetic books. But it is difficult to believe that a poet of his scope chose the initiation structure because he had read a number of books on that subject. And, furthermore, it is significant that Nerval has felt the necessity to express his real or imaginary experiences in an initiatory language.

The critics have also discovered similar themes in writers unacquainted with occult literature. This is the case, for instance,

33. Hedwig von Beit, *Symbolik des Märchens* (Berne, 1952); *Gegensatz und Erneuerung im Märchen* (Berne, 1956). See our observations in *Critique*, no. 89 (October 1954), pp. 904–7.
34. Quoted by Jean Richer, *Nerval*, p. 512.

with Jules Verne; some of his novels — especially *Le voyage au centre de la terre, L'Ile mystérieuse, Le chateau des Carpathes* — have been interpreted as initiatory novels. And one has only to read the essay of Léon Cellier on the initiatory novels in France during the period of Romanticism to understand the contribution that literary criticism is able to bring to our investigations.[35]

American critics have also gone quite far in this direction. One can even say that a great number of critics interpret literary creations in a perspective borrowed from the historians of religions. Myth, ritual, initiation, heroes, ritual death, regeneration, rebirth, etc., belong now to the basic terminology of literary exegesis. There are a considerable number of books and articles analyzing the initiation scenarios camouflaged in poems, short stories, and novels. Such scenarios have been identified not only in *Moby Dick*,[36] but also in Thoreau's *Walden*,[37] in the novels of Cooper [38] and Henry James, in Twain's *Huckleberry Finn*, and in Faulkner's *The Bear*.[39] And in a recent book, *Radical Innocence* (1963), the author, Ihab Hassan, consecrates an entire chapter to the "dialectics of initiation," using as examples the writings of Sherwood Anderson, Scott Fitzgerald, Wolfe, and Faulkner.

It is probable that the biographies of some important writers — i.e., their crises, sufferings, and trials — have been interpreted in the light of such "dialectics of initiation." As we have seen, the initiation pattern deciphered by Richer in *Aurélie* may indicate that Gerard de Nerval traversed a crisis comparable in depth to a *rite de passage*. The case of Nerval is not exceptional. I do not know if Goethe's youth, for example, has been analyzed and interpreted from a similar perspective. But in *Dichtung und Wahrheit* the old Goethe described the turbulent experiences of his *Sturm und Drang* in terms which remind one of a "shamanistic" type of initiation. Goethe speaks of the instability, eccentricity, and irresponsibility of those years. He admits that he wasted both

35. Léon Cellier, "Le Roman initiatique en France au temps du romantisme," *Cahiers Internationaux de Symbolisme*, no. 4 (1964), pp. 22–40.
36. Cf. Newton Arvin, *Herman Melville* (New York, 1950).
37. Stanley Hyman, "Henry Thoreau in our Time," *Atlantic Monthly*, November, 1946, pp. 137–76; cf. also R. W. B. Lewis, *The American Adam* (Chicago, 1955), pp. 22 ff.
38. Cf. Lewis, *American Adam*, pp. 87 ff., 98 ff.
39. R. W. B. Lewis in *Kenyon Review*, Autumn, 1951, and *The Picaresque Saint* (New York, 1961), pp. 204 ff.

his time and his gifts, that his life was purposeless and meaning-less. He lived in a "state of chaos," he was "dismembered and cut into pieces" ("*in solcher vielfachen Zerstreuung, ja Zerstückelung meines Wesens*"). As is well known, the dismemberment and cutting into pieces, and also the "state of chaos" (i.e., psychic and mental instability), are characteristic traits of the shamanistic initiation. And just as the would-be shaman reintegrates, through his initiation, a stronger and more creative personality, one can say that after the *Sturm und Drang* period Goethe conquered his immaturity and became the master both of his life and of his creativity.

Meanings for the Modern World

We do not intend to judge here the validity or the results of such enterprises. But, to repeat, it is significant that certain literary works, both ancient and modern, have been interpreted — by his-torians, critics, and psychologists — as having direct, though un-conscious, relations to the process of initiation. And it is significant for several reasons. First of all, in their most complex forms, initia-tions inspire and guide spiritual activity. In a number of tradi-tional cultures, the poetry, the spectacles, and the wisdom are direct results of an initiatory apprenticeship. It will indeed be worthwhile to investigate the relations between initiation and the most "noble" and most creative expressions of a culture. We have pointed out elsewhere the initiatory structure of the Socratic maieutics.[40] One could make a similar rapprochement between the function of initiation and Husserl's phenomenological endeavor. Indeed, the phenomenological analysis intends to suppress the "profane" experience, that is to say, the experience of the "natural man." Now, what Husserl called man's "natural attitude" corre-sponds, in the traditional cultures, to the "profane," preinitiation stage. Through the puberty rites, the novice gains access to the sacred world, that is to say, to what is considered *real* and *mean-ingful* in his culture, just as through phenomenological reduction the subject-as-cogito succeeds in grasping the reality of the world.

But such research is also significant for an understanding of modern Western man. The desire to decipher initiatory scenarios

40. Cf. Eliade, *Birth and Rebirth*, p. 114.

in literature, plastic arts, and cinema denotes not only a reevalua-
tion of initiation as a process of spiritual regeneration and transformation, but also a certain nostalgia for an equivalent experience.
In the Western world, initiation in the traditional and strict
sense of the term has disappeared long ago. But initiatory symbols
and scenarios survive on the unconscious level, especially in
dreams and imaginary universes. It is significant that these sur-
vivals are studied today with an interest difficult to imagine fifty
or sixty years ago. Freud has shown that certain existential tendencies and decisions are not conscious. Consequently, the strong
attraction toward literary and artistic works with an initiatory
structure is highly revealing. Marxism and depth psychology have
illustrated the efficacy of the so-called demystification when one
wants to discover the *true* — or the *original* — significance of a behavior, an action, or a cultural creation. In our case, we have to
attempt a demystification in reverse; that is to say, we have to
"demystify" the apparently profane worlds and languages of literature, plastic arts, and cinema in order to disclose their "sacred"
elements, although it is, of course, an ignored, camouflaged, or
degraded "sacred." In a desacralized world such as ours, the
"sacred" is present and active chiefly in the imaginary universes.
But imaginary experiences are part of the total human being, no
less important than his diurnal experiences. This means that the
nostalgia for initiatory trials and scenarios, nostalgia deciphered
in so many literary and plastic works, reveals modern man's longing for a total and definitive renewal, for a *renovatio* capable of
radically changing his existence.

It is for this reason that the recent research which we have
rapidly reviewed does not represent only contributions interesting
to such disciplines as history of religions, ethnology, orientalism,
or literary criticism; they can also be interpreted as characteristic
expressions in the cultural configuraton of modern times.

8

Prolegomenon to Religious Dualism: Dyads and Polarities

History of a Problem

Religious and philosophical dualism has had a long history, both in Asia and in Europe. I will not attempt to discuss this immense problem here. But from the beginning of the century, dualism and other connected problems, such as polarity, antagonism, and complementarity, have been approached in a new perspective, and we are still drawn toward the results of these researches, especially to the hypotheses that they have raised. The modification of the perspective was certainly begun by the monograph of Durkheim and Mauss, "De quelques formes primitives de classification: contribution à l'étude des représentations collectives." [1] The authors did not consider the problems of dualism or polarity directly, but they did bring forward certain types of social classification ultimately grounded in a similar principle, namely the bipartite division of nature and society. This article had an exceptional resonance, expecially in France. As a matter of fact, it illustrates one of the first, and most brilliant, manifestations of what may be called sociologism, i.e., a sociology elevated to the rank of a totalitarian doctrine. Durkheim and Mauss believed they had proved that ideas are organized according to a model furnished by society. For them there exists an intimate solidarity between social system and logical system. If the universe is divided into more or less complex zones (heaven and earth, high and low, right and left, the four

1. *Année Sociologique*, 6 (1903): 1–72.

cardinal points, etc.), the reason is that society is divided into clans and totems.

We do not need to discuss this theory. It suffices to say that Durkheim and Mauss did not — as a matter of fact, they could not — prove that society has been the cause, or the model, of the bipartite and tripartite classification.[2] One can only say that the same principle informs both the classification of the universe and of the society. If one wants to find the "origin" of the principle which establishes order in a preexistent chaos, it is rather in the primary experience of *orientation* in space that one ought to search for it.

Be that as it may, Durkheim and Mauss' monograph had a considerable echo. In his introduction to the English translation of "De quelques formes primitives de classification," R. Needham cites a great number of authors and works inspired or guided by this text. Among the best known, it should be recalled, is the article by Robert Hertz on the preeminence of the right hand. The author arrives at the conclusion that dualism, which he considers to be a basic principle in the thinking of the primitives, dominates their entire social organization; accordingly, the privilege granted to the right hand has to be explained by the religious polarity which separates and opposes the sacred (sky, male, right, etc.) and the profane (earth, female, left, etc.).[3] As for the brilliant sinologist Marcel Granet, he did not hesitate to write, in 1932, that "the few pages of this (i.e., Durkheim and Mauss') monograph ought to mark a date in the history of sinological studies." [4]

In the first quarter of the century, thanks to the growing knowledge of social and political institutions, scholars were impressed

2. In his introduction to the English translation of this essay, Rodney Needham has summarized the most important objections (*Primitive Classification* [Chicago, 1963], pp. xvii–xviii, xxvi–xxvii).

3. Robert Hertz, "De la prééminence de la main droite," *Revue Philosophique*, 48 (1909): 553–80, especially pp. 559, 561 ff. The problem of right and left in "primitive" symbolic classification has recently occasioned a series of illuminating studies; see, among others, T. O. Beidelman, "Right and Left Hand among the Kaguru: A Note on Symbolic Classification," *Africa*, 31 (1961): 250–57; Rodney Needham, "The Left Hand of the Mugwe: An Analytical Note on the Structure of Meru Symbolism," *Africa*, 30 (1960): 20–33, and "Right and Left in Nyoro Symbolic Classification," *ibid.*, 36 (1967): 425–52; John Middleton, "Some Categories of Dual Classification among the Lugbara of Uganda," *History of Religions*, 7 (1968): 187–208. A book edited by R. Needham, to be published shortly, has the title *Right and Left: Essays on Dual Symbolic Classification*.

4. Marcel Granet, *La Pensée chinoise* (Paris, 1934), p. 29 n. 1.

and intrigued by the considerable number of social organizations of a binary type and by the multiple forms of "dualities." Concomitant with the sociologism of Durkheim and his followers, a "diffusionist" school rose to dominance in England. According to its adherents, social organizations of a binary type are the result of historical events, specifically of the intermixture of two different peoples, one of whom, the victorious invader, would have elaborated a social system in cooperation with the aboriginal inhabitants of the territory. In this manner W. H. R. Rivers explained the origin of dual organization in Melanesia.[5]

I do not intend to analyze here the ideology and the methods of the British diffusionist school. It was not, however, an isolated phenomenon. A whole movement, anticipated by Ratzel but articulated and developed by F. Graebner and W. Schmidt, endeavored to introduce the temporal dimension, and consequently historical methods, into ethnology. Rivers and his disciples associated themselves with this movement, though without sharing the historico-cultural methodology of Graebner and Schmidt. Two fundamental considerations inspired these researches: on the one hand was their conviction that the "primitives" do not represent *Natur-völker*, but are formed by history; on the other hand, postulating as a principle a poor, almost nonexistent creativity of archaic and traditional societies, the similarities between different cultures were explained almost exclusively by diffusion.

In England, after the death of Rivers, diffusionism took the form of panegyptianism under the influence of G. Elliot Smith and W. J. Perry. In his *Children of the Sun* (1925), Perry construes the unfolding of universal history as follows: in India, Indonesia, Oceania, and North America the earliest form of social organization was the dual organization, except for the food gatherers, who were agglutinated in family groups. The tribal bipartition was integrated with a complex of specific cultural elements, the most important being the totemic clan system, the irrigation technique, megaliths, polished stone implements, etc. According to Smith and Perry, all these cultural elements were of Egyptian origin. From the Fifth Dynasty on, they argued, the Eyptians had undertaken long voyages in search of gold, pearls, copper, spices, etc. Every-

5. W. H. R. Rivers, *The History of Melanesian Society*, 2 vols. (Cambridge, 1914), vol. 2, chap. 38, and *Social Origins* (London, 1924).

where they went, these "children of the Sun" brought with them, and imposed upon the original inhabitants, their social organization and their civilization (i.e., irrigation, megaliths, etc.). In sum, according to the panegyptianists, the uniformity of the most archaic world, characterized by the economy of food collecting and hunting, illustrates the poor creativity of the primitives; at the same time, the quasi-uniformity of the traditional societies, with their dual structure, betrays their direct or indirect dependence on Egyptian civilization, thus again indicating the indigent character of human creativity.

It would be instructive to analyze someday the reasons for the striking, though ephemeral, vogue of the panegyptian diffusionist school. With G. Elliot Smith and W. J. Perry, the "historicization" of primitive cultures reached its apogee. All the archaic worlds from Oceania to North America, in all their rich variety, were now provided with a "history," but it was everywhere the *same history*, effectuated by the *same human groups* — the "children of the Sun," or their representatives, imitators, or epigones. This "history," uniform from one end of the world to the other, was supposed to have had as its only center and only source the Egypt of the Fifth Dynasty. And, for Perry, one of the most convincing proofs of this unity was the presence of the dual organization, implying an antagonistic bipartition of the society.

Historicism and Reductionism

In short, by the twenties, the dual classification of society and the world, with all the cosmologies, mythologies, and rituals which the dual classification sustained, was considered to have had either a *social origin* (Durkheim and his followers) or a *"historical"* *origin*; in this later case, it resulted from the mingling of two ethnic groups: a minority of civilized conquerors and a mass of aborigines lingering in a primitive stage (Elliot Smith and the panegyptianists). Not all "historicists" fell in with the excesses of these extreme diffusionists. But confronted with a certain form of "duality," they were tempted to explain it "historically," i.e., as a consequence of the meeting of two different peoples followed by their intermingling. Thus, for instance, in his book *Essai sur les origines de Rome* (1916), A. Piganiol explained the formation of the Roman nation as the union of Latins, i.e., the Indo-Europeans, with Sabines, the latter being, in the opinion of the French scholar, a Mediterranean ethnic group.

As to their religion, the Indo-Europeans would have been responsible for the cremation burial, the Sabines for tomb inhumation. . . . The Indo-Europeans would have introduced in Italy the fire altar, the cult of the male fire, of the Sun and of the bird, and the aversion to human sacrifices; the Sabines would have had for their altars stones which they smeared with blood, they would have venerated the moon and the snake, and immolated human victims.[6]

From 1944 on, Georges Dumézil has patiently dismantled this construction.[7] We know now that the two modes of burial — cremation and inhumation — do not reflect an ethnic duality. In fact, these two modes often coexist.[8] With regard to the war between Romulus and his Romans and Titus Tatius and his Sabines, Dumézil has shown that such a war is a recurrent theme of Indo-European mythology; he compared it with another mythical war, the one between the two divine groups of the Scandinavian tradition, the Ases and the Vanes. As in the case of the Romans and Sabines, the war between the Ases and Vanes did not come to an end by a decisive battle. Weary of their alternating semivictories, the Ases and Vanes concluded a peace. The chief Vanes — the gods Njördhr and Freyr and the goddess Freja — were received into the society of the Ases, to whom they brought fertility and richness, of which they were the divine representatives. Thenceforward, there was never again conflict between the Ases and Vanes. (We may add that this Scandinavian mythical war was also "historicized" by some scholars who explained the long combat between the two divine groups as a drastically mythicisized souvenir of a war between two different populations that ultimately merged into one single nation, just as the Sabines and the Latins did in ancient Italy.)

Thus, as these few examples suffice to emphasize, scholars have sought a concrete "origin" — social organization or historical events — for all forms of duality, polarity, and antagonism. Recently, however, efforts have been made to go beyond these two approaches, which may be called sociological and historicistic.

6. Summarized by Georges Dumézil, *La Religion romaine archaïque* (Paris, 1966), p. 72.
7. Cf. G Dumézil, *Naissance de Rome* (Paris, 1944), chap. 2.
8. G. Dumézil, *Religion romaine archaïque*, pp. 75 ff.

Structuralism, for instance, interprets the various types of opposition as expressions of a rigorous and perfectly articulated system, although this system operates at the unconscious level of the mind. With Troubetzkoi, phonology becomes the study of the unconscious structure of language. Claude Lévi-Strauss has applied the linguistic model to the analysis of family, starting from the principle that kinship is a system of communications comparable to language. The pairs of opposites (father/son, husband/ wife, etc.) are articulated into a system that becomes intelligible only in a synchronic perspective. Lévi-Strauss utilizes the same linguistic model in his structural study of myth. According to him, "the aim of myth is to furnish a logical model for solving a contradiction." Furthermore, "mythical thought proceeds from the *prise de conscience* of certain contradictions and leads to their progressive mediation." [9]

In sum, for the structuralists, polarities, oppositions, and antagonisms do not have a social origin nor are they to be explained by historical events. Rather, they are expressions of a perfectly consistent system which informs the unconscious activity of the mind. Ultimately, what is involved here is a structure of life, and Lévi-Strauss asserts that this structure is identical with the structure of matter. In other words, there is no solution of continuity between the polarities and oppositions grasped at the level of matter, life, deep psyche, language, or social organization and those grasped at the level of mythological and religious creations. Sociologism and historicism are replaced by a materialistic reductionism much more ambitious, though also more subtle, than the classical or positivist materialisms.

Being a historian of religions, I will use a different approach. Understanding the function of polarities in the religious life and thought of archaic and traditional societies demands a hermeneutical effort, not a demystification. Our documents — be they myths or theologies, systems of space divisions or rituals enacted by two antagonistic groups, divine dualities or religious dualism, etc. — constitute, each according to its specific mode of being, so many creations of the human mind. We do not have the right to treat them differently from the way we treat, let us say, the Greek tragedies or one of the great religions. We do not have the right

9. Claude Lévi-Strauss, *Anthropologie structurale* (Paris, 1958), pp. 254, 248.

to reduce them to something other than what they are, namely spiritual creations. Consequently, it is their meaning and significance that must be grasped. For this reason, I shall present a certain number of documents chosen from different cultures. I have selected them in such a way as to illustrate the amazing variety of solutions offered to the enigmas of polarity and rupture, antagonism and alternance, dualism and the union of opposites.[10]

Two Types of Sacrality

Let us recall first that the religious experience presupposes a bipartition of the world into the *sacred* and the *profane*. The structure of this bipartition is too complex to be conveniently discussed here; besides, the problem is not directly related to our subject. Suffice it to say that it is not a question of an embryonic dualism, for the profane is transmuted into the sacred by the dialectics of hierophany. On the other hand, numerous processes of desacralization retransform the sacred into the profane. But we find the exemplary opposition of sacred and profane in the numberless lists of binary antagonisms, together with the oppositions male-female, heaven-earth, etc. To look at it more closely, it is evident that when the sexual antagonism is expressed in a religious context, it is less a question of the opposition sacred-profane than it is of the antagonism between two types of sacralities, one exclusive to men, the other proper to women. Thus, in Australia, as elsewhere, the goal of the puberty initiation is to separate the adolescent from the world of the mother and women, and to introduce him to the "sacred world," whose secrets are jealously withheld by men. However, all over Australia the women have their own secret ceremonies, which are sometimes considered to be so powerful that no man can spy upon them with impunity.[11] Moreover, according to certain mythical traditions, the most secret cultic objects, today accessible only to men, originally be-

10. We will not discuss certain important aspects of the problem — for instance, myths and rituals of bisexuality, the religious morphology of the *coincidentia oppositorum*, the mythologies and gnoses centered on the conflict between gods and demons, God and Satan, etc. — which have already been studied in my *Méphistophélès et l'Androgyne* (Paris, 1962), pp. 95–154 (English translation: *Mephistopheles and the Androgyne* [New York, 1965], pp. 78–124).

11. R. M. and C. H. Berndt, *The World of the First Australians* (Chicago, 1964), p. 248.

long to women; such myths imply not only a religious antagonism between the sexes, but also an avowal of the original superiority of feminine sacrality.[12]

Similar traditions are to be found in other archaic religions, and their significance is the same; that is, there is a qualitative difference and hence antagonism between the specific sacralities exclusive to each sex. For instance, at Malekula the term *ileo* designates the sacredness specific to men; however, its contrary, *igah*, does not denote the "profane," but describes another form of sacrality, that exclusive to women. The objects imbued with *igah* are carefully avoided by men, for such objects paralyze, or even annihilate, their reserve of *ileo*. When women celebrate their sacred ceremonies, they are so saturated with *igah* that if a man should catch sight even of their headdress he would become "like a child" and would lose his rank in the male secret society. Even the objects touched by women during their rituals are dangerous and for this reason are taboo for men.[13]

This antagonistic tension between two types of sacredness ultimately expresses the irreducibility of the two modes of being in the world, those of man and woman. But it would be a misrepresentation to explain such religious tension between the sexes in psychological or physiological terms. Certainly, there are two specific modes of existing in the world, but there is also the jealousy and the unconscious desire of each sex to penetrate the "mysteries" of the other sex and to appropriate its "powers." On the religious level, the solution of the sexual antagonism does not always imply a ritual reenactment of the *hieros gamos*; in many cases, the antagonism is transcended by a ritual androgynization.[14]

South American Divine Twins

I shall begin the inquiry with some South American material, and this for two reasons: first, the tribes which will be considered belong to archaic stages of culture; second, one finds here, more or less clearly articulated, a certain number of the "classical solu-

12. Cf. M. Eliade, "Australian Religions, Part III: Initiation Rites and Secret Cults," *History of Religions*, 7 (1967): 61–90, especially pp. 87 and 89; H. Baumann, *Das doppelte Geschlecht* (Berlin, 1955), pp. 345 ff.
13. A. B. Deacon, *Malekula* (London, 1934), pp. 478 ff.
14. Cf. Eliade, *Méphistophélès et l'Androgyne*, pp. 121 ff.

3

tions" to the problem raised by the discovery of dichotomy and antagonism. Needless to add, these few examples do not exhaust the richness of the South American material. Roughly speaking, the themes which interest us are: (1) the binary division of space and habitat; (2) the myths of the Divine Twins; (3) the dichotomy generalized to the whole world, including man's spiritual life; and (4) the divine antagonism, reflecting rather an occult complementarity, which supplies the model for human behavior and institutions. Frequently, several or even all of these motifs are attested in the same culture.

I shall not recall, for every tribe, its specific configuration of sacred space and its cosmography; to this problem I have devoted a monograph which will be published shortly. It suffices to keep in mind that the mythologies and the cosmological conceptions which will be examined presuppose an *imago mundi*. As for the myth of the Divine Twins, it is widespread in South America. Usually, the father of the Twins is the Sun; when their mother is treacherously murdered, the boys are extracted from her corpse, and after a number of adventures they succeed in avenging her.[15] The Twins are not always rivals. In some variants, one of the heroes is resuscitated by his brother from his bones, his blood, or fragments of his body.[16] Nevertheless, the two culture heroes express the universal dichotomy. The Kaingang of Brazil relate their entire culture and all their institutions to their mythical ancestors, the Twins. Not only have they divided the tribe into two exogamous moieties, but all nature is distributed between the two heroes. Their mythology, which furnishes the exemplary model for the Kaingang, dramatically illustrates this universal bipartition, made intelligible and meaningful by the activity of the two heroes.[17]

15. A Bakairi myth narrates that the celestial god, Kamuscini, after creating human beings, marries a woman to the mythical jaguar, Oka. Miraculously, the wife becomes pregnant but is killed by her mother-in-law's intrigues. The twins, Keri and Kame, are extracted from the lifeless body and avenge their mother, burning the plotter. The old sources are collected by R. Pettazzoni, *Dio*, 1 (1922): 330–31. See also Paul Radin, "The Basic Myth of the North American Indians," *Eranos Jahrbuch*, 17 (1949): 371 ff.; A. Métraux, "Twin Heroes in South American Mythology," *Journal of American Folklore*, 59 (1946): 114–23; Karin Hissing and A. Hahn, *Die Tacana, Erzählungsgut* (Frankfort, 1961), pp. 111 ff.
16. Cf. Otto Zerries in W. Krickeberg, H. Trimborn, W. Müller, O. Zerries, *Les Religions amérindiennes* (Paris, 1962), p. 390.
17. Egon Schaden, *A mitologia héroica de tribos indígenas do Brasil*, 2d ed. (Rio de Janeiro, 1959), pp. 103–16, utilizes Telemaco Borba, *Atualidade*

Moreover, certain traits indicate a difference in the natures of the Divine Twins. Thus, among the Cubeo of inner Guyana, Hö-manihikö, who created the earth, does not intervene in human affairs; he dwells in the sky, where he receives the souls of the dead. His brother, Mianikötöibo, who is misshapen, inhabits a mountain.[18] According to the Apinayé, in the beginning the Sun and Moon lived on earth in human form. They begot the two ancestral groups of the tribe and installed them in a village divided into two zones, the Sun group in the north, the Moon group in the south. The myths indicate a certain antagonism between the brothers; for instance, the Sun is said to be intelligent while the Moon is rather stupid.[19]

The antagonism is more conspicuous among the Caliñas, Caraibes of the northern coast of Guyana. Amana, goddess of the waters, simultaneously a mother and a virgin, and reputed to be "without navel" (i.e., not born),[20] brought forth twins, Tamusi at dawn and Yolokantamulu at sunset. Tamusi is anthropomorphous and is considered to be the mythical ancestor of the Caliñas; he created all things that are good and useful to men. Tamusi dwells in the luminous part of the moon, and he is the lord of a paradise, the land without evening, where the souls of the pious go to rejoin him. But nobody can see him because of the dazzling light that surrounds him. Tamusi fights heroically against the hostile powers that have annihilated the world several times and will destroy it again, but after every destruction the world has been created anew by Tamusi. His brother also inhabits the celestial regions, but at the opposite end of the paradise, in the land without morning. He is the creator of obscurity and author of all evils inflicted upon mankind. In a certain sense, he symbolizes the active powers of the mother-goddess Amana. Haekel sees in him the necessary complement of the luminous aspect of the world, personified by

indigena (Curitiba, Brazil, 1908), pp. ii ff., 20 ff., 70 ff., and H. Baldus, *Ensaios de Etnologia brasileira* (Saõ Paolo, 1937), pp. 29 ff., 45 ff., 60 ff.
18. Koch-Grünberg, summarized by Zerries in *Religions amerindiennes*, pp. 361–62.
19. Curt Nimuendaju, *The Apinayé*, The Catholic University of America, Anthropological Series no. 9 (Washington, D.C., 1939), pp. 158 ff.
20. Amana, the beautiful woman whose body terminates in a snake's tail, symbolizes both time and eternity, for though she resides in the celestial waters, she regenerates herself periodically by molting like a snake. The process is repeated by the souls of the dead and by the earth itself. Amana has engendered the entire creation and can take any form.

Tamusi. Nevertheless, Yolokantamulu is not the absolute adversary of his brother; the Evil Spirit of the Caliñas is another personage, Yawané. But of the Divine Twins, Tamusi plays the more important role and becomes a sort of supreme being.[21]

Often such a total dichotomy of nature extends itself as well to the spiritual aspect of man.[22] According to the Apapocuva, a Tupi-Guarani tribe from southern Brazil, every child receives a soul which descends from one of the three celestial regions — East, Zenith, and West —where it preexisted beside a deity ("Our Mother" in the East; "Our Elder Brother" at the Zenith; Tupan, the younger twin brother, in the West). After death, the soul goes back to its place of origin. It is this soul, called by Nimuendaju the "plant-soul," that establishes the connection with the superior world. To make this soul "light," man must refrain from eating meat. But some time after birth, the child receives a second soul, the "animal soul," which will determine his character. Various temperaments of different individuals are decided according to the species present in the "animal soul," and only the shamans are able to discern the species type.[23]

According to Nimuendaju, the conception of the two souls reflects the dichotomy of nature, illustrated in exemplary fashion by the mythical Twins, whose opposed and antagonistic characters are transmitted to the members of the two moieties. This is certainly correct, but there is something more: we are confronted with a creative reinterpretation of a widely diffused cosmological schema and mythical theme. The ideas, familiar to the primitives, that the source of the soul is divine and that the supreme cosmogonic deities are of a celestial nature or inhabit the sky, have added another religious value to the concept of the universal dichotomy. Furthermore, one can decipher in this example a new religious valorization of the world: the antagonism between the Twins is reflected in the antagonism of the souls, but only the "plant-

21. Josef Haekel, "Purá und Hochgott," *Archiv für Völkerkunde,* 13 (1958): 25–50, especially p. 32.

22. It would be useless to multiply the examples. We may mention the Timbira, for whom the cosmic totality is divided into two halves: on one hand, east, sun, day, dry season, fire, the color red; on the other, west, moon, night, rain season, water, the color black, etc. Curt Nimuendaju, *The Eastern Timbira,* University of California Publications in Archaeology and Ethnology, vol. XLI (Berkeley and Los Angeles, 1946), pp. 84 ff.

23. Curt Nimuendaju, "Religion der Apapocuva-Guarani," *Zeitschrift für Ethnologie,* 46 (1914): 305 ff.

soul" is reputed to have a divine origin, and this implies a religious devalorization of the animal. But animal sacrality constitutes an essential element of archaic religions. One can decipher here the effort of isolating, among many other "sacralities" present in the world, the purely "spiritual," i.e., divine, element of a celestial origin.

This conception may be compared with the basic idea of the Caliñas that everything which exists on earth has a spiritual replica in heaven.[24] In this case also we have an original and audacious use of the theme of universal dichotomy, one which defines a spiritual principle capable of explaining certain contradictions of the world. The Caliña theory of celestial duplicates is not exceptional; it is to be found in both Americas, as well as elsewhere. As a matter of fact, the idea of a "spiritual replica" has played an important role in the general history of dualism.

Polarity and Complementarity among the Kogi

The conceptions related to our theme are probably more nuanced and better articulated into a general system than one can infer from some of our older sources. When a qualified fieldworker takes the trouble to report not only behavior and rituals but also the significance that they have for the aborigines, a whole world of meaning and values is revealed to us. I shall cite as an example the usage made by the Kogi from Sierra Nevada of the ideas of polarity and complementarity in their explanation of the world, society, and the individual.[25] The tribe is divided between the "people from above" and the "people from below," and the village, as well as the cultic hut, is separated into two halves. The world is equally divided into two sections, determined by the sun's course. Furthermore, there are many other polar and antagonistic couples: male/female, right hand/left hand, warm/cold, light/darkness, etc. These pairs are associated with certain categories of animals and plants, with colors, winds, diseases, and, likewise, with the concepts of good and evil.

24. Haekel, "Purá und Hochgott," p. 32.
25. We are following very closely the article of G. Reichel-Dolmatoff, "Notas sobre el simbolismo religioso de los Indios de la Sierra Nevada de Santa Marta," *Razón y Fabula, Revista de la Universidad de los Andes*, no. 1 (1967): 55–72, especially pp. 63–67.

The dualistic symbolism is evident in all magico-religious practices. However, the contraries coexist in every individual as well as in certain tribal deities. The Kogi believe that the function and the permanence of a principle of good (identified in an exemplary way with the right direction) are determined by the simultaneous existence of a principle of evil (the left). The good exists only because the evil is active; if the evil would disappear, the good would equally cease to be. A conception dear to Goethe, but known also in other cultures: one must commit sins, thus proclaiming the active influence of evil. According to the Kogi, the central problem of the human condition is precisely how to bring these two contraries to equilibrium and yet maintain them as complementary forces. The fundamental concept is *yulúka*, a term that can be translated "being in agreement," "being equal," "being identified." Knowing how to balance the creative and destructive energies, "being in agreement," is the guiding principle of human behavior.

This scheme of complementary oppositions is integrated in its turn into a quadripartite system of the universe: to the four cardinal directions correspond other series of concepts, mythical personages, animals, plants, colors, and activities. The antagonism reappears in the quadripartite general system (for example, red and white, "light colors," correspond to South and East, and are opposed to the "evil side," formed by the "dark colors" of North and West). The quadripartite structure informs both macrocosmos and microcosmos. The world is sustained by four mythical giants; Sierra Nevada is divided into four zones; the villages built on a traditional plan have four points of entrance where there are four sacred sites for offerings. Finally, the cultic house has four hearths around which the members of the four principal clans take their places. (But here again there reappears the antagonistic bipartition: the "right side" — red — is reserved for "those who know less," while on the "left side" — light blue — sit "those who know more," for the latter are more often confronted with the negative forces of the universe.)

The four cardinal directions are completed by the "central point," which plays an important role in the life of the Kogi. It is the Center of the World, the Sierra Nevada, whose replica is the center of the cultic house where the principal offerings are buried; there, the priest (*máma*) sits down when he wants to "speak with the gods."

Finally, this schema is developed in a tridimensional system with seven guiding marks: North, South, East, West, Zenith, Nadir, and Center. The last three constitute the cosmic axis that traverses and sustains the world, which is conceived of as an egg. As Reichel-Dolmatoff points out, it is the cosmic egg that introduces the dynamic element, namely the concept of the nine stages. The world, and man as well, have been created by the Universal Mother. She has nine daughters, each one representing a certain quality of arable soil: black, red, clayish, sandy, etc. These arable soils constitute as many layers inside the cosmic egg, and also symbolize a scale of values. Men live on the fifth earth — the black soil — which is the one in the Center. The great pyramid-like hills of Sierra Nevada are imagined to be "worlds" or "houses" of a similar structure. Likewise, the principal cultic houses are their microcosmic replicas; consequently, they are situated at the "Center of the World."

The associations do not stop here. The cosmic egg is interpreted as the uterus of the Universal Mother, in which mankind lives. The earth is equally a uterus, as is Sierra Nevada and each cultic house, home, and tomb. The caves and crevices of the earth represent the orifices of the mother. The roofs of the cultic houses symbolize the sexual organ of the Mother; they are the "doors" which give access to the higher levels. During the funeral ritual the deceased returns to the uterus; the priest lifts the corpse nine times to indicate that the dead goes again, but backwards, through the nine months of gestation. But the tomb itself represents the cosmos and the funerary ritual is an act of "cosmicization."

I have insisted on this example because it admirably illustrates the function of polarity in the thinking of an archaic people. As we have seen, the binary division of space is generalized to the entire universe. The pairs of opposites are at the same time complementaries. The principle of polarity seems to be the fundamental law of nature and life, as well as the justification for ethics. For the Kogi, human perfection does not consist in "doing good," but in securing the equilibrium of the two antagonistic forces of good and evil. On the cosmic level, this interior equilibrium corresponds to the "central point," the Center of the World. This point is to be found at the intersection of the four cardinal directions and the vertical Zenith-Nadir axis, in the middle of the cosmic egg, which is identical with the uterus of the Universal Mother. Thus the different systems of polarities express the structures of the world and of life, as well as man's specific mode of being. Human existence is understood and assumed as a "recapitulation" of the universe; conversely, the cosmic life is rendered intelligible and significative by being grasped as a "cipher."

I do not intend to add other South American examples. I think I have, on the one hand, sufficiently emphasized the variety of spiritual creations occasioned by the effort of "reading" nature and human existence through the cipher of polarity, and, on the other hand, shown that the particular expressions of what have sometimes been called binary and dualistic conceptions disclose their profound significance only if they are integrated in the all-encompassing system of which they are a part.

We encounter a similar, though more complex, situation among the North American tribes. There also one finds the bipartition of the village and the world, and the resulting cosmological system (the four directions, the Zenith-Nadir axis, the "Center," etc.), as well as various mythological and ritual expressions of religious polarities, antagonisms, and dualisms. Of course, such conceptions are neither universally nor uniformly distributed. A number of North American ethnic groups know but a rudimentary bipartite cosmology, and many other tribes ignore the "dualistic" conceptions though they utilize systems of classification of a binary type. Now, it is precisely this problem which is of interest, namely, the diverse religious valorizations, in various cultural contexts, of the basic theme of polarity and dualism.

Combat and Reconciliation: Mänäbush and the Medicinal Hut

Among the central Algonkians, the culture hero — Nanabozho (Ojibway and Ottawa), Mänäbush (Menomini), or Wisaka (Kri, Saux, etc.) — plays a preeminent role.[26] He restores the earth after the flood and gives it its actual shape; he establishes the seasons and procures the fire.[27] Mänäbush is famous particularly for his

26. Cf. Werner Müller, *Die Blaue Hütte* (Wiesbaden, 1954), pp. 12 ff.
27. Indeed, when the earth disappeared under water, Mänäbush sent an ani-

combat with the (inferior) Powers of the Waters, a conflict that initiated the cosmic drama whose consequences still bear upon men.[28] The struggle reached its culminating point when the aquatic Powers succeeded in murdering Mänäbush's younger brother, the Wolf, thus introducing death into the world. The Wolf reappeared after three days, but Mänäbush sent him back to the Land of the Sunset, where he became the lord of the dead. To avenge his brother's murder, Mänäbush slew the chief of the Water Powers; his adversaries then released a new flood followed by a terrific winter, yet without success in overthrowing the hero. Alarmed, the Powers proposed a reconciliation: the erection of the medicinal hut, in whose mysteries Mänäbush would be the first initiate.

It is significant that the theme of reconciliation is known only in esoteric myths, revealed exclusively to the initiates in the secret *midēwiwin* cult.[29] According to this esoteric tradition, the Great Spirit (the Supreme Manitu) advised the aquatic Powers to appease Mänäbush, since they had committed the first crime; following this advice, the Powers built the initiation cabin in heaven and invited Mänäbush. Ultimately the hero accepted, knowing that the ceremonies revealed by the Powers would be beneficent to men. Indeed, after his initiation in heaven, Mänäbush returned to earth and with the help of his grandmother (the Earth) carries out for the first time the secret rites of *midēwiwin*.

Thus, according to the esoteric version of the myth, the cosmic catastrophe was avoided because the inferior Powers — who, having slain the Wolf, introduced death on earth — offered to Mänä-

mal to bring some slime from the bottom of the abyss (on this motif, see M. Eliade, "Mythologies asiatiques et folklore sud-est européen: le plongeon cosmogonique," *Revue de l'Histoire des Religions*, 160 [1961]: 157–212; the American variants are found on pp. 194 ff.). Mänäbush re-created the earth and made anew the animals, plants, and man; see the essential bibliography in Mac Linscott Ricketts, "The Structure and Religious Significance of the Trickster-Transformer-Culture Hero in the Mythology of the North American Indians" (Ph.D diss., University of Chicago, 1964), vol. 1, p. 195, n. 35.

28. Let us add that Mänäbush presents certain characteristic traits of the trickster; for example, he is provided with an excessive and grotesque sexuality, and in spite of his heroism, he sometimes appears surprisingly narrow-minded.

29. The myths with their bibliographies are in Ricketts, "*Structure and Religious Significance*," vol. 1, pp. 196 ff.; Müller, *Die Blaue Hütte*, pp. 19 ff., and *Die Religionen der Waldlandindianer Nordamerikas* (Berlin, 1956), pp. 198 ff.

bush a secret and powerful ceremony capable of ameliorating the mortals' lot. Certainly, the initiation in the *midēwiwin* does not pretend to change the human condition, but it assures, here below, health and longevity and a new existence after death. The initiation ritual follows the well-known scenario of death and resurrection: the novice is "killed" and immediately resuscitated through the sacred shell.[30] In other words, the same Powers that robbed man of his immortality have ultimately been forced to provide him with a technique capable of fortifying and prolonging his life, at the same time insuring him a "spiritual" postexistence. During the secret ceremonies, the novice impersonates Mänäbush and the priests represent the Powers. The initiation hut emphasizes the dualistic symbolism. The cabin is divided into two sections: the north, painted in white, is the site of the inferior Powers; on the southern half, painted in red, are to be found the superior Powers. The two colors symbolize day and night, summer and winter, life and death (followed by resurrection), etc. The association of these two polar principles represents the totality of cosmic realities.[31]

We have here an excellent example of what may be called the valorization of the negative elements of a polarity. The creative genius of the Menomini succeeded in finding a new and effective solution to the existential crisis provoked by the awareness of the dreadful omnipresence of suffering, adversity, and death. I will discuss shortly other solutions of varying similarity, but for the moment it will be instructive to situate the mythico-ritual complex of the Menomini initiation cabin in the general Algonkian religion so that we may know the common religious ideas from which the Menomini have evolved their particular system. Indeed, as Werner Müller has pointed out, other Algonkian tribes have a different tradition, probably more ancient, in which the culture hero does not play any role in the ritual of the initiation cabin.

The Ojibway of Minnesota, for example, assert that the hut was erected by the Great Spirit (Manido) in order to secure eternal life for men.[32] Manido is symbolically present in the initiation cabin

30. W. J. Hoffman, "The Midewiwin or 'Grand Medicine Society' of the Ojibwa," *Seventh Annual Report of the Bureau of American Ethnology*, 1855–86 (Washington, D.C., 1891), pp. 143–300, especially pp. 207 ff.; Müller, *Die Blaue Hütte*, pp. 52 ff.
31. Müller, *Die Blaue Hütte*, pp. 81 ff., 117, 127.
32. *Ibid.*, pp. 38 ff., 51.

(*midēwigan*). The cabin reproduces the world: its four walls symbolize the four cardinal directions, the roof represents the celestial vault, the floor symbolizes the earth.[33] In the two types of initiation cabins — those of the Menomini and the Ojibway — the cosmic symbolism emphasizes the fact that the first initiation has had for its stage the entire universe. But to the dualistic structure of the hut erected by Mänäbush on earth, following his reconciliation with the inferior Powers, is opposed the quaternary symbolism of the cabin built by Manido: four doors, four colors, etc. In the ritual complex of Mänäbush, the Great God is absent or almost obliterated; inversely, the Culture Hero does not play any role in the ceremony of the *midēwigan*. But in both types of initiation the central issue is the personal destiny of each initiate: among the Ojibway, eternal life after death, bestowed by the Great God; in the case of the Menomini, health and longevity (and probably a new existence after death), obtained from Mänäbush as a consequence of a series of dramatic events which took place at a time when the world was nearly destroyed. It should also be noted that in the esoteric myth it is the Great Manitu who advises the inferior Powers to seek a reconciliation; without his intervention, the battle would most probably have gone on until both the world and the inferior Powers were totally annihilated.

High God and Culture Hero

One can see what is new in the mythico-ritual complex of the Menomini in comparison to the initiation cabin of the Ojibway: according to the Ojibway, the Great God built the cabin in order to grant eternal life to men; for the Menomini, the hut is received, through Mänäbush, from the inferior Powers, and the initiation bestows health, longevity, and a postmortem existence. The quaternary symbolism of the Ojibway cabin, reflecting a well-balanced universe without fissures, whose rhythms continue in an orderly way under the control of the Great God, is replaced by the dualist symbolism of the Menomini. This symbolism likewise reflects the cosmos, but it is a world torn by all sorts of antagonisms and dominated by death, a world on the point of destruction due to

33. *Ibid.*, pp. 80 ff. The same symbolism is found in the structure of the sweat hunt of the Omaha (*ibid.*, p. 122), in the initiation cabins of the Lenape, the Prairie Algonkians (*ibid.*, p. 135), and elsewhere.

the conflict between Mänäbush and the aquatic Powers, a world where the Great God is absent and where man's only protector is the Culture Hero, himself rather akin to man, as we see from his fierce combativeness and ambiguous behavior. Certainly, the dualist symbolism of the Menomini cabin also expresses the integration of the opposites in the cosmic totality as well as in human existence. But in this case, the integration represents a desperate effort to save the world from its final destruction, to assure the continuity of life, and, above all, to find a meaning to the precariousness and the contradictions of human existence.

To better understand the sense in which the religious conceptions of the Algonkians have unfolded, we may compare the cosmic symbolism of the Big House of the Delaware (Lenape), an Algonkian people of the Atlantic coast, and the theology implicit in the ceremonies of the New Year. The Big House is erected every year, in October, in a forest glade. It is a rectangular hut with four doors and, in the middle, a wooden post. The floor symbolizes the earth, the roof the sky, and the four walls the four horizons. The Big House is an *imago mundi* and the ritual displayed celebrates the new beginning (the re-creation) of the world. It is the Supreme God, the Creator, who is reputed to have established the cult. He inhabits the twelfth heaven; he keeps his hand on the central post or *axis mundi*, which has its replica in the Big House. But the god is also present in the two faces carved on the post. Every new festival of the Big House has as one of its results the re-creation of the earth; it also prevents the earth from being destroyed by a cosmic catastrophe. Indeed, the first Big House was erected after an earthquake. But the annual re-creation of the earth, brought about through the New Year ceremony, insures the continuity and the fertility of the world. Contrary to the initiation effected in the cabins of the Menomini and Ojibway, which concerns separate individuals, the ceremony of the Big House regenerates the cosmos in its totality.[34]

Thus, the Algonkian ethnic group presents three types of cultic houses and three categories of ritual, dependent on three different religious systems. It is significant that the most archaic system,

---

34. Frank G. Speck, *A Study of the Delaware Big House Ceremonies* (Harrisberg, Pa., 1931), pp. 9 ff.; Müller, *Religionen der Waldandindianer*, pp. 259 ff.; see also Josef Haekel, "Der Hochgottglaube der Delawaren in Lichte ihrer Geschichte," *Ethnologica*, n.s., 2 (1960): 439–84.

that of the Delaware, is centered on the periodic regeneration of the cosmos, while the most recent one, dominated by the Culture Hero and the dualist symbolism, aims chiefly at an amelioration of the human condition. In this second case, the "dualism" is the consequence of a mythical history, but it was not predetermined by any essential characteristics of the protagonists. As we have seen, the antagonism between Mänäbush and the inferior Powers was exacerbated as a consequence of an event — the murder of the Wolf — which could very well have not taken place.

Iroquois Dualism: the Mythical Twins

With the Iroquois, one can speak of a "dualism" proper. First of all, there is the idea that everything which exists on earth has a prototype — an "elder brother" — in heaven. The cosmogonic process begins in heaven, but, one may say, it begins somewhat accidentally. A young girl, Awenhai ("Fertile Earth"), asked for the Chief of Heaven in marriage. He married Awenhai and rendered her pregnant by his breath. However, not understanding the miracle and being jealous, the god uprooted the tree whose flowers illuminate the celestial world (for the sun did not yet exist), and hurled his wife through the hole. He also threw the prototypes of some animals and plants, and these became the animals and plants that exist today on earth, while their "elder brothers," the prototypes, remained in heaven. Then the god put the tree back in its place.

The muskrat brought some mud from the bottom of the primordial ocean and spread it out on the back of a tortoise. Thus the earth was created, and Awenhai gave birth to a daughter who grew up miraculously fast. Soon the girl married, but the bridegroom put an arrow beside her belly and disappeared. Pregnant, Awenhai's daughter heard twins quarreling in her womb. One wished to descend, the other, on the contrary, wanted to come out through the upper part. Finally, the elder was born in the normal way while his brother emerged through the armpit, thus causing the death of his mother. He was made of flint, and for this reason was named Tawiskaron ("Flint"). Awenhai asked the twins who had killed her daughter. Both swore their innocence; Awenhai, however, believed only "Flint" and drove away his brother. From her daughter's body, Awenhai made the sun and the moon, and suspended them on a tree near the hut.

While Awenhai devoted herself to Tawiskaron, the elder brother was helped by his father. One day he fell into a lake and, on the bottom, encountered his father, the great tortoise. He received from him a bow and two ears of corn, "one ripe, to be sown, the other raw, to be roasted." Returning to the surface, he spread out the earth and created animals. He then proclaimed: "henceforth men shall call me Wata Oterongtongnia" ("Young Maple-tree"). Tawiskaron tried to imitate his brother, but in seeking to create a bird, he made a bat. Likewise, seeing Oterongtongnia modeling men and animating them, he attempted to do the same, but his creatures were pitiful and monstrous. Then Tawiskaron, with the help of the great mother, enclosed the animals created by his brother in a cave, but Oterongtongnia succeeded in setting a number of them free. Unable to create, Tawiskaron strove to destroy the creation of his brother. He facilitated the arrival of monsters from another world, but Oterongtongnia succeeded in driving them back. Oterongtongnia hurled the sun and the moon into the firmament, and since then they shine for all men, while Tawiskaron brought the hills and cliffs into being in order to make men's life more painful.

The twins then lived together in a hut. One day, Oterongtongnia kindled such a mighty fire that small splinters began to detach themselves from the flint body of his brother. Tawiskaron rushed out of the hut, but Oterongtongnia pursued him, throwing stones, until the other collapsed. The Rocky Mountains are the remains of Tawiskaron.[35]

This myth establishes and at the same time justifies the entire religious life of the Iroquois. It is a dualist myth, the only North American myth susceptible to comparison with the Iranian dualism of zurvanite type. The cult and the calendar reflect in detail the

---

35. J. N. B. Hewitt, *Iroquoian Cosmology. First Part*, Twenty-first Annual Report of the Bureau of American Ethnology, 1899–1900 (Washington, D.C., 1903), pp. 127–339, especially pp. 141 ff., 285 ff. Cf. Müller, *Religionen der Waldlandindianer*, pp. 119 ff. (who also utilizes other sources), and the résumé given by the same author in *Les Religions amérindiennes*, pp. 260–62. A certain number of variants are summarized by Ricketts, "Structure and Religious Significance," vol. 2, pp. 602 ff. One of the versions collected by Hewitt among the Onondaga relates that the Good Brother ascended to Heaven together with "Flint" (Ricketts, *ibid.*, p. 612).

opposition of the mythical Twins. Nevertheless, as we shall presently see, such an irreducible antagonism does not reach the Iranian paroxysm, and this for the simple reason that the Iroquois refuse to identify in the "bad" twin the essence of "evil," the *ontological evil* that obsessed Iranian religious thought.

The Cult: Antagonism and Alternation

The "long house" is the cultic cabin. It has two doors: through the north-east the women enter, taking places in the east; through the south-west come the men, who sit in the west. The feast calendar comprises two semesters: winter and summer. The winter ceremonies are celebrated by men: they give thanks for the gifts received. The summer rituals are the women's responsibility, and call for rains and fertility. The antagonism is evident even in the ceremonial details. The two clan moieties, the Deer and the Wolf, representing the mythical Twins, play at dice, a game that symbolizes the conflict between the Twins. The sacred dances, celebrated in honor of the "Great Spirit," belong to Oterongtongnia and to that half of the day when the sun ascends toward the zenith. The so-called social dances, carried out for distraction, are related to Tawiskaron and the evening.[36]

Werner Müller has shown that the actual monotheistic aspect of these ceremonies is the result of a reform which goes back to the beginnings of the nineteenth century. A prophet of the Seneca tribe, Handsome Lake, decided to reform the religion of his people after an ecstatic revelation. He substituted for the couple of the mythical Twins that of the Great God, Haweniyo (the "Great Voice"), and the Devil, Haninseono ("Who Dwells in the Earth"). But the prophet endeavored to concentrate the religious life on the Great God; for this reason he forbade the rituals consecrated to the bad Twin and transformed them into "social dances."

This reform, with its strong monotheistic tendency, can be partly accounted for by the ecstatic experience that decided the vocation of Handsome Lake, but there were also other aspects. The Europeans reproached the Iroquois because they "adored the Devil." Evidently, however, there was no question of an adoration

---

36. On the liturgical calendar, see Müller, *Religionen der Waldlandindianer*, pp. 119 ff., 256 ff.

of the Devil, since the bad Twin does not incarnate the idea of "evil" but only the negative, dark aspect of the world. As we have just seen, the mythical Twins reflect and rule the two modes, or two "times," which together constitute the living and fertile universe. One encounters again the complementary couples day and night, winter and summer, sowing and harvesting, as well as the polarities man and women, sacred and profane, etc.

To understand how rigorously the dualistic principle articulates the total religious conception of the Iroquois, let us recall one of their most important rites: the wearing of the Masks in spring and autumn, and their healing function.[37] The members of one of the confraternities, the "False Faces," enter the houses and expel disease. The other confraternity, the "Faces of Maize Straw," celebrate their rites during the ceremonies in the Long House. The Masks sprinkle the assistants with "medicine water" and scatter ashes as a defense against disease.

Now, according to the myths, sicknesses and other afflictions have been produced by a superhuman being, the double of Tawiskaron.

At the origin of the world, he fought against the Creator, but he was defeated and was given the task of curing and helping people. He lives in the rocks which border the world, there where fever, tuberculosis, and headaches are born. Among his attendants are the False Faces, deformed beings with big heads and simian features who, like their master, dwell far from men and haunt desert places. Myths represent them as the abortive creations of Tawiskaron, who try to imitate the human beings produced by his brother; in rituals they are impersonated by masked men who, in spring and autumn, drive away maladies from villages.[38]

In other words, though the adversary has been defeated by the Great God, his works, the "evil," persist in the world. The Creator does not seek to, or perhaps he cannot, annihilate the "evil," but neither does he permit it to corrupt his creation. He accepts it as an inevitable negative aspect of life, but at the same time he compels his adversary to combat the results of his own work.

This ambivalence of "evil" — considered a disastrous innovation but accepted as a henceforth inevitable modality of life and of

37. On the Masks, see the essential bibliography in Müller, *Les Religions amérindiennes,* p. 271, n. 1 .
38. Müller, *Les Religions amérindiennes,* p. 272.

human existence — is equally evident in the Iroquois conception of the world. The universe is imagined to have a central portion, i.e., the village and the cultivated fields, inhabited by men; this central portion is surrounded by an exterior desert full of stones, swamps, and False Faces. Such an *imago mundi* is well known in archaic and traditional cultures. This conception of the world is fundamental to the Iroquois mind, and it did not disappear once the tribe was installed in a reservation. "Inside the Iroquois Reservation the 'good' brother rules; there are the houses and the fields, there one is safe; but outside reign the 'bad' brother and his agents, the white men; there is the desert of the factories, the buildings, and the paved streets." [39]

Pueblos: Antagonistic and Complementary Divine Couples

Among the Pueblos, the Great God yields his place to divine pairs, sometimes antagonistic but always complementary. With these maize cultivators we witness the passage from the archaic dichotomy — applied to society, habitat, and all of nature — to a real and rigorous "dualistic" articulation of the mythology and the religious calendar. The agricultural rhythm reinforces the already present division between women's labor (food gathering, gardening) and man's work (hunting), and systematizes the cosmic-ritual dichotomies (two seasons, two classes of gods, etc.). The few examples which follow will allow us to grasp not only the degree of "dualistic specialization" of the agrarian populations of New Mexico, but also the variety of their mythico-ritual systems.

The Zuni myth can serve as a point of departure and also as a model. According to Stevenson and Cushing, the primordial being Awonawilona, called "He-She" or "Container of All," transformed himself into the sun, and out of his own substance produced two seeds with which he impregnated the Great Waters, from which came into existence "All-covering Father-Sky" and "Four-fold Containing Mother-Earth." From the union of these cosmic Twins came forth all forms of life. But the Earth-Mother kept all these creations within her body, in what the myth calls the "Four-fold Womb of the World." Men, that is, the Zuni, were born in the

39. *Ibid.*, p. 272.

deepest of these cavernous wombs. They emerged at the surface only after being guided and helped by another couple of divine Twins, the two war gods, Ahayutos. These were created by the (Father-) Sun in order to lead the Zuni's ancestors to light and finally to the "Center of the World," their present territory.[40]

During this voyage toward the center, different gods came into being: the Cocos (Katchinas) — gods of the rain — and the animal gods, the chiefs of the medicine societies. Now, the characteristic feature of the Zuni myth is that the Twins are not adversaries. Besides, they do not play an important role in the ritual. On the contrary, religious life is dominated by a systematic opposition between the cults of the *rain gods* (in summer) and of the *animal gods* (in winter).[41] The two cults are supervised by numerous religious confraternities. Zuni "dualism" is evident in the calendar of the festivals. The two classes of gods succeed each other in the religious actuality, following the course of the seasons. The opposition between gods — realized through the alternating dominance of the two categories of religious confraternities — reflects the cosmic rhythm.

Another Pueblo tribe, the Acoma, interprets differently the opposition of the divinities and the cosmic polarities. For the Acoma, as for the Zuni, the supreme god is a *deus otiosus*. In fact, the primordial being Uchtsiti is supplanted in the myths and in the cult by two sisters, Jatiki and Nautsiti. They oppose each other from the moment they emerge from the subterranean world. Jatiki discloses a mystical solidarity with agriculture, order, the sacred, and time; Nautsiti is associated with hunting, disorder, indifference to the sacred, and space. The two sisters separate, thus dividing mankind into two categories: Jatiki is the mother of the Pueblos, Nautsiti the mother of nomad Indians (Navaho, Apache, etc.). Jatiki creates the cachique, who performs the role of priest, while Nautsiti founds the category of war chiefs.[42]

40. See the sources utilized in M. Eliade, *Mythes, Rêves et Mystères* (Paris, 1957), pp. 211–14 (English translation: *Myths, Dreams and Mysteries* [London and New York, 1961], pp. 158 ff.)
41. On the Katchinas, see Jean Cazeneuve, *Les Dieux dansent à Cibola* (Paris, 1957).
42. Cf. M. V. Stirling, *Origin Myth of Acoma and Other Records*, Smithsonian Institution Bureau of American Ethnology, Bulletin CXXXV (Washington, D.C., 1942); Leslie White, *The Acoma Indians*, Annual Report of American Bureau of Ethnology (Washington, D.C., 1932). According to

It suffices to compare only briefly the religious conceptions of the Pueblos with those of the Iroquois to measure the profound difference. Though belonging to the same type of culture, that of maize cultivators, and thus partaking of an analogous conception of the world, each people has differently valorized the dualist structure of their religion. The myths and cult of the Iroquois are centered on the antagonism of the divine Twins, whereas for the Zuni the Twins are not rivals and their cultual role is very modest. In contrast to the Iroquois, the Zuni have laboriously systematized the polarities in their religious calender, with the result that the antagonism between the two classes of gods is manifested in the cyclic alternation of cosmic forces and religious behaviors, concurrently opposed and complementary. Furthermore, the Zuni formula does not exhaust the creativity of the Pueblos. Among the Acoma, the two divine Sisters divide men and the ensemble of realities into two categories which contrast and at the same time complete each other.

If we are allowed to widen the comparative horizon we can distinguish in the Iroquois system a replica of the Iranian dualism in its most rigid expression, while the Zuni system calls to mind the Chinese interpretation of the cosmic polarity, translated into the rhythmic alternation of the two principles *yang* and *yin*.

the mythology of another Pueblo group, the Sia, the creator, the spider Sussistinnako, existed originally in the lower world. Sussistinnako made a sand painting and began to chant, thus creating two women, Utset ("East") and Nowutset ("West"), who eventually became the mothers of the Indians and of all other people (or, according to other variants, of the Pueblo and the Navahos). Spider continued to create by chanting, but the two women likewise manifested their creative powers, and their antagonism became increasingly accentuated. They engaged in numberless contests in order to prove who was superior. Consequently, the peoples belonging to the two women began to fight each other. Ultimately, Utset assailed Nowutset, killed her and cut out her heart. From her heart came rats (or a squirrel or a dove), who ran away into the desert, followed by the people of Nowutset. Spider sent the Sun and the Moon and also some animals to the world above, and set up a reed to permit men to emerge. Indeed, men climbed the reed and emerged at the surface of a lake. Utset gave them pieces of her own heart to plant, and thus corn came into being. She said: "This corn is my heart, and it shall be for my people like milk from my breasts." Finally, Utset organized the priests and promised to help them from her subterranean home (Matilda Coxe Stevenson, *The Sia*, Eleventh Annual Report of the American Bureau of Ethnology, 1889–90 (Washington, D.C., 1894), pp. 26 ff.; Ricketts, "Structure and Religious Significance," vol. 2, p. 544.

Californian Cosmogonic Myths: God and His Adversary

A totally different form of dualism is found among certain archaic tribes of central California (food collectors and hunters). Their myths present a High God, creator of the world and of man, and a mysterious and paradoxical supernatural being, Coyote, who sometimes intentionally opposes God's work, but more often corrupts the creation by blunder or boasting. Occasionally Coyote is described as existing from the beginning, in God's proximity, and systematically opposing his work.

The cosmogonic myth of the Northwest Maidu begin with this preamble: the supreme being, Wonomi ("Without Death") or Kodoyambe ("Who Names the Earth"), and Coyote are together on a boat floating on the primordial ocean. God creates the world by chanting, but Coyote raises the hills. After the formation of man, the adversary too tries his powers and produces blind beings. God has insured men's return to life thanks to a "fountain of youth," but Coyote destroys it. Moreover, Coyote glorifies himself in front of the Creator: "We are chiefs both of us," and God does not contradict him. Coyote also proclaims himself "the oldest in the world," and boasts that men will say about him: "he has vanquished the Great Chief." In another variant, Coyote calls the Creator "brother." When God imparts to men the rules of birth, marriage, death, etc., Coyote modifies them, but later on reproaches the Creator that he did not do anything for the happiness of men. Finally, God admits: "Without willing so, the world will know death," and he departs, but not before preparing the punishment of the adversary. Indeed, Coyote's son is killed by a rattlesnake; in vain the father asks the Creator to abolish death, promising that he will no more behave as an adversary.[43] Following the rules of the archaic religious logic, that which came into being at the beginning, while Genesis was not yet completed, cannot be suppressed. So long as the Creation is still in process, all that takes place, and all that is said, constitute ontophanies, found modalities of being, in sum belong to the cosmogonic activity.

43. Ronald B. Dixon, *Maidu Myths*, Bulletin of American Museum of Natural History, XVII (Washington, D.C., 1902), pp. 33–118, especially pp. 46–48, and *Maidu Texts*, Publications of the American Ethnological Society, IV (Leiden, 1912), pp. 27–69; Ricketts, "Structure and Religious Significance, vol. 2, pp. 504 ff. See also Ugo Bianchi, *Il Dualismo religioso* (Roma, 1958), pp. 76 ff.

Maidu myths, especially the northeastern variants, are characterized by the decisive role they concede to Coyote. One can say that the systematic opposition to God's projects betrays, on the part of Coyote, the pursuit of a precise aim: he labors to ruin the almost angelic condition of man, such as it was conceived by the Creator. In fact, thanks to Coyote, man ends by obtaining his actual mode of being, which implies effort, work, suffering, and death, but which also renders possible the continuation of life on Earth.[44]

I will come back to the role of Coyote in the establishment of the human condition, for it is a mythological theme susceptible to unexpected elaborations. For the moment, I will cite other Californian cosmogonic myths of a dualist structure which illustrate even more vividly the hostility between Coyote and the Creator. According to a Yuki myth, the Creator, Taikomol ("He Who Comes Alone") formed himself on the primordial sea in the aspect of a piece of fluff. While still surrounded by foam, he spoke, and Coyote — who, according to the narrator, had already long existed — heard him. "What shall I do?" asked Taikomol, and began to chant. Little by little he takes on human form, and calls

44. Among another Californian tribe, the Wintun, the creator, Olelbis, decides that men will live like brothers and sisters, that there will be neither death nor birth, and that life will be easy and happy. He charged two brothers to build a "stone road" up to heaven: upon growing old, men will be able to climb to heaven to bathe in a miraculous spring and become young again. But while they were working, Sedit, the adversary of Olelbis, appeared and convinced one of the brothers that it would be better if marriages, births, deaths, and even work existed in the world. The brothers destroy the nearly completed road, are transformed into vultures, and fly away. But soon Sedit repents, for he senses himself now to be mortal. He tries to fly to heaven with the help of an engine made of leaves, but falls and dies. Olelbis beholds him from the sky and exclaims: "This is the first death; from now on, all men will die." (The documents are analyzed by Wilhelm Schmidt, *Ursprung der Gottesidee*, 12 vols. vol. 2 [Münster, 1929], pp. 88–101). A similar myth is attested among the Arapaho, an eastern Algonkian tribe: while the Creator ("The Man") was achieving his work, an unknown personage Nih'asa ("Bitter Man"), arrived with a stick and asked for the creative power and a piece of land. The Creator granted him the first demand, and then Nih'asa, raising his stick, produced mountains and rivers. Afterwards the Creator threw a piece of skin in the water and declared: "Just as this piece of skin sank but reascended to the surface, so men, dying, will come back to life." But Nih'asa remarked that the earth would be quickly overpopulated; he threw a pebble, and declared that just as it sank to the bottom and disappeared, so man's destiny would be from then on (cf. Schmidt, *ibid.*, pp. 707–9, 714–17; Bianchi, *Dualismo religioso*, pp. 108–9).

Coyote "brother of my mother." He extracts food from his body and gives it to Coyote, and similarly creates the Earth by pulling out from his body the necessary material. Coyote helps him to make man, but he also determines man's mortality. Indeed, Coyote's son dies, and when Taikomol offers to resuscitate him Coyote refuses.[45]

It is possible, as Wilhelm Schmidt surmises,[46] that Taikomol does not represent the genuine type of the Californian creative god. But it is significant that it is precisely this myth, where Coyote plays an important part, that has retained the attention of the Yuki. The obliteration of the supreme and creator God is a process rather frequent in the history of religions. The majority of supreme beings end by becoming *dii otiosi*, and this is true not only with primitive religions. In our example, it is interesting to note that God gives way before such an ambivalent and paradoxical personage as Coyote, the trickster *par excellence*. Among the Coast Pomo, Coyote takes the place of the Creator; as a matter of fact, God is not present in the cosmogonic work. But Coyote creates the world by accident. Being thirsty, he uproots aquatic plants, thus provoking the violent eruption of subterranean waters. The torrent projects him very high in the air, and soon the water covers the earth as an immense sea. Coyote succeeds in damming the waters, and then starts to create men from specks of down. But, furious that men give him nothing to eat, he starts a fire and immediately after releases a flood to extinguish the conflagration. He creates a second humanity, which mocks him, and Coyote threatens to bring on a new catastrophe. Nevertheless, he continues his demiurgic activity, but because men do not take him seriously he transforms a number of them into animals. Finally, Coyote makes the sun and entrusts a bird to bear it through the sky; he establishes the cosmic rhythms and institutes the ceremonies of the Kuksu cult.[47]

45. A. L. Kroeber, "Yuki Myths," *Anthropos*, 27 (1932): 905–39, especially pp. 905 ff., and *Handbook of the Indians of California*, Smithsonian Institution, Bureau of American Ethnology, Bulletin 78 (Washington, D.C., 1925), pp. 182 ff.

46. *Ursprung der Gottesidee*, vol. 5, pp. 44, 62, quoted by Bianchi, *Dualismo religioso*, pp. 90 ff.

47. E. M. Loeb, "The Creator concept among the Indians of North Central California," *American Anthropologist*, n.s. 28 (1926): 467–93, especially pp. 484 ff.

I have cited this myth to illustrate the specific style of a cosmogony completed under the sign of Coyote. The creation of the world and of man seems to be the work of a demiurge *malgré lui*, and it is significant that men, his creation proper, laugh at him and even refuse to give him food. Whatever may be the historical explanation of this substitution of Coyote for the Creator, it is evident that, in spite of his prominent position and his creative powers, his character of Trickster-demiurge did not change. He behaves and acts, even in the position of a unique creator, like the unforgettable Trickster who delights the audiences of so many North American Indian folk tales.

The Trickster

It is significant that the extreme type of dualism found among the North American Indian tribes gives an emphatic role to Coyote, the Trickster *par excellence*. But the Trickster performs a function far more complex than may be guessed from the Californian cosmogonic myths just mentioned.[48] His personality is ambivalent and his role equivocal. It is true that in the majority of mythological traditions the Trickster is responsible for the advent of death and for the present condition of the world. But he is also a transformer and a culture hero, since he is said to have stolen fire and other useful objects and to have destroyed the monsters who ravaged the earth. Nevertheless, even when he acts as a culture hero, the Trickster preserves his specific traits. For instance, when he steals the fire or some other object indispensable to man, jealously withheld by a divine being (the Sun, the Water, the game, the fish, etc.), he succeeds not heroically, but by cunning or fraud. Often the success of his enterprises is endangered by his blunders (for example, the earth is destroyed by fire or by flood, etc.). And it is always by stratagem or dissimulation that he delivers mankind from his monstrous cannibal adversaries.

Another characteristic trait is the Trickster's ambivalent attitude toward the sacred. He parodies and caricatures shamanistic

48. The Trickster appears as Coyote in the Great Plains, the Great Basin, the Plateau, the Southwest, and California. But on the Northwest Coast he is Raven or Mink, and in the Southeast and probably among the ancient Algonkian he was the Hare. Among modern Algonkians, Sioux, and some other tribes, he has a human appearance and is known by a specific proper name, such as Gluskabe, Iktomi, Wisaka, Old Man, Widower, etc.

experiences or priestly rituals. The shaman's guardian spirits are grotesquely identified by the Trickster with his excrements,[49] and he parodies the shaman's ecstatic flight, though he always ends by falling down. It is clear that this paradoxical behavior has a double significance: the Trickster mocks the "sacred," the priests, and the shaman, but the ridicule also turns against him. When he is not the obstinate and deceitful adversary of the Creator God (as in the Californian myths), he proves to be a personage difficult to define, both intelligent and stupid, near the gods by his "primordiality" and his powers, but even nearer men by his gluttonous hunger, his exorbitant sexuality, and his amorality.

Ricketts sees in the Trickster the image of man in his efforts to become what he must become — the master of the world.[50] Such a definition can be accepted with the condition that the image of man be situated in an imaginary universe impregnated by sacredness. It is not a question of an image of man in a humanistic, rationalistic, or voluntaristic sense. In fact, the Trickster reflects what can be called a *mythology of the human condition*. He opposes God's decision to make man immortal and to assure him an existence somehow paradisiacal, in a pure and rich world free of all contraries. And he makes fun of "religion," or, more exactly, of the techniques and pretensions of the religious elite, i.e., of priests and shamans, though the myths always emphasize that mockery is not enough to annul the powers of such religious elites.

But certain traits are characteristic of the human condition as it is today, as a consequence of the Trickster's interference in the work of creation. For example, he triumphs over monsters without acting as a hero; he succeeds in many enterprises but fails in others; he organizes and completes the world, but with so many errors and blunders that ultimately nothing comes out perfectly. In this respect, one may see in the figure of the Trickster the projection of man searching for a new type of religion. The decisions and adventures of the Trickster constitute a sort of a radically secularized mythology, parodying the gestures of divine beings but at the same time mocking the Trickster's own revolt against the gods.

49. Cf. M. L. Ricketts, "The North American Indian Trickster," *History of Religions*, 5 (1966): 327–50, especially pp. 336 ff.
50. *Ibid.*, pp. 338 ff.

To the degree that one can recognize a real dualism in the Californian myths that radically oppose Coyote to the Creator, one could say that this dualism — which is not reducible to a system of polarities — equally reflects man's opposition to the Creator. But we have seen that the revolt against God develops under the sign of precariousness and parody. We can recognize here a certain embryonic philosophy. But do we have the right to recognize it only here?

Some Remarks

It is needless to summarize the foregoing analyses of the North American documents. It suffices to recall briefly the different types of antagonism and polarity attested in the area to realize their character as "spiritual creations." It is true that a certain type of dualism seems to be the systematic elaboration of agricultural societies, but the most radical dualism is found among the Californian tribes which ignore agriculture. Sociogenesis, like any other "genesis," cannot explain the functions of an existential symbolism. For instance, the bipartition of the inhabited territory and of the village, together with the antagonism between two polar principles, is attested among many tribes, and yet their mythologies and religions do not present a dualist structure. These tribes have simply applied the territorial bipartition as an immediate datum of experience, but their mythological and religious creativity express itself on other planes of reference.

As for the tribes which have actually faced the enigma of polarity and have tried to resolve it, we recall the surprising variety of solutions that have been proposed. There is, among the central Algonkians, the *personal* antagonism between the Culture Hero and the inferior Powers, which explains the origin of death and the installation of the initiation hut. But such antagonism was not inevitable: it is the result of an accident (the murder of Mänäbush's brother). In regard to the initiation cabin, we have seen that it existed already among some other Algonkian tribes, namely the Ojibwa. They claim to have received the hut from the Great God, and its symbolism expresses the cosmic polarities as well as their integration. Among the maize cultivators, the dualism receives totally different expressions. With the Zuni, dualism is weak in mythology while it dominates the ritual and the liturgical calendar; among the Iroquois, on the contrary, both mythology and cult are articulated in such a rigorous dualism that one is even reminded of the classical Iranian type. Finally, among the Californians the antagonism between God and his adversary, Coyote, open the way to a "mythologization" of the human condition, comparable to — and yet different from — that effectuated by the Greeks.

Indonesian Cosmologies: Antagonism and Integration

In Indonesia, the idea of creation and the conception of cosmic life and of human society unfold themselves under the sign of polarity. In certain cases, the polarity presupposes a preceding stage of unity/totality. But the creation is the result of the encounter — "offensive" or "conjugal" — of two divinities. There exists no cosmogony by the will and power of a creator or a group of supernatural beings. At the beginning of the universe and of life, there is a couple. The world is either the product of a *hieros gamos* between a god and a goddess or the result of a conflict between two deities. In both cases, there is an encounter between the principle, or the representative, of the sky, and the principle, or the representative, of the lower regions, conceived either as the underworld or as the region which later on, after the creation, will become the earth. In both cases, there is, at the beginning, a "totality" in which one conjectures the two principles united in *hieros gamos* or as not yet differentiated.[51]

51. Cf. W. Münsterberger, *Ethnologische Studien an Indonesischen Schöpfungsmythen* (The Hague, 1939). Almost everywhere in East Indonesia and in the Mollucas and Celebes, the cosmogonic myth implies the marriage between Sky (or Sun) and Earth (or Moon). Life — that is, plants, animals, and men — is the result of this marriage (cf. Walder Stöhr in *Die Religionen Indonesiens*, ed. W. Stöhr and Piet Zvetmulder, [Stuttgart, 1965], pp. 123–46). Since the cosmogonic *hieros gamos* establishes the model for any other "creation," in certain islands, like Leti and Lakor, the marriage between the Sky and the Earth is celebrated at the beginning of the monsoon: during the ceremony, Upulero, the sky god, descends and fertilizes Upunusa, the earth (H. Th. Fischer, *Inleiding tot de culturele Anthropologie van Indonesie* [Haarlem, 1952], p. 174; cf. Stöhr, *Religionen Indonesiens*, p. 124). On the other hand, every human marriage reactualizes the *hieros gamos* between the Sky and the Earth (Fischer, *Inleiding tot de culturele Anthropologie*, p. 132). The cosmogony resulting from a *hieros gamos* seems to be the most diffused mythical theme and also the most ancient (Stöhr, *Religionen Indonesiens*, p. 151). A parallel theme explains the creation by the separation of Sky and Earth previously united in *hieros gamos* (cf. Her-

In a previous chapter I have presented in some detail the cosmogony and the religious pattern of the Ngadju Dayak (see p. 77). I will recall now only some of the most important elements of the myth: from the primordial cosmic totality, undivided in the mouth of the coiled watersnake, came forth the two principles, manifested in succession in the forms of two mountains, of a god and a goddess, and of two hornbills. The world, life, and the primeval human couple came into being as a result of the combat of the two polar divine principles. But the polarity represents only an aspect of divinity. No less important is the godhead's manifestation as a *totality*. As we have seen (p. 80), this divine totality constitutes the fundamental principle of Dayak religion, and it is repeatedly reintegrated through the various individual and collective rituals.[52]

Also among the Toba-Batak the creation is the result of a combat between the higher and lower powers. But here the fight does not end — as in the case of the two hornbills of Dayak mythology — with the reciprocal destruction of the adversaries, but with their reintegration through a new creation.[53] In Nias, the two supreme deities, Lowalangi and Lature Danö, though opposed to each other, are at the same time complementary. Lowalangi is associated with the upper world; he incarnates good and life, his colors are yellow or gold, his symbols and cultic emblems are the cock, the eagle, the sun, and light. Lature Danö belongs to the lower world; he incarnates evil and death, his colors are black or red, his emblems the snakes, his symbols the moon and darkness. But the antagonism between the two deities implies equally their com-

mann Baumann, *Das doppelte Geschlecht* [Berlin, 1955], p. 257; Stöhr, *Religionen Indonesiens*, p. 153). In many cases, the name of the Indonesian supreme being is constituted by the agglutination of the names "Sun-Moon" or "Father-Mother" (cf. Baumann, *Das doppelte Geschlecht*, p. 136); in other words, the primordial divine totality is conceived as the nondifferentiation of Heaven and Earth while joined together in *hieros gamos*.

52. Hans Schärer, *Die Gottesidee der Ngadju Dayak in Süd-Borneo* (Leiden, 1946), pp. 70 ff. (English translation: *Ngaju Religion* [The Hague, 1963], pp. 32 ff.).

53. W. Stöhr, *Religionen Indonesiens*, p. 57. According to Ph. L. Tobing, the supreme being represents the cosmic totality, since he can be grasped under three aspects, each one representing one of the three worlds (superior, inferior, intermediary). The cosmic tree which rises from the inferior regions to heaven symbolizes concurrently the totality of the universe and the cosmic order (cf. Tobing's *The Structure of the Toba-Batak Belief in the Highgod* [Amsterdam, 1956], pp. 27–28, 60–61).

plementarity. The myths relate that Lature Danö came into the world without head and Lowalangi without rear; in other words, togethery they constitute a totality. Moreover, each one possesses some attributes that seem more appropriate to the other.[54]

In Indonesia, the cosmic dualism and complementary antagonism are expressed in the structure of villages and houses, in clothing, ornaments, and weapons, as well as in the rites of passage (birth, initiation, marriage, death).[55] To refer only to a few examples: in Ambryna, one of the Molucca Islands, the village is divided in two halves; the division is not only social, but also cosmic, for it comprises all the objects and the processes of the world. Thus, left, woman, seacoast, lower, spiritual, exterior, west, young, new, etc., are opposed to right, male, land or mountain, superior, heaven, mundane, high, interior, east, old, etc. Nevertheless, when the Ambrynas refer to this system, they speak of three rather than two divisions. The third element is the "superior synthesis" which integrates the two antithetical elements and keeps them in equilibrium.[56] The same system is found hundreds of miles from Ambryna, for example, in Java and Bali.[57]

The antagonism between contraries is emphasized chiefly in cul-

54. P. Suzuki, *The Religious System and Culture of Nias, Indonesia* (The Hague, 1959), p. 10; Stöhr, *Religionen Indonesiens*, p. 79.
55. P. Suzuki, *Religious System* p. 82.
56. J. P. Duyvendak, *Inleidung tot de Ethnologie van den Indischen Archipel*, 3d ed. (Groningen-Batavia, 1946), pp. 95–96. Cf. Claude Lévi-Strauss, *Anthropologie Structurale* (Paris, 1958), pp. 147 ff.
57. The Badung of Java divide their society in two categories: the Badung of the interior represent the sacred half, the Badung of the exterior the profane half; the first dominates the second (cf. J. van der Kroef, "Dualism and Symbolic Antithesis in Indonesian Society," *American Anthropologist*, n. s. 56 [1954]: pp. 853–54). In Bali, the antitheses between life and death, day and night, luck and misfortune, benediction and malediction, are made in relation to the geographical structure of the island, namely the mountains and the waters, respectively symbolizing the superior and the inferior worlds. The mountains represent the beneficial direction, since the rains come from there; on the contrary, the sea symbolizes the inferior direction and thus is associated with misfortunes, diseases, and death. Between the mountains and the sea — i.e., between the superior and the inferior worlds — is situated the inhabited land, the island Bali; it is named *madiapa*, the intermediary zone, and belongs to the two worlds. Consequently, it supports their antagonistic influences. As Swellengrebel puts it, *madiapa* (Bali) "is the unity of polar antitheses" (quoted by van der Kroef, "Dualism and Symbolic Antithesis," p. 856). Of course, the cosmological system is more complicated, for the directions north and east, as opposed to south and west, are associated with different colors and divinities (*ibid.*, p. 856).

tic objects and rituals,[58] which, in the last analysis, aim at the conjunction of the contraries. Among the Minangkabau of Sumatra,
the hostility between the two clans is expressed by a cockfight on
the occasion of marriage.[59] As P. E. de Josselin de Jong puts it: "The
whole community is divided into two parts which are mutually
antagonistic, yet complementary; the total community can only
exist if both occur and if both actively come into contact with each
other. A marriage is the occasion for them to do just this." [60] According to Josselin de Jong, all Indonesian festivals resemble a
secret or even declared war. Their cosmic significance is undeni-
able; the antagonistic groups represent certain sections of the
universe, and consequently their contest illustrates the opposition
of the primeval cosmic forces: the ritual constitutes a cosmic
drama.[61] Among the Dayak, this is clearly emphasized during the
collective festival of the dead, which is concluded by a mock
combat between two masked groups around a barricade erected
in the village. The festival is a dramatic reactualization of the cosmogony. The barricade symbolizes the Tree of Life, the two rival
groups represent the two mythical hornbills which killed each
other and destroyed at the same time the Tree of Life. But destruction and death produce a new creation and thus the misfortune brought into the village by death is exorcized.[62]
    In sum, one could say that Indonesian religious thought inces-

58. The knife, the *kris*, and the sword are masculine symbols; cloth is a
feminine symbol (cf. Gerlings Jager, quoted by van der Kroef, *ibid.*, p.
857). Among the Dayaks, the cloth attached to a spear symbolizes the
union of the two sexes. The flag — i.e., the staff (the spear) and the cloth —
represents the Tree of Life, the expression of divine creativity and of immortality (cf. Schärer, *Die Gottesidee*, p. 18–30).
    59. J. van der Kroef, "Dualism and Symbolic Antithesis," p. 853. In mar-
riage as well as in commerce the totem of the bridegroom's clan is united
to the totem of the bride's clan, thus signifying the cosmic unity of human
groups through their antithesis (*ibid.*, p. 850).
    60. Quoted in *ibid.*, p. 853. In another work, the author remarks that the
antitheses between sky and earth, male and female, the center and the two
contiguous sides are expressed by a monotonous but suggestive insistence in
the social categories and the distinctive titles (*ibid.*, p. 847).
    61. J. P. B. de Josselin de Jong, "De Oorsprong van den goddelijken Bed-
rieger," pp. 26 ff., quoted by F. B. J. Kuiper, "The Ancient Aryan Verbal
Contest," *Indo-Iranian Journal*, 4 (1960): p. 279.
    62. Cf. Waldemar Stöhr, *Das Totenritual der Dayak* (Cologne, 1959), pp.
39–56, and *Religionen Indonesiens*, pp. 31–33. For an exhaustive description
of the funerary ritual, and of the related myths, see Hans Schärer, *Der Toten-
kult der Ngadju Dayak in Süd-Borneo*, 2 vols. (The Hague, 1966).

santly elaborates and elucidates the intuition grasped by the cosmogonic myth. Since the world and life are the result of a disjunction which breaks the primordial conjunction, man must repeat this exemplary processus. The polar antagonism is elevated to the rank of a cosmological principle; not only is it accepted, but it becomes the cipher through which the world, life, and human society disclose their significance. Moreover, by its own mode of being, the polar antagonism aims to annul itself in a paradoxical union of contraries. The polarities, by clashing together, produce what could be called a "third term," [63] which can be either a new synthesis or a regression to a previous situation. One seldom encounters in the history of presystematic thought a formula which recalls more emphatically the Hegelian dialectics than the Indonesian cosmologies and symbologies. Nevertheless, there is this difference: for the Indonesians, the synthesis of the polarities, the "third term," though representing a new creation in regard to the immediately preceding stage, that of polar antagonism, is at the same time a regression, a return to the primordial situation when the contraries coexisted in a nondifferentiated totality.[64]

One could say that the Indonesian mind, after identifying the mystery of life and creativity in the mythical junction and disjunction of the opposites, did not seek to go beyond this biological model, as did, for example, Indian thought. In other words, the Indonesians have chosen wisdom, not philosophy, artistic creation, not science. Of course, they are not alone in this choice, and who would declare them right or wrong at this point.

Cosmogony, Ritual Competitions, and Oratorical Contests: India and Tibet

Ancient India permits us to grasp in process the passage from a mythico-ritual scenario to a paleotheology that will later inspire different metaphysical speculations. Moreover, India illustrates better than any other culture the resumption on multiple levels,

63. It is especially this aspect of the problem of dualist organizations that has interested Cl. Lévi-Strauss; see *Anthropologie structurale*, pp. 166 ff.

64. In a considerable monograph, *Das doppelte Geschlescht*, H. Baumann has attempted to trace the passage of the sexual antagonism (representing an archaic stage) to the idea of divine and human bisexuality considered by the author to be posterior. See my observations in *Revue de l'Histoire des Religions*, January–March, 1958, pp. 89–92.

164 PROLEGOMENON TO RELIGIOUS DUALISM

and the creative reinterpretation, of an archaic and well-diffused theme. The Indian documents help one to understand that a fundamental symbol, pursuing the revelation of a profound dimension of human existence, is always "open." In other words, India admirably illustrates that such a symbol may inaugurate what could be called a *chain-symbolization of all experiences laying bare man's situation in the universe*, thus influencing a sort of presystematic reflection and articulating its first results. Of course, it is impossible to recall here all the important creations of Indian genius. I shall begin with an example of ritual valorization of the motif of antagonism between two polar principles. I shall quote afterwards a few examples of elaboration and creative reinterpretation of this familiar motif on the planes of mythology and metaphysics.

The vedic mythology is dominated by the theme of the exemplary combat between Indra and the dragon Vṛtra. I have insisted elsewhere on the cosmogonic structure of the myth.[65] Releasing the waters imprisoned by Vṛtra in the mountains, Indra saves the world; symbolically, he creates it anew. In other variants of the myth, the decapitation and dismemberment of Vṛtra express the passage from virtuality to the actuality of creation, for the Snake is a symbol of the nonmanifest. The exemplary myth *par excellence*, this combat between Indra and Vṛtra furnishes the model for other forms of creation and many types of activities. "He verily slays Vṛtra who is a victor in the battle," says a vedic hymn.[66] Kuiper has recently pointed out two series of convergent facts. First, he has shown that the verbal contests in vedic India reiterate the primordial struggle against the forces of resistance (*vṛtāni*). The poet compares himself to Indra: "I am a slayer of my rivals, unhurt and uninjured like Indra" (*Rig Veda*, X, 166, 2). The oratorical contest, the competition between poets, represents a creative act and consequently a renovation of life.[67] Second, Kuiper has shown that there are reasons to believe that the mythico-ritual scenario centered on the combat between Indra and Vṛtra constituted, in fact, the New Year festival. All forms of contest and combat — chariot courses, struggles between two groups, etc. — were considered likely to stimulate the creative

65. Mircea Eliade, *The Myth of the Eternal Return* (New York, 1955), p. 19.
66. *Maitrāyaṇi-Saṃhitā*, II, 1, 3, quoted by F. B. J. Kuiper, "Ancient Aryan Verbal Contest," p. 251.
67. *Ibid.*, pp. 251 ff.

forces during the winter ritual.[68] Benveniste has rendered the Avestan term *vyāxana* as "oratorical contest" having a "military quality" that secures the victory.[69]

Thus, it seems that there existed a rather archaic Indo-Iranian conception which exalted the renovating and creative virtues of the verbal contest. Moreover, this view was not exclusively Indo-Iranian. Violent verbal confrontations are attested, for example, among the Eskimos, the Kwakiutl, and the ancient Germans. As Sierksma has recently pointed out, verbal contests were highly esteemed in Tibet.[70] The public debates of the Tibetan monks, whose aggressiveness and cruelty were not only verbal, are well known. Though the disputes bear upon problems of Buddhist philosophy and follow, at least in part, the rules established by the great Indian Buddhist doctors, especially Asaṇga, the passion with which the public controversy is carried out seems to be characteristic of the Tibetans.[71] Moreover, Rolf Stein has shown that in Tibet the verbal contest falls among other forms of competition, such as horse races, athletic games, wrestling, competition in archery, cow milking, and beauty contests.[72] On the occasion of the New Year, the most important competition besides the horse races took place between the members or representatives of different clans, who recited the cosmogonic myth and exalted the tribal ancestors. The essential theme of the New Year mythicoritual scenario was the combat between the Sky God and the demons, represented by two mountains. As in similar scenarios, the god's victory assured the victory of new life in the following year. As for the oratorical contests, they were, according to Stein, part of

an ensemble of competitions which, on the social plane, exalt the prestige, and on the religious plane fasten the social group to its habitat. The gods are present at the spectacle and laugh in common with men. The contest of enigmas and the recitation of tales, like the Epic of Gesar, have an effect on the crops and cattle. Gods and men being reunited at

68. *Ibid.*, p. 269.

69. Quoted in *ibid.*, p. 247.

70. F. Sierksma, "*Rtsod-pa*: the Monacal Disputations in Tibet," *Indo-Iranian Journal*, 8 (1964): 130–52, especially pp. 142 ff.

71. A. Wayman, "The rules of debate, according to Asaṇga," *Journal of the American Oriental Society*, 78 (1958): 29–40; Sierksma, "*Rtsod-pa*."

72. R. A. Stein, *Recherches sur l'épopée et le barde au Tibet* (Paris, 1959), p. 441.

the occasion of the great festivals, the social oppositions are reaffirmed and appeased at the same time. And the group, connected again with its past (origin of the world and of the ancestors) and with its habitat (ancestors — sacred mountains) feels invigorated.[73]

Rolf Stein has also indicated the Iranian influences in the Tibetan New Year festival.[74] But this does not mean that the entire scenario has been borrowed. Most probably, Iranian influences have reinforced certain indigenous elements already in existence. The New Year scenario was certainly archaic, since it disappeared quite early in India.

Devas and Asuras

But in India, such schemes have been continuously taken up again and developed on different plans of reference and in multiple perspectives. I have discussed elsewhere the opposition between Devas and Asuras, that is to say, between gods and "demons," powers of light and of darkness. But as early as vedic times this conflict — which constituted an extremely diffused mythological theme —has been interpreted in a rather original sense: namely, it was completed by a "prologue" which disclosed the paradoxical consubstantiality, or fraternity, of Devas and Asuras.

One has the impression that the Vedic doctrine is at pains to establish a double perspective: although, as an immediate reality, and as the world appears to our eyes, the Devas and the Asuras are irreconcilable, different by nature and condemned to fight one another, at the beginning of time, on the other hand, that is to say before the Creation or before the world took its present form, they were consubstantial.[75]

Moreover, the gods are, or have been, or are able, to become Asuras, i.e., nongods.

We have here, on the one hand, a daring formula of the divine ambivalence, an ambivalence expressed equally by the contradictory aspects of the great vedic gods such as Agni and Varuṇa.[76] But we perceive also the effort of the Indian mind to arrive at a

73. *Ibid.*, pp. 440–41.
74. *Ibid.*, pp. 390–91, etc. Cf. Sierksma, "Rtsod-pa," pp. 146 ff.
75. Mircea Eliade, *Méphistophélès et l'Androgyne* (Paris, 1962), p. 109 (English translation: *Mephistopheles and the Androgyne* [New York, 1965], p. 89).
76. Cf. *ibid.* pp. 111–13.

unique *Urgrund* of the world, life, and the spirit. And the first stage in the discovery of such an all-embracing perspective has been to recognize that what is true in eternity is not necessarily true in time. I shall not pursue this problem here, since I have already discussed it in a previous work.

Mitra-Varuṇa

No less significant is the development of an ancient Indo-European theme concerning the two complementary aspects of the divine sovereignty, designated in India by the names of Varuṇa and Mitra. Georges Dumézil has shown that the couple Mitra-Varuṇa belongs to the Indo-European trifunctional system, since it has homologues among the ancient Romans and Germans. But Dumézil has also indicated that this conception of the divine sovereignty underwent, in India, a philosophical elaboration unknown elsewhere in the Indo-European world. To put it briefly, for the ancient Indians Mitra is "the sovereign under his rational, calm, benevolent, sacerdotal aspect, while Varuṇa is the sovereign under his somber, inspired, violent, terrible, warrior-like aspect." [77] The same dyptic is found in Rome, with the same oppositions and same alternations; there is, on the one hand, the opposition between the Luperci and the flamins: "tumult, passion, imperialism of a *iunior* let loose" over against "serenity, exactitude, moderation of a sacerdotal *senior*." [78] There are, in the same vein, the different structures and behaviors of the first two Roman kings: Romulus and Numa. Their contrast corresponds to the opposition between Luperci and flamins, and likewise to the polarity Mitra-Varuṇa, which is evident not only in the religious and mythological frames of reference, but also on the cosmic level (day and night, etc.) and in the epic history (Manu, the legislator-king, corresponding to Numa, is said to be a descendant of the Sun and inaugurates the "solar dynasty"; Purûravas, the Gandharva-king, analogous to Romulus, is the grandson of the Moon and establishes the "lunar dynasty").

But it suffices to compare the elaborations of this Indo-European mythico-ritual theme made by the Romans and Indians to realize the differences between their two kinds of genius. While India

77. Georges Dumézil, *Mitra-Varuna*, 2d ed. (Paris, 1948), p. 85.
78. *Ibid.*, p. 62.

developed theologically and philosophically the complementarity and the alternation symbolized by these two aspects of divine sovereignty,[79] Rome historicized her gods as well as her myths. The principles of complementarity and rotation remained, in Rome, on the level of rituals, or served to build up a fabulous historiography. On the contrary, in India the two principles, understood somehow as incarnated in Mitra and Varuṇa, furnished an exemplary model for the explanation of both the world and of the dialectical structure of man's mode of being, for the human condition mysteriously comprises a masculine modality and a feminine one, life and death, bondage and freedom, etc.

Indeed, Mitra and Varuṇa are set one against the other as day and night, and even as male and female (*Śatapatha Brāhmaṇa*, II, 4, 4, 9 tells us that "Mitra discharges his seed in Varuṇa"), but they are also opposed as "the one who comprehends" (*abhigantṛ*) and "the one who acts" (*karta*), and as brahman and *kshatra*, i.e., "spiritual power" and "temporal power." Moreover, the dualism elaborated by Sāmkhya, with a passive and placid "self" (*purusha*) as spectator, and an active and productive "Nature" (*prakriti*), has been sometimes understood by the Indians as an illustration of the opposition between Mitra and Varuṇa.[80] And a similar correspondence has been worked out in Vedanta with regard to Brahman and *māyā*, for as the old liturgical texts assert, "Mitra is Brahman," and in the Vedas *māyā* is the characteristic technique of Varuṇa the magician.[81] Moreover, as early as the *Rig Veda* (I, 164, 38), Varuṇa has been identified with the manifest.

Polarity and *Coincidentia Oppositorum*

Of course, the couple Mitra-Varuṇa was not the original model of all the other polarities, but only the most important expression, on the religious and mythological planes, of this principle in which Indian thought has recognized the fundamental structures of the

79. Cf. Ananda K. Coomaraswamy, *Spiritual Authority and Temporal Power in the Indian Theory of Government* (New Haven, 1942); M. Eliade, "La Souveraineté et la Religion Indo-Européennes," *Critique*, no. 35 (April, 1949): 342–49.
80. See, for example, *Mahābhārata*, XII, 318, 39, quoted by Dumézil, *Mitra-Varuna*, p. 209.
81. *Ibid.*, pp. 209–10.

cosmic totality and of human existence. Indeed, later speculation has distinguished *two* aspects of Brahman: *apara* and *para*, "inferior" and "superior," visible and invisible, manifest and nonmanifest. In other words, it is always the mystery of a polarity, all at once a biunity and a rhythmic alternation, that can be deciphered in the different mythological, religious, and philosophical "illustrations": Mitra and Varuṇa, the visible and invisible aspects of Brahman, Brahman and *māyā*, *purusha* and *prakriti*, and later on Shiva and Shakti, or *saṃsāra* and Nirvāna.

But some of these polarities tend to annul themselves in a *coincidentia oppositorum*, in a paradoxical unity-totality, the *Urgrund* of which I spoke of a moment ago. That it is not only a question of metaphysical speculations but also of formulas with the help of which India tried to circumscribe a peculiar mode of existence, is proved by the fact that *coincidentia oppositorum* is implied in *jivan mukta*, the "liberated in life," who continues to exist in the world even though he has attained final deliverance; or the "awakened one" for whom Nirvāṇa and *saṃsāra* appear to be one and the same thing; or the situation of a tantric yogin able to pass from asceticism to orgy without any modification of behavior.[82] Indian spirituality has been obsessed by the "Absolute." Now, however one may conceive the Absolute, it cannot be conceived except as beyond contraries and polarities. This is the reason why India includes the orgy among the means of attaining deliverance, while deliverance is denied to those who continue to follow the ethical rules depending on social institutions. The "Absolute," the ultimate liberation, the freedom, *moksha*, *mukti*, is not accessible to those who have not surpassed what the texts call the "couples of contraries," i.e., the polarities we have discussed.

This Indian reinterpretation recalls certain rituals of archaic societies which, though related to mythologies of a polar structure, pursue the periodic abolition of the contraries by means of a collective orgy. We have seen that the Dayaks suspend all rules and interdictions during the New Year festival. It will be useless to insist on the differences between the Dayak mythico-ritual scenario and the Indian philosophies and "mystical" techniques aiming at the abolition of contraries; the differences are evident. Nevertheless, in both cases the *summum bonum* is situated beyond

82. I have discussed these problems in *Techniques du Yoga* (Paris, 1948) and *Le Yoga. Liberté et Immortalité* (Paris, 1954).

polarities. To be sure, for the Dayaks the *summum bonum* is represented by the divine totality, which alone can insure a new creation, a new epiphany of the fullness of life, while for the yogins and other contemplatives the *summum bonum* transcends the cosmos and life, for it represents a new existential dimension, that of the *unconditioned*, of absolute freedom and beatitude, a mode of existence known neither in the cosmos nor among the gods, for it is a human creation and accessible exclusively to men. Even the gods, if they desire to obtain absolute freedom, are obliged to incarnate themselves and to conquer this deliverance by the means discovered and elaborated by men.

But, to come back to the comparison between the Dayaks and the Indians, something must be added: the creativity of a specific ethnic group or of a particular religion does not manifest itself solely in the reinterpretation and the revalorization of an archaic system of polarities, but also in the significance given to the *reunion of contraries*. The Dayak orgiastic ritual and the tantric orgy achieve a sort of *coincidentia oppositorum*, but the significance of the transcending of contraries is not the same in the two cases. In other words, neither the experiences made possible by the discovery of the polarities and by the hope of their integration nor the symbolization that articulates and sometimes anticipates these experiences are susceptible of *exhaustion*, even if, in certain cultures, such experiences and symbolizations seem to have exhausted all their possibilities. It is in a total perspective, encompassing the totality of cultures, that we must judge the fecundity of a symbolism which expresses the structures of cosmic life and concurrently renders intelligible man's mode of existing in the world.

Yang and Yin

I have purposely left for the end the example of China. As in the archaic societies of the Americas and Indonesia, the cosmic polarity, expressed by the symbols *yang* and *yin*, was "lived" through the rites, and it also furnished quite early the model for a universal classification. Besides, as in India, the couple of contraries *yang* and *yin* was developed into a cosmology which, on the one hand, systematized and validated innumerable bodily techniques and spiritual disciplines, and on the other hand inspired rigorous and systematic philosophical speculations. I will not present the

morphology of *yang* and *yin* nor will I retrace its history. It suffices
to remark that polar symbolism is abundantly attested in the icon-
ography of Shang bronzes (1400–1122 B.C., according to the traditional Chinese chronology). Carl Hentze, who has devoted a
series of important works to this problem, points out that the polar
symbols are disposed in such a way as to emphasize their conjunction; for instance, the owl, or another figure symbolizing the darkness, is provided with "solar eyes," while the emblems of light are
marked by a "nocturnal" sign.[83] Hentze interprets the conjunction of polar symbols as illustrating religious ideas of renewal of
time and spiritual regeneration. According to Hentze, the symbolism of *yang* and *yin* is present in the most ancient ritual objects,
long before the first written texts.[84]

This is also the conclusion of Marcel Granet, though he reached
it from other sources and by utilizing a different method. Granet
recalls that in *Che King* the word *yin* evokes the idea of cold and
cloudy weather, and also of what is internal, whereas the term
yang suggests the idea of sunshine and warmth.[85] In other words,
yang and *yin* indicate the concrete and antithetical aspects of the
weather.[86] In *Kouei tsang*, a lost manual of divination known only
from some fragments, it is a question of "a time of light" and "a
time of obscurity," anticipating the saying of Tchouang tseu: "a
(time of) plenitude, a (time of) decrepitude . . . a (time of)
refining, a (time of) thickening . . . a (time of) life, a (time of)
death." [87] Thus, the world represents "a totality of a cyclical order
(*tao, pien, t'ong*) constituted by the conjugation of two alternate
and complementary manifestations." [88]

Granet thinks that the idea of alternation seems to have entailed
the idea of opposition.[89] This is clearly illustrated by the structure
of the calendar. "*Yang* and *yin* have been summoned to organize
the calendar because their emblems evoked with a particular force

83. Cf. Carl Hentze, *Bronzegerät, Kultbauten, Religion im ältesten China
der Shangzeit* (Anvers, 1951), pp. 192 ff. See also our observations in *Critique*,
no. 83 (April, 1954): 331 ff.
84. Carl Hentze, *Das Haus als Weltort der Seele* (Stuttgart, 1961), pp. 99
ff. For a general exposition of the problem of polarity see Hermann Köster,
Symbolik des chinesischen Universismus (Stuttgart, 1958), pp. 17 ff.
85. Marcel Granet, *La Pensée chinoise* (Paris, 1934), p. 117.
86. *Ibid.*, p. 118.
87. *Ibid.*, p. 132.
88. *Ibid.*, p. 127.
89. *Ibid.*, p. 128.

the rhythmic conjugation of two concrete antithetic aspects." [90] According to the philosophers, during the winter the *yang*, overcome by *yin*, undergoes below the frozen soil a kind of an annual trial from which it emerges invigorated. The *yang* escapes from its prison at the beginning of spring; then the ice melts and the sources reawaken.[91] Thus the universe shows itself to be constituted by a series of antithetic forms alternating in a cyclical manner.

Fascinated by the sociologism of Durkheim, Marcel Granet was inclined to deduct the conception and the systematic articulation of cosmic rotation from the ancient formulas of Chinese social life. We do not need to follow him on this path. But it is important to notice the symmetry between the complementary alternation of the activities of the two sexes and the cosmic rhythms governed by the interplay of *yang* and *yin*. And because a feminine nature was recognized in everything that is *yin*, and a masculine nature in everything that is *yang*, the theme of hierogamy — which, according to Granet, dominates the entire Chinese mythology — discloses a cosmic as well as religious dimension. The ritual opposition of the two sexes, carried out, in ancient China, as that of two rival corporations,[92] expresses simultaneously the complementary antagonism of two modes of being and the alternation of two cosmic principles, *yang* and *yin*. In the collective feasts of spring and autumn, the two antagonistic choirs, arrayed in lines face to face, challenged each other in verse. "The *yang* calls, the *yin* answers." These two formulas are interchangeable; they signify conjointly the cosmic and social rhythms.[93] The antagonistic choirs confront each other as shadow and light. The field where they meet represents the totality of space, just as the group symbolizes the totality of human society and of the realities belonging to natural realm.[94] A collective hierogamy ended the festivity. As we have noticed, such ritual orgies are well known in many parts of the world. In this case, too, the polarity, accepted as a fundamental rule of life during the year, is abolished, or transcended, through the union of contraries.

90. *Ibid.*, p. 131.
91. *Ibid.*, p. 135.
92. *Ibid.*
93. *Ibid.*, p. 141.
94. *Ibid.*, p. 143.

We do not need to recall the elaboration of such categories, which was carried out in the systematic work of the philosophers. We may only add that the comparison of the notion of *tao* with the different primitive formulas of the "third term" as a solution of polarities, constitutes a fascinating theme for the historian of ideas. Hopefully, this work will be undertaken soon.

Final Remarks

To conclude, I would like to return to a point which I consider decisive in any comparative analysis, namely the irreducibility of the spiritual creation to a preexistent system of values. In the mythological and religious universe, every *creation* re-creates its own structures, just as every great poet reinvents his language. The different types of bipartition and polarity, duality and alternation, antithetical dyads and *coincidentia oppositorum*, are to be found everywhere in the world and at all stages of culture. But the historian of religions is ultimately interested in finding out what a particular culture, or group of cultures, has done with this immediate datum. A hermeneutics which pursues the comprehension of cultural creations hesitates before the temptations of reducing all the species of dyads and polarities to a single fundamental type reflecting certain unconscious logical activities. For, on the one hand, the dichotomies allow themselves to be classified in multiple categories, and, on the other hand, some typical systems are susceptible of being entrusted with an amazing number of functions and values. There is no question of presenting here a complete and detailed morphology of all the species and varieties of religious dichotomies, dyads, and polarities. As a matter of fact, such a considerable undertaking would go far beyond our subject. But the few documents which we have analyzed, and which have been purposely chosen as the most representative, suffice to illustrate our argument.

Roughly, one can distinguish: (1) the groups of cosmic polarities and (2) those polarities related directly to the human condition. Certainly, there is a structural solidarity between the cosmic dichotomies and polarities and those connected with man's specific mode of being. Nevertheless, our preliminary distinction is useful, for it is mainly the polarities of the second type that have opened the way, in certain cultures and certain historical moments, to systematic philosophical speculations. Among the cosmic polarities, one may discern those of spatial structure (right/left, high/low, etc.), of temporal structure (day/night, the seasons, etc.) and finally those expressing the process of cosmic life (life/death, the rhythms of vegetation, etc.). As to the dichotomies and polarities related to the human condition, which somehow serve as a cipher of this condition, they are more numerous and, one could say, more "open." The fundamental pair is that of male/female, but there are also ethnic dichotomies ("we"/the foreigners), mythological dichotomies (the antagonistic Twins), religious dichotomies (sacred/profane, which, as a matter of fact signifies a total dichotomy, relating concurrently to cosmos, life, and human society; gods/adversaries of gods; etc.), and ethical dichotomies (good/evil, etc.).

What strikes one first in this provisory and incomplete classification is the fact that a great number of dichotomies and polarities *imply each other mutually*, as, for example, the cosmic polarities and the sexual or religious dichotomy. Ultimately, they express the modalities of life comprehended in rhythm and rotation. As we have already noticed apropos of Kogi and the Indonesians (and the same can be said about the Chinese), the polar antagonism becomes the "cipher" through which man unveils both the structures of the universe and the significance of his own existence. At this stage one cannot speak of religious or ethical "dualism," since the antagonism does not presuppose "evil" or the "demonic." Rigorously dualistic ideas arise from those pairs of contraries in which the two antagonists do not mutually imply each other. This is evident in some cosmogonic myths of California where Coyote continuously and successfully interferes with God's work of creation. A similar situation is to be found in Mänäbush's mythology: his conflict with the inferior Powers was not predestined, but broke out as a consequence of a fortuitous event (the murder of his brother, the Wolf).

It will be interesting to determine precisely in what cultures, and at what epochs, the negative aspects of life, until then accepted as constitutive and unexceptionable moments of the cosmic totality, lost their initial function and began to be interpreted as manifestations of *evil*. For it seems that in the religions dominated by a system of polarities, the *idea of evil* arises slowly and with some difficulty; in certain cases the notion of evil even leaves out of its sphere many negative aspects of life (for example, suffering, disease, cruelty, bad luck, death, etc.). We have seen that among the Kogi the *principle of evil* is accepted as an inevitable and necessary moment in the cosmic totality.

Finally, it is important to note that the mediation between the contraries also presents a great variety of solutions. There is opposition, clash, and combat, but in certain cases the conflict is resolved in a union which produces a "third term," while in others the polarities seem to coexist paradoxically in a *coincidentia oppositorum*, or they are transcended, i.e., radically abolished or rendered unreal, incomprehensible, or meaningless. (I refer especially to certain Indian metaphysics and "mystical" techniques.) This variety of solutions to the problems raised by the mediation between the contraries — and we must add also the radically "dualistic" positions, which refuse any mediation — merits a special investigation. For if it is true that any solution found to the crisis provoked by the awareness of polarities implies somehow the beginning of wisdom, the very multiplicity and the extreme variety of such solutions arouse the critical reflection and prepare for the coming of philosophy.

Index